Cosmopolitan Aesthetics

ALSO AVAILABLE FROM BLOOMSBURY

Aesthetics, Arts, and Politics in a Global World, Daniel Herwitz

Aesthetics: Key Concepts in Philosophy, Daniel Herwitz

Aesthetic Theory, Abstract Art, and Lawrence Carroll, David Carrier

Contemporary Chinese Art, Aesthetic Modernity and Zhang Peili, Paul Gladston

Introducing Aesthetics and the Philosophy of Art, Darren Hudson Hick

The Philosophy and Art of Wang Guangyi, edited by Tiziana Andina and Erica Onnis

Cosmopolitan Aesthetics

Art in a Global World

DANIEL HERWITZ

BLOOMSBURY ACADEMIC
LONDON • NEW YORK • OXFORD • NEW DELHI • SYDNEY

BLOOMSBURY ACADEMIC
Bloomsbury Publishing Plc
50 Bedford Square, London, WC1B 3DP, UK
1385 Broadway, New York, NY 10018, USA

BLOOMSBURY, BLOOMSBURY ACADEMIC and the Diana logo are trademarks
of Bloomsbury Publishing Plc

First published in Great Britain 2020

Copyright © Daniel Herwitz, 2020

Daniel Herwitz has asserted his right under the Copyright, Designs and Patents
Act, 1988, to be identified as Author of this work.

For legal purposes the Acknowledgments on p. vii constitute an extension
of this copyright page.

Cover design: Maria Rajka
Cover image: Clifford Possum Tjapaltjarri and Tim Tjapaltjarri, Warlugulong,
1976, Gallery of New South Wales, Sydney. Rights courtesy of
Aboriginal Artists Agency Limited.

All rights reserved. No part of this publication may be reproduced or
transmitted in any form or by any means, electronic or mechanical,
including photocopying, recording, or any information storage or retrieval
system, without prior permission in writing from the publishers.

Bloomsbury Publishing Plc does not have any control over, or responsibility for,
any third-party websites referred to or in this book. All internet addresses given
in this book were correct at the time of going to press. The author and publisher
regret any inconvenience caused if addresses have changed or sites have ceased
to exist, but can accept no responsibility for any such changes.

A catalogue record for this book is available from the British Library.

A catalog record for this book is available from the Library of Congress.

ISBN: HB: 978-1-3500-7523-8
PB: 978-1-3500-7524-5
ePDF: 978-1-3500-7525-2
eBook: 978-1-3500-7526-9

Typeset by Newgen KnowledgeWorks Pvt. Ltd., Chennai, India
Printed and bound in Great Britain

To find out more about our authors and books visit www.bloomsbury.com
and sign up for our newsletters.

Contents

List of Figures vi
Acknowledgments vii
How to Use This Book ix

1 Introduction to Globalization 1
2 The Global Art World Today: Prospects and Problems 13
3 Aesthetic Cosmopolitanism 51
4 Cultural Property and Aesthetic Synergy 85
5 Meaning, Medium, and History in Art 107
6 Taste in Its Eighteenth-Century Context 133
7 Aesthetic Judgment from a Cosmopolitan Perspective 161

Notes 197
Bibliography and Suggestions for Further Reading 205
Index 211

Figures

1. William Kentridge, *Felix in Exile*, 1993–4 19
2. Alexander Rodchenko, *At the Telephone {Na telefone}*. From a series on the production of a newspaper. 1928 23
3. Cindy Sherman, *Untitled Film Still #84*, 1978 25
4. George Gittoes, *The Preacher*, 1995 30
5. Irma Stern, *Paradise: The Journal and Letters of Irma Stern, 1917–1933* 34
6. Thomas Heatherwick Design Studio, Zeitz MOCAA, 2017 42
7. Thomas Heatherwick Design Studio, Zeitz MOCAA, 2017 43
8. Thomas Heatherwick Design Studio, Zeitz MOCAA, 2017 44
9. Clifford Possum Tjapaltjarri and Tim Tjapaltjarri, *Warlugulong*, 1976 76
10. Judy Watson, *Our Bones in Your Collections*, 1997 81
11. Marcel Duchamp, *Étant donnés* 113
12. Thomas Daniell, *Ruins of the Naurattan, Sasaram, Bihar*, 1811 151
13. Pablo Picasso, *Les Demoiselles d'Avignon*, Paris, June–July 1907 155

Acknowledgments

Akeel Bilgrami read this book in draft and greatly contributed to its integration of themes. Albie Sachs offered his scrupulous and trenchant eye for visual detail and political connotation. Thanks also to Michael Steinberg and Lydia Goehr for a lifetime of conversation about aesthetics and cultural politics. And to Imraan Coovadia, George Gittoes, Lucia Saks, Sarah Nuttall, Derek Peterson, and the two anonymous readers of my manuscript, all of whom helped with this book's bettering.

I had the luck to present the third chapter at the Department of Philosophy's Aesthetics Seminar and received all kinds of useful remarks from the group, whom I thank collectively. Parts of the second chapter were presented at a workshop in Maputo, Mozambique, thanks to the Andrew Mellon Foundation, the University of Michigan's African Studies Center, and WISER (the University of Witwatersrand Institute for Social and Economic Research). The comments were again very helpful.

This book came into being at the prompting of my editor at Bloomsbury Press, Colleen Coalter, who suggested that rather than updating an earlier book on aesthetics I wrote and published with Bloomsbury in 2008, *Aesthetics: Key Concepts in Philosophy*, I should write something new: rethinking aesthetics in the light of the globalization of culture. Or put the other way around, rethinking the globalization of culture in the light of what is necessary from the history of aesthetics to do it. The earlier book had been written not only as an introduction to aesthetics for advanced students but also as an essayistic attempt to say something new in the philosophy of art. I took her hint, and I have worked closely with her in pitching the timbre and themes of this book, which share with the earlier one the double purpose of being a textbook and a book of (I hope) new ideas. Her advice has proved invaluable.

The voice of Ted Cohen, my teacher and friend, has remained in my head throughout the writing of this and every other book I've written. It is the clarion call of one who lived a life in philosophy in what Ludwig Wittgenstein called the "rough ground." Ted wrote about sporting events, ceramic vases, Eastern European cities, Hollywood films, middle American food, jokes, metaphors, the moral imperatives of visiting concentration camps, the writings of Tolstoy, the question of art in relation to human intimacy, about rules and the stakes of their violation in everything from baseball to music. He believed philosophy begins in the whirl of life in a way that should cause one to stand aside from theories and books enough to let the world seep in. For him the values of art were similarly understood in relation to these wider frames of life, not simply in relation to the pages of Immanuel Kant. Ted is my ideal of what it is to be brilliant, supple, and humane. My own writing is more political than his, and perhaps more cosmopolitan, which he would only have applauded, since his belief was that the role of a teacher is to train a student to find their own voice, not to channel that of the teacher's. There are no words adequate to the thanks I owe him, which is why this book is dedicated to the late Ted Cohen.

How to Use This Book

This book is about the contemporary culture of globalization in which we all variously live, and some of the ways it demands a rethinking of key ideas in aesthetics. A central theme of this book is the intersection among art, art markets, and aesthetics. The book urges that these be studied together rather than separately. I have organized the book along four related themes. The book proceeds from the present back to the nineteenth century and then to the eighteenth century, when the discipline of aesthetics arose in philosophy. It has four parts, distributed across seven chapters.

First, the book explores the contemporary nature of global art markets and their variable effects on the making of art across unequally resourced places in what has been called the global north and the global south. Chapter 1 is a very short course on globalization. Chapter 2 is about the way art markets today impose demands on the making and character of art and the ways in which new opportunities for the global distribution of art also arise thanks to these markets. Opportunity is linked to a challenge, namely, for whom is an artist now creating, given the fact that the person who buys or follows art could now be living anywhere with little real knowledge of the conditions of place under which a work is made. This production for a disembodied audience leads to a number of problems in the making and reception of art. Then there is the issue of brand uniformity and stylistic homogenization imposed by the market, along with an interest in diversity on the part of some artworld players.

The first part of the book might be called more art historical or cultural than philosophical, although I find that the distinctions between these disciplines ought to be blurred when an aesthetician gets to work. For if aesthetics does not address events in the art of our time—or in earlier times—then it tends to lose its point.

Chapters 3 and 4 are the heart of the book. They revisit an idea as old as the ancient world, an idea given its Enlightenment formulation (in the eighteenth century) by Immanuel Kant. That is the idea of cosmopolitanism, which I hope to convince the reader is the best/most fruitful attitude to embrace in a global world of aesthetics, and one deeply fused with global stances on morals and politics. These chapters are framed as a long conversation with the work of the Ghanaian/British/American philosopher Anthony Appiah. The point is to free cosmopolitanism from its Enlightenment claims of universality and understand it as the position in aesthetics that recognizes and seeks to learn from human diversity as well as human interconnectedness without overall rankings of culture or taste. Cosmopolitanism demands a particular capacity of the imagination I identify as *synergy*: the ability to synthesize disparate cultural forms into new and integral patterns in the absence of rules.

A second purpose of the cosmopolitan discussion is to work through the conundrum of cultural property in a world where culture circulates globally and is endlessly transplanted.

Cosmopolitanism is an approach to art and morals of long-standing value, as old as classical Greece and Rome. But it is especially called for in our global world where commodities are designed and made from multiple cultural traditions, where we live and work with people from across the world on a daily basis, where cultures daily intersect thanks to global markets, and where questions of moral and aesthetic judgment (about right and wrong, better or worse) arise in the context of diversity.

The first two chapters call for cosmopolitanism in yet another way. Global art markets tend to homogenize genuine differences between peoples and cultural traditions into common brands and styles. The irony is that in our day globalization is a threat to genuine diversity, not simply a way of encountering it. Everyone ends up wearing Nike sneakers and making similar kinds of art. And so, cosmopolitanism also has the purpose of trying to rescue art and culture from this homogenizing tendency central to markets, by seeking to acknowledge deeper diversity than the market may sometimes allow.

The third part of the book travels back into the nineteenth century to the aesthetic theory of G. W. F. Hegel, where the importance of a medium in the making of artistic meaning finds its greatest articulation. For Hegel, art is the expression of the guiding aspirations of an historical age, and its purpose is to bring about progressive history by giving expression or embodiment to those ideas in the context of a suitable medium. But Hegel believed only Europe was capable of generating art history. The rest of the world, meaning the colonial world, was consigned to a kind of dormancy, endlessly repeating its past without any exit strategy into modernity. Hegel's ideas about history demand cosmopolitan revision.

Hegel's great successor is the twentieth-century philosopher Arthur Danto, who brings Hegel into the twentieth century by rewriting him in the light of the rise of the art markets, the artworld, and modernist art, furthering the link between this chapter and the opening sections of the book. One might say that Chapter 5, the chapter on Hegel and Danto, philosophically amplifies the discussion of contemporary art in Chapters 1 and 2.

However, Danto's is also a colonial story, restricting the modernist history in the light of which he frames his thesis of the end of art, to what is happening in Europe and America. Danto too wants cosmopolitan rewriting.

Suitably expanded to encompass the globe, we are then free to focus on the philosophical power of both Hegel and Danto.

This section of the book also highlights how Danto is representative of a tendency in late-twentieth-century art theory and aesthetics, which is to focus on meaning, rhetoric, and politics in art, or what he calls art's ability to "make a statement"—this at the expense of acknowledging the importance of sensuous, aesthetic aspects of art. These sensual/aesthetic features Danto believes are irrelevant to the definition of art. Such a point of view fails to adequately understand even contemporary art. For this we need to go back a century more, to the eighteenth.

This is the fourth section of the book, which returns to the eighteenth century when the discipline of aesthetics was founded as an exploration of the importance of taste. The eighteenth century identifies taste first and foremost as pleasure taken in objects experienced as beautiful and/or sublime. With the birth of aesthetics, the philosophical interest in art changed by foregrounding taste and judgment and sidelining other dimensions to art and aesthetic experience such as expression, meaning, communal solidarity, and religious celebration. This had the great virtue of highlighting the sensuous elements of art, and the quality of pleasure taken in an art object. The eighteenth century was the first to give voice to the values of aesthetic *experience*.

What the eighteenth century got wrong was its own sidelining of meaning, rhetoric, and politics from art and aesthetic experience. If contemporary art theory sidelines beauty and the sublime, then the eighteenth century sidelined the opposite: meaning, social engagement, and politics. These centuries are dialectically opposed in their approach to art. Neither provides an adequate picture of even the art of its time, much less other art.

The final two chapters (Chapters 6 and 7) serve as an introduction to thinking on taste characteristic of the eighteenth century. This introduction also brings up a fault line central to the eighteenth century's thinking about taste, namely, the eighteenth century's commitment to *universality of judgment and ranking*. I spend some time in both chapters unpacking this fault line. A question framing both chapters is what caused the eighteenth century to marginalize meaning and use? And at the same time to believe its judgments were universal? The answer is complex, but I believe—and argue—it involves a *global* discussion of nationalism, empire, and the birth of the institutions of the museum and the concert hall.

Once these new ideas from the eighteenth century are freed from the ideology of their time and given a more cosmopolitan rewriting, we are free to understand why that century's thinking about art remains of vital importance today, in part as a corrective to the ideology that the sole role of art today is representational, rhetorical, and political, an ideology that derives from the legacy of the avant-gardes at the beginning of the twentieth century, which linked experimentation in art to its putative political force.

You could read any one section of this book without reading the others and get something from it. But reading the book from cover to cover will enhance each chapter. For the book seeks to relate its four sections together in terms of a paradox. Art requires a certain autonomy from the rest of the world to deliver its experiences of absorption and happiness. There is something deeply right about the eighteenth-century insight that with art, we seem to leave the world in an experience that feels transcendent—if only temporary, which the eighteenth century called pleasure taken in a subject or object for its own sake. To review the eighteenth century is to learn a great deal about aesthetic experience of a kind that is subdued in the present artworld but remains vital for the understanding of art, in particular, the approach to art that treats art as an encomium of exalted and autonomous pleasure rather than a way of embodying meaning in a medium. Without this idea, we lose much of the distinctiveness and importance of art.

And yet art also delivers meaning, addresses history, speaks politically, and *engages* the world—this the nineteenth and twentieth centuries understood.

It is in the *tension* between these aspects of art—between its transcendent side and its engagement with the world—that art lives. You need to read the entire book to get this point. For it took philosophy three hundred years to make it.

1

Introduction to Globalization

Globalization and Aesthetic Ideas

It has been a central idea guiding the aesthetics of the twentieth century that new art demands new aesthetic ideas. One finds this idea in the writing of the American aestheticians John Dewey, Stanley Cavell, and Arthur Danto; the British thinkers Robin Collingwood and Richard Wollheim; and the French philosophers Jacques Derrida and Michel Foucault, all of whom produced major aesthetic innovation in the light of modernist, avant-garde, and contemporary art and its boundary-shattering creativity. I myself wrote a book called *Making Theory/Constructing Art: On the Authority of the Avant-Gardes* some time ago (1993), which endeavored to fit that mold.

But there is also the idea central to the German nineteenth-century philosophers of history G. W. F. Hegel and Karl Marx that it is the wider domain of new historical, social, political, and economic realities that catalyzes change in both art and aesthetic ideas. New aesthetic ideas are the result both of new art and of the shifting Hegelian world in which new art arises. Aesthetics arises in conversation with new art, not simply trailing behind it, and in conversation with the culture and society through which that art arises. Indeed, since new aesthetic ideas are part of what drives the making of new art, aesthetic innovation does not merely follow art and reflect on it; new aesthetic ideas are part of what empower the making of art for new times.

This book is not only about the way the profound changes in society, economy, politics, and life that have occurred over the past thirty years thanks to globalization have made their mark on art and on art markets—in ways that demand new aesthetic ideas and revision of older ones—but also about the importance of older ideas, suitably refined, for the understanding of contemporary life and art.

The globalization of the past thirty years has happened at a velocity perhaps unparalleled in history, affecting every aspect of life.

Fordist capitalism—the form of manufacturing and industrial production that was in place during the first half of the twentieth century, the capitalism of the assembly line, and the film studio—has given way to globally extended modes of production in which an automobile or computer's parts are fabricated in Bangladesh, Brazil, and Arizona; assembled in Texas; and designed in Silicon Valley by a company whose corporate headquarters may be located (for tax purposes!) in Ireland, Luxembourg, or the Channel Islands.[1]

Families that two generations ago would have only had to drive twenty miles at most to congregate at church, for weddings, funerals, Thanksgiving meals, Boxing Day, or other occasions now have children living in Vancouver, Seattle, Denver, London, Singapore, Shanghai, and São Paulo. They communicate thanks to Skype, WhatsApp, and Twitter.

When people wish to find romantic companions, they tend to go online to various dating websites and take it from there. When they divorce, they do so thanks to law firms with branches in New York, Los Angeles, Beijing, and Doha. When they wish to shop, they go online and purchase goods whose origins are as complicated as their own lives. When they wish to visit their parents, they get on planes and change time zones. My wife, child, and Pomeranian dog live and work in Cape Town, South Africa, while I teach in Ann Arbor, Michigan. This book has partly been written on planes.

This is not merely true of the middle classes but the poor and disenfranchised, whose families may be split between Syria and Norway, Guatemala and the United States thanks to ancient immigrant desire to improve one's life elsewhere, or the pressures that turn citizens into refugees.

Globalization has also significantly shifted the mode of production from manufacturing to service industries, healthcare, and investment banking, generating new kinds of wealth that are as profound as those of the gilded age when the mega-rich emerged in America thanks to railroads (Vanderbilt, Crocker), oil (Getty, Rockefeller), steel (Carnegie), real estate (Astor), and banking (Mellon). The emergence of wealth has been of the greatest importance for the history of the arts since it is these persons, and before them the Third Estate of Europe, the Medici of Florence, and Doges of Venice not to mention the Roman Popes, who were the ones who commissioned art for their villas, built the churches and palaces. In our time, new wealth is as liable to emerge in Russia, China, India, and Singapore as it is in Europe or America, leading to decentered art markets and a global system of art production.

The world has become more homogeneous thanks to globalization, with everyone wanting the same Nike sneakers and iPhones. But ours is also a world of conversation and politics around the recognition of diversity. This double condition of enhanced conformity and enhanced recognition of diversity should be pressed. As the world grows smaller thanks to new technologies, including relatively affordable jet travel, social media, and the like, two things happen. First, a kind of flattened English-speak takes over—call it the prose of neoliberalism. People across the world are forced to learn English—an English of declarative sentences, blogs, and tweets—draining the English language of vocabulary and grammatical complexity. Would that it were not so! But sadly, the subjunctive mood is much attenuated in use—and with it the daily recognition (since the subjunctive is the mood of uncertainty or possibility) of Socratic skepticism that is the better part of humane intelligence. Do not doubt, we declare. We declare in blogs, tweets, text messages, e-mails, on social media sites. Global English serves this aggressive politics of assertion. It is the language of making deals, asserting facts, or, equally, alternative facts (meaning propaganda). Such communication leaves little space for the recognition of the diversity of persons who are communicating across the globe nor, for the uncertainty, is it the better part of wisdom to bring to the understanding of diverse peoples: open ears rather than dominating bombast. The chapters on Cosmopolitanism (Chapters 6 and 7) are about this.

And yet, there is probably greater knowledge and interest in human diversity today than ever before in history. And greater recognition of its importance as a source of knowledge, a human reality requiring negotiation, a conundrum for politics. Persons across the globe experience the realities of globalization in profoundly different ways.[2] A worker in Bangladesh earning subsistence wages from a US or Chinese corporation or a factory associated with mega-production has a quite different view of globalization than the person who buys a shirt in a mall, happily at a discount. With inequality spiraling, virulent nationalism raising its ugly face, and automation rusting the manufacturing sectors of the United States, leaving people out of jobs and stranded, many people find globalization disastrous. In its search for cheap labor, globalization picks up new people then discards them when conditions become unstable or a cheaper yet efficient workforce is found. A consequence of the disenfranchisement of the working class is the politics of resentment, and, with it, the return of nationalism, sometimes racist, anti-immigrant, seeking national pride through closure of the global, something about as easy to do as to stop breathing.

And so, the mixed sword of globalization leads to economic growth in parts of the world that have never seen it while abandoning others in search of cheap labor elsewhere or for political reasons, disenfranchising those who have only just emerged from centuries of impoverishment. It leads to not only enhanced human recognition but also greater exploitation and nationalist contempt of those in distant parts of the world.

Globalization has in certain respects vitalized art markets, which are on the rise in many parts of the world. With their rise, access and opportunity for formerly marginalized parts of the globe are expanded. Art markets (and this will be explored in Chapter 2) continually seek new products and search the globe for them. This leads to enhanced inclusivity, which is a good thing. It also leads to problems of branding, homogeneity, and voice, which we will turn to in that chapter. As the super-rich seek liquid capital, flipping it for quick profit in a rising market, or hanging on to it as investment, often in some tax-free region of the world, prices soar, galleries open, entire markets arise in places in the world where they would have been unimaginable forty years ago. These markets are linked in an endless system of biennales and art fairs through global auction houses and museum acquisitions.

And yet a great deal of the world suffers what I would like to call market insufficiency in their cultural markets (again the topic of the next chapter). Insufficiency means an excess of supply (artists) over infrastructure (galleries, museums, print media), human capital (critics, art dealers), and consumers (museums, collectors). This is the condition of supply trumping not only demand but also the capacity of local markets to acquire and circulate "goods" (artwork). It forces art in the direction of disembodied, global markets and consumers, in a way that can mitigate the power of art to bespeak local place and people who disappear from its radar screen thanks to the global buyer. This continues a cycle of inequality framed in the days of colonialism, about which this book will have a great deal to say. These conditions were extraction of goods and claiming of cultural objects from the colonies to the nations of the colonizers, thus enriching European and American resources at the expense of native resources. This colonial fault line has been retained in globalization where resource-poor places end up contributing to first-world markets in a way that continues to drain culture as well as raw materials from former colonies to well-resourced nations. Added to the mix is often a lack of state funding for art and culture in resource-middling or poor nations. (This will be taken up in Chapter 2.)

A Very Brief History of Globalization

European globalization predates the late twentieth century by nearly a millennium. In 1260, Marco Polo, the first to write about his travels (although not the first Venetian to reach Asia by ship), set sail for the Orient from Venice, that sea-fearing colloquy of tiny islands connected by bridges that was for a thousand years an empire whose ships ruled the Mediterranean. Marco Polo reached China and remained for twenty-four years, writing (while imprisoned thereafter in Genoa) of a wealth of spices, silks, and treasures that Europe has never seen before, nor even dreamed. His father and uncle had already established trading relations with Asia. Without these initial gestures of globalization, Europe would have had no corn, potato, or tomato, and practically no spices. Salt was so rare in Europe that it was said a man was "worth his salt," meaning *worthy* of it. Marco Polo visited the Silk Road, already a long-standing form of Chinese globalization, for China invented globalization, along with firecrackers and social philosophy well before Europe. This vast trading route stretched from China through the deserts of the Indian subcontinent into what is now Afghanistan and Iran, and then into the Middle East, and along it goods were bartered, traded, and transported.

Venice was the first explorer of the seas, but in the fifteenth century the ships of Spain, Portugal, and Genoa began their transatlantic voyages with the goal of reaching China by sea. Columbus famously thought he'd arrived there when his three ships bumped into what is now Santo Domingo, and so accidentally discovered the Americas. Later, in 1612, the English landed at what would become Jamestown, Virginia, with the hope of navigating a land route across the continent of North America to China. They had, of course, no idea of the size of the landmass onto which they'd secured their toehold.

A few years before Columbus, the Portuguese sailor Bartolomeu Diaz steered his ship down the West Coast of Africa with the intention of finding a route around that continent toward the East. He was the first European to discover the tip of Africa, or what would be called the Cape of Good Hope, although he named it Cape of Storms because of the fierce tides that would over time wreck many a sailing ship. His discovery (which was likely predated in ancient times by the Phoenicians and others) proved that there could be a way to get to Asia around Africa, something soon thereafter accomplished by Vasco da Gama who in 1497–9 managed to reach India by sailing around the African continent.

Thus, the great game of mercantile capitalism arose in early modern Europe, the seeking of trade routes by sailing ship. Over time, this led to the settling of foreign lands, the domination of native populations, and the extraction of goods to be sent back to Europe. Colonialism took hold in the ensuing centuries: the expansion of empire, the conquest of the world. The Dutch East India Company laid claim to the Indian subcontinent until it reverted to British hands and became their jewel in the crown, the Dutch established the Cape Colony and a stronghold over what is now Indonesia, Spain settled Latin America, the French West Africa and Indo-China, the Germans South-West Africa and parts of what is now Kenya, and on it went. By the eighteenth century, much of the world was in the hands of European powers. The ongoing scramble for every inch of unclaimed territory would last until the First World War, with Africa being the last and perhaps most vicious point of contest between European powers.

Emblematic of the scramble for Africa in the nineteenth century was the rush to find the source of the Nile, something that had captivated Europe since Roman times. The longest river in the world, the Nile's source was believed by the ancient astronomer Ptolemy to originate in a place called "the mountains of the moon." To find this place, clouded in obscurity and drenched in fantasy, would mean, Europe believed, to discover and tame even the most impenetrable corners of the earth. Drawn by the prospect of a trade route that would allow for the extraction of goods from "deepest darkest Africa" straight to the Mediterranean Sea courtesy of this river, English, French, and other expeditions set off into the southern African interior, usually from Zanzibar: the center of the slave trade.

And this is another reason why Europe, and especially England, wanted to find this river's source. For a missionary like David Livingstone who died in the search for it along with his wife, slavery was a scourge. Livingstone believed that by finding the source of the Nile he could clear the "dark continent" of those slave routes still very much in place in the mid- to late nineteenth century, slave routes that led from the Southern African interior through Zanzibar to the Middle East and were controlled by Arab traders with the help of local African chiefs. Slogging through the underbrush, wretched with disease, prey to the arrows of local tribes, knee-deep in mud: this suffering was for Livingstone the work of redemption. It was not for all, and the bandwagon of explorers included swashbucklers, weirdos, macho freaks, men wishing to chart the limits of geography, men funded by the newspapers, the explorer's clubs, the governments, the philanders, and robbers.

As it happened, the finding of the Nile's source was no easy matter. For while this river begins in Lake Victoria, it then meanders into Lake Albert before continuing up the continent until it, the White Nile, merges with the Blue Nile at Omdurman in the Sudan and then flows upward to the Mediterranean Sea. Livingstone, whom John Morton Stanley found at Lake Tanganyika, got it wrong, confusing the Lualaba River with the Nile, until he realized the Lualaba flowed into Lake Congo.

Stanley was the one who confirmed the Nile's correct source, something that had earlier been discovered, without being proved, by the explorer John Hanning Speke, who after all the labor of his discovery seems to have accidentally shot himself while climbing over a fence at his English property, where he promptly died.

Europe and America were so fascinated by these expeditions that in 1874 Stanley was commissioned by two newspapers, the *New York Herald* and the *Daily Telegraph*, to find Livingstone. Stanley sent dispatches to these New York and London papers from various African locations as he made his way toward Livingstone and his dispatches made for whopping good reading, being highly inflated in factual value for the benefit of his readers. In the course of this he became an international celebrity: people bought the newspapers simply to read the next installment of his fabulous (in every sense of the word) story. *He* was the news. Stanley's famous "Dr. Livingstone I presume" was a perfect instance of his bending fact to suit the demands of British rag journalism. His readers found the remark unforgettable. The newspapers expanded their circulation.

Colonialism hit its apogee in the eighteenth and nineteenth centuries at exactly the moment Europe was evolving into the modern system of nation-states and this is crucial for this book's story. The rise of the European nation-state began with the Treaty of Westphalia in 1648, which ended Europe's disastrous wars of religion between Catholics and Protestants. What had been a continent organized along conflicted religious lines would now become one defined by national borders. The treaty set the terms of national sovereignty, making what happens within each nation entirely its own affairs, a refusal of international intervention that would remain in place until the end of the Second World War. Until the Treaty of Westphalia, England was split between Protestant and Catholic, and at various moments could have become an adjunct of France or Spain, as Scotland veered between independence and British vassal-dom. Now the nation-state was by virtue of international law (treaty) absolutely sovereign. With this shift to internal sovereignty, the modern European nation-state needed to find new ways for diverse and antagonistic populations to imagine themselves as *belonging*. Since religion could not serve as the basis for national unity, that is, the sense of nationalism, new forms of belonging needed to be created. As Benedict Anderson famously put it in *Imagined Communities*,³ the work of nationalism was the creation of newly minted "imagined communities" whereby partisan allegiances would be replaced, or at least bettered, by a new sense on the part of citizens of being part of a national community most of whose members would never meet or know one another but who all were meant to feel in solidarity.

The focus of nationalism became one of linguistic unity (the English-speaking people, the French), of race (to the point where each nation began to think of itself as its own unique race with "English" or "French" blood), of culture, and also of the modern instrument of heritage, invented for the purpose of nationalism and nation building. The institutions of the nation; its courts of law, religious churches, and shrines; its universities and museums all became the guardians of the nation's traditions, social practices, and moral codes, a past now understood as the inheritance and binding force of the nation, its claim to power, prominence, and glory.

A word on heritage—that crucial instrument of the nation-state. The modern idea and practice of heritage have two parts. First, the past comes to be understood as the legacy from which the new nation arises, giving it a myth of historical longevity and, if you will, destiny, as if all prenational history conspired to produce it. Nothing is more flexible than the past when the present comes to reinvent it for its own purposes. As the philosopher Friedrich Nietzsche said, the past is written by the present and for it.⁴

The heritage turn of the modern nation-state rewrites the past as its cultural capital and as its origin.

On the idea of cultural capital: The past becomes understood as a national *bank* of values that unify and exalt the nation. The past becomes a currency of values built up over time and held in trust for the nation's future. "In God We Trust" becomes synonymous with "In the Nation We Trust," because the nation has a moral value that is worthy of secular religion. In their ritual and religion, museums, courts of law, poetry and politics, ideals, sciences, and liberal arts, in their civilized ways and god-fearing decency the citizens of the nation inherit these values, are bound together by them, and will march into the future on account of them. For he is an Englishman, yes, he is an Englishman, Gilbert and Sullivan incant, meaning there is rock solid decency, stability, and futurity in this particular "race." Gilbert and Sullivan are ironic, but they are making theatre out of an attitude central to Victorianism, which is the attitude of the nation as founded on platinum-grade heritage.

But heritage as it begins to be thought in the nineteenth century also has a second significance for the nation. This begins in discontent with the detritus of modernity: the grime, the factories, the disenfranchised, utilitarian, mercantile society, the furious rate of industrialization, occluding nature, that society lambasted by Marx and Engels as the worst ever for the "proletariat." As a lament against what modern Europe (modernity) has become, Romanticism preaches return: Modern life had lost sight of its true origins; it has lost its way. Foundering in the desert, unaware that it lacked a road map or destination, modern society required reminding of what it really was and where it had gone wrong. This turn to origins/deepest values became the stern stuff of moralizing. Only the return to and appropriation of a people's virtues and ideals would set the people again on the right historical road, supply them their destination: their destiny. This return inevitably lands Europe in Ancient Greece, which for the nineteenth-century Romantic represents the Golden Age whose noble ideals and high-minded culture and character need to be interpolated back into the present in order to renew it.

Both Matthew Arnold and Friedrich Nietzsche believed the origin of what is best in their nations was to be found in Ancient Greece, along with many others. Ancient Greek heritage has been lost, demanding to be found again and reinscribed in modern life. This idea that the true origin of the modern European nation is in the ideals of Ancient Greece has another, further implication. By finding again the source of all that is good in European heritage Europe will find again its true destiny—the destiny to live in accordance with the lessons of the past.

Nationalism and the heritage that is meant to catalyze it have always been fraught with difficulty. Every nation is at war between competing national narratives, some of which are highly virulent and aim to marginalize or exclude whole sectors of the population in the name of adulating others. Minorities, the poor, women, immigrants, blacks, Jews, nowadays Muslims, those people suffer under the yoke of violent nationalism, which periodically impels populations to burn houses, murder civilians, and push groups into exile. At worst is extermination. The very words "American," "French," "British," and other national titles quickly become badges of honor justifying brutality in the name of the nation-state. National heritage creation, aiming to create citizens who identify with being members of the relevant national tribe, is therefore a matter of sometimes brutal and racist cultural politics.

There is one heritage instrument of special importance for this book, namely the museum. The museum is an artifact of the eighteenth century and the rise of nations. There was no public museum, not even the *idea* of such a public institution, until the nation-state came into being, demanding it. Until the Treaty of Westphalia and the rise of nations, collections of art and culture were housed either in religious institutions (churches) or in the palaces of the royals. The museum is a bourgeois creation, open to the (usually paying) public, where art and culture are exhibited as a proclamation of national power and patrimony. The museum is a symbol of the nation's empire and authority, of its wealth and grandeur. In its halls are the accretions of conquest and capital.

The museum was a repository of secular religion, celebrating the patrimony of empire, proclaiming the glory of France, England, Habsburg Vienna, Russia. Much of the stuff in the museum was stolen from elsewhere, making the museum an institution that could only have arisen in tandem with colonialism. Napoleon arrived in Egypt to bring back the obelisk for the glory of France, Elgin the marbles of Greece, where through a feat of national imagination/prestidigitation these suddenly became "French" or "English," that is, the property of the European nation and a symbol of its lordship, prestige, and authority. As objects were removed across the globe from their original sites, their social meanings and purposes did not transfer. Europe was not interested in the role of objects in native culture, and certainly did not consider this relevant to their aura or fascination. And so, these objects grabbed and collected from around the globe and exhibited in the rarefied halls of the museum became mute, mere "sights" for the rapt contemplation of the viewer.

The museum was the conduit for this process and arose at the intersection of colonial empire and nationalism. England created the British Museum in 1753; France opened the Louvre, formerly a fortress and then palace, as a museum in 1793; Russia opened the Hermitage Museum of St. Petersburg founded by Catherine the Great in 1764.

The museum demonstrated to its citizens that the global world was *the European world*: that Europe authorized and curated the goods of the world as its own patrimony, that it *owned* the world, owned its culture and claimed sovereignty over global politics. These things demonstrated the glory of the nation to its citizens. The importance of the museum for this book's story is that as an institution it played a central role in articulating practices of *aesthetics*. By this I mean the practice of contemplation predicated on *disinterest* in the meaning of the work of art contemplated and instead foregrounding the viewer's imagination and pleasure. In this way, the museum was part of a larger movement in the eighteenth century to treat art and, with it, nature, as an object of abstract contemplation apart from meaning or social purpose, as an experience *in and for itself*, as that century liked to put it. This new way of treating art was theorized by that century with a new term and that term was "taste." The theory of taste was what the eighteenth century created when it created the discipline of *aesthetics*. We shall return to it at the end of the book.

First, we explore the contemporary art world and the conditions it imposes on the making of art.

2

The Global Art World Today: Prospects and Problems

In this chapter, I will try to limn some of the basic conditions of the art of our time and think about how these conditions variously affect the production, circulation, and nature of art. These are not eternal conditions, they are of the *now*. As times change the kind and character of art also changes, along with the kind of aesthetic principles foregrounded. I am foregrounding here not only the intersection between art markets, stylistic choices, and how art today "makes a statement," to use the words of the great aesthetician of the second half of the twentieth century: Arthur Danto,[1] but also how a globalized art market offers special opportunities and puts special pressures on places in the world that remain in an underresourced state. This thanks in part to legacies of colonialism and global inequality between north and south.

Let us begin with the way globalization has changed the conditions under which art is made and circulated. This material returns to some of the things discussed in the previous chapter.

I have seven points to make:

1. Globalization has led to the decentering of art markets from their former concentration in Europe and America. Art markets now extend across the globe, from the Biennale

in Sao Paolo to the gallery in Shanghai, from the museum is Oslo to the art foundation in Cape Town. They are highly decentered, with robust markets centered around India, others in China, across Europe, in Russia, in the United States, Brazil, and so on. My cousin who is a director of a major gallery in New York City is literally never off planes. One week he is at Art Basel Miami, the next at Art Basel, Basel, the week following in Beijing where the city's designated art area, 733, is a full square mile of galleries and studios. Pace Gallery there has forty thousand square feet of gallery space and is chock-full of art exhibited and marketed. Collectors now approach art as a form of liquid capital, easily hidden from the taxman, and so stashed in Swiss vaults and the back rooms of Panamanian law firms. Art collections sometimes reside on different continents from those who own them.

2. This decentering of art markets has led to enhanced access and circulation for formerly marginalized places across the "global south," which is a good thing. It has also led to stylistic branding and homogenization thanks to the flattening of real cultural differences into more saleable product differences by international markets. International styles proliferate. Everyone from Cape Town to Algeria to Vancouver makes performance photography, in which the trope is the presence of the photographer or a proxy who appears from one photo to the next in the manner of a motif. Everyone installs, creating rooms from video, projected language (usually polemical), ambient sound, a sculpture or two, and various items on walls. Some of this work is stunning, some routine, the point being that international legitimacy is sought through the taking on of these branded forms. There is considerable similarity with the manufacturing sector, where running shoes are now a universal brand, which have been expanded from sport to hip-hop urban hangout and luxury wear. Automobiles, once the purview of the individualizing automaker, now resemble each other to the point of indistinguishability.

Film shares with manufacturing the condition of what David Harvey calls "flexible capitalism," with productions being financed, shot, edited, and distributed through alliances between production companies in Hollywood, the UK, France, China, and other countries. And film, at least in its American production, has reduced to two categories. First the mega-blockbuster that costs upward of two hundred million dollars and relies extensively on CGS (digital simulation and special effects), usually containing huge amounts of violence and following more or less the same plot (e.g., a young woman in the FBI fighting terrorism while sinking into her own overwrought mind and fighting with colleagues as drones take out terrorists in a Middle Eastern location). Versus second, the independent film that costs less than 5 million dollars to make and comes into being thanks to actors cutting their fees and often raising money for the production because they are desperate to appear in movies of quality rather than schlock mostly created for the Chinese market.

3. Central to the globalized art market is its continual search for *new product*, product with sufficient difference from what has come before to allow for the sense of innovation and give buyers a reason to buy more when they already have more than enough. New product must announce itself as new while remaining close enough to preexistent brands so as to fit the market, allowing for easy "recognition" and therefore salability.

The current darling of the international art market is contemporary African art. Formerly considered of museological or anthropological interest, according to which modern African art was judged in accord with tradition, craft, or as second-rate imitation of Western modernism, African art is now a hot commodity. A lot of this art is vibrant, creative, and sourced to deep cultural and visual roots. And this also sometimes matters for the consumer who wants to acknowledge their own interest in the wider world by reaching out to new cultural objects and encountering new and distant continents while perhaps also enhancing monetary value by getting in early on a new product that will, it is hoped, only increase in price. This is like the person who takes the risk of investing in real estate in those parts of the city that are currently underdeveloped or dilapidated. Markets run on calculated risk: too much risk, and trust is lost, leading to collapse; too little and the market fails to expand. And so new art is essential to international markets, which is what my grandmother would have called "another country heard from" in her broken English.

4. Globalization has also led to a *basic problem of voice*. To whom is an artist talking to when they make work that sits uneasily between an abstracted global consumer and the demands of local acknowledgment? It takes luck—being in the right place at the right time—and genius to pull off a reconciliation or resolution of these tensions, as Salman Rushdie managed with *Midnight's Children*, a novel of the Indian partition that both reveled in Indian linguistic patois (especially from the Bombay high rises he knows well) and spoke to an international audience by fusing the comic British novel with the American Jewish writer's capacity to write between registers of language (Shakespeare and Yiddish schtick) in single, fabulous sentences. And with the Latin American magic realist form.

Or William Kentridge, whose work brings a poetry of mourning, memory, violence, and ambivalent longing for (his) Johannesburg past to completely original fusions of drawing (at which he is so good as to compare with Michelangelo) with film, theatre, dance, and a variety of African processional forms. Kentridge's sense of theatre is joyous and somber at once, in the way black South African funeral or political demonstrations can become an occasion for singing and dancing, as well as fear and mourning.

Kentridge is worth spending some time on, to see how successfully he fuses avant-garde and modernist style with film, drawing, and theatre in ever innovative ways. And this is a feat, considering that the problem with fame is that one is in demand everywhere, making it almost impossible to keep up, thereby causing even the best artists to repeat themselves, homogenizing their work into a "brand" in the way that starchitects create signature buildings that the world then wants endlessly repeated, each resembling the one before so the consumer can say: I too own a building by so and so. Kentridge has astonishingly managed to avoid this, he is protean. But he shows how hard it is to do it.

The work of William Kentridge began as painting, in a German expressionist figurative mode with emphasis on the intensity of drawing. In the early 1980s, he left South Africa to attend L'École Internationale de Théâtre Jacques Lecoq in Paris, with the intention of becoming an actor. Upon return to South Africa, he began to toy with a new form of film that would arise from drawing, which led to a series of masterpieces created during the early days of the South African democratic transition from the repressive and racist Apartheid state to the current dispensation: the early and mid-1990s. The films represented an ongoing drama, if not battle, between two characters, Soho Eckstein, a mineowner/capitalist boss with a central European/Jewish background, and Felix, the beautiful soul who adores and steals his wife. The films are set in the old days of Johannesburg rogue capitalism in the first decades of the twentieth century, when "randlords" could own the mines and rule the city like bosses of old, and when racial capitalism depended on the exploitation of black miners, who threaded their hushed way throughout his films.

The films are built up from drawing and variation, in the manner of animated Disney features of old like *Fantasia*, whose every frame was meticulously painted. Since there are twenty-four frames per second in a normally paced film, it means that twenty-four paintings were required for a single second of film. The key is, of course, to sync the frames so that each painting follows the next in a way that leads to continuous motion for the viewer, no easy task. For Kentridge the problem became one of drawing. Working at an enormous easel, he drew a frame, then rubbed it out and varied it, so as to yield a silent film generated by the micro-changes in the drawing, allowing figures to move frame to frame and narrative action to take place. In his case the rubbing of each image left a residue of opacity to the succeeding frame, since a rubbed drawing is a somewhat vague one. And in this visual opacity seemed to reside the aura of the past, the strange opacity of memory, remembrance, the haunted nature of things gone before and remaining in the mind. At the moment of democratic transition, Kentridge's work not only bespoke narratives of the old days of big capital and racial exploitation but also resonated with mourning, nostalgia, and the suffusion of memory. This came from the technique of film created through drawing.

Equally important is Kentridge's use of montage, of cutting between moments in time, space, and narrative that suddenly shift perspective, seeming to still time and narrative into tableaux. There is a love of old technology in his work, of silent film with its simplicity of message, its profound lighting, its love of human physiognomy and landscape.

Among his most powerful works of that time was *Felix in Exile* (1993–4), about the same Felix from his Soho Series, a character physically modeled on Kentridge himself (see Figure 1). Felix is confined in a safe house, somewhere in exile. He longs for his lover, a black woman (Felix is white, making their relationship an Apartheid crime), literally drawing her into proximity, while (although the sense of time is obscure) she probably already lies dead, a death shown at the end of the short film, the woman abandoned to an empty, haunted landscape of discard, covered in newspapers.

Since that time Kentridge has turned to theatre, to the construction of glass and wood objects resonant with the Russian avant-gardes and their abstract sculpture, to a montage of images layered onto newspaper clippings (resonant of Picasso's collage and Russian lithography), to opera design, theatre with puppets, and more recently the fusion of drawing, film, theatre, dance, and music in parades of history with African township jazz, of vibrancy and lamentation. These large theatrical projections dance even at the moment of suffering, with the panoply of South African history in all its dispossession. His cast of players include the sick, the corrupt, the politicians, the fierce comrades, the joyous children, the dying, the mourned, and the invisible, all of which he makes visible. And so Kentridge manages to speak a distinctly South African language while making art in accord with the principle of multimedia avant-garde invention internationally a norm today. And to do it in a way no one else can pull off. When commissioned by the city of Rome to create a huge installation along the walls of the city fronting the Tiber river, Kentridge created a parade of such forms, projected from a boat in the middle of the river, as if shining a light on the city from within, and in a way that fuses the ancient story of Rome with, as ever, South Africa.

FIGURE 1 William Kentridge, Felix in Exile, 1993–4.
Color video, transferred from 35 mm film, with sound, 8 min., 43-second edition 7/10. Dimensions variable. Purchased with funds contributed by The Peter Norton Family Foundation. Courtesy of The Solomon R. Guggenheim Foundation / Art Resource, NY.

Geniuses like Kentridge are few, and everyone wants a piece of them. They are the success stories of negotiating the conundrum of voice (to whom is one speaking, and of what, a local audience, national, international, embodied, disembodied, market driven, for experts, for the populace at large?): the condition of aesthetics in our time. This shows how hard it is to really succeed today, given the contradictory tensions impelling art and its markets. And to stay creative, since given the success everyone wants a piece of you.

For most others there is a constant and unresolved tension between the demands of locality and of international style, an uncertainty as to whether one is creating for a local community or a disembodied consumer.

This tension is, I venture to say, an existential condition especially for young people who are more promptly and thoroughly globalized than my generation and think nothing about spending a year working crops in Guatemala followed by a summer in Turkey, study abroad in Canada, and perhaps relocation for some years. I think it is fair to say young people of this kind are less tied to nation and locality and more to the globe. For these persons the issue of voice is caught up with the issue of identity: where and to what do I belong, to my country, to the world of art, to the global market, to what is happening on the internet, where is my home?

There is no single way of resolving this. It is an existential question for each individual.

5. According to the art critic and theorist Rosalind Krauss, the past half-century has favored multimedia artistic creation over the earlier modernist ideal of the purity and purification of the single medium. Kentridge's work is a perfect example. Krauss formulated this idea in the 1970s, when some of the best art was already being produced in multimedia formats.[2] This is indeed a legacy of the avant-gardes in the first half of the twentieth century, when, for example, the Bauhaus fashioned itself as a laboratory for creating the new, working across architecture, interior design, furniture design, tapestry, craft, theatre, painting, mounting multimedia shows featuring all elements.

Multimedia art today tends to work between digital and plastic formats, with not only video, internet, or projection but also drawing, painting, and photography. It tends to fuse multiple and diverse styles. Its statements (about politics, race, culture, whatever) tend to arise from the interplay of these media types and globally synergized forms. The juxtaposition between media bespeaks an unresolved tension at the heart of life, an inability to dissolve differences into a single framework, and rather to make their tension productive of new kinds of form and meaning. Alternately it celebrates diversity, synergy between media and styles, and simultaneity (we live simultaneously in real and digital worlds, sometimes in transit, with globally extended daily communications, and in a world where style, product, and culture are created from a global domain).

Multimedia art can be traced to the avant-gardes. The avant-gardes dedicated themselves to two kinds of experimentation: first with *new* media explored as singular items—abstract painting, new architecture, film, photography, new musical instruments, and sounds; second with multimedia forms. The goal of both forms of experimentation with the new was to generate a sense of forward thrust in the history of art, as if history were grasping the contradictory forces and/or new technologies inherent in its fabric and urging them forward with art in its forward flank (the avant-garde is originally a military term for those on the front lines, leading the troops). The eruption or clash that came with expanded uses of new media, or between one medium and another, was meant to defamiliarize the viewer from his or her complacent, habitualized, and unconscious ways of seeing and knowing the world, to whisk the viewer away from their comfort zone so that the most ordinary things, a building, a woman sitting on a bench, a day in the life of a city, could be reframed not only as strange, distant, anthropological, unfamiliar, but also fresh and magical, as if reality, the most ordinary reality were suddenly encountered for the first time. The key was to make the viewer's perspective opaque, demanding reflection by that viewer about where they stand in relation to the world they now see so differently. This reflection was meant to sharpen, and free perception and knowledge from its encrustations and cause the viewer to realize they are capable of reframing their world in new and magical ways, ways that seem to make that world into a process of *becoming*. And with the right prompting, this recognition was meant to be revolutionary: the viewer would now become aware that the world is capable of being known and constructed afresh in some radically new way, and the viewer, through a process of self-reflection, was part of that process.

This was a tall order. Not easily accomplished.

To take an example: Alexander Rodchenko, a photographer associated with the revolutionary constructivist movement in the Russia of the revolutionary 1920s, would photograph an ordinary building from a nearly inscrutable visual angle of such shock and beauty that the viewer of his photo finds their perception of what should have been a totally ordinary scene disrupted. A high-rise building is shot upward from between the vertical fire escape and the building's side with a man curled on the ladder. One cannot easily tell on which side of the ladder the figure is located, because the man twists through both sides.

Or he would photograph a woman at the telephone from an angle above the woman and tilted toward her, positioning her against the edge of a wall so that she appears lopsided and foreshortened, while the wooden floor on which she stands seems to be tilted on a downward slope as if she will slide off it, against all logic (see Figure 2). And so, what the mind knows about the scene (that the floor is not tilted, the woman is not sliding down it) clashes with what the eye says, causing a disruption of consciousness around even such an ordinary scene.

These photos were meant to enthrall the viewer, disorient the viewer, and uplift the viewer with the feeling the ordinary world is, seen otherwise, from a new perspective, vibrantly strange. The work of working out perspective was meant to sharpen the viewer's senses. And the larger point in that was to expand the viewer's capacity to think otherwise, by experiencing a kind of contradiction between eye and mind demanding resolution. The work of resolution was meant to teach the viewer a lesson of history: that quotidian reality can and must be known differently, that one's very relation to the world can and must be inhabited, differently.

The constructivist movement dedicated itself to the creation of art that foregrounded incomplete process, as if we should wake up to the fact that we are in the middle of a great historical battle, which was the political message.[3]

The avant-garde work sought to be a beacon of change in a time of ashes: the ashes of the First World War when everything wonderful about Europe, its national treaties, its science, its technology, its population growth, had led to mustard gas, bombs, trench warfare,

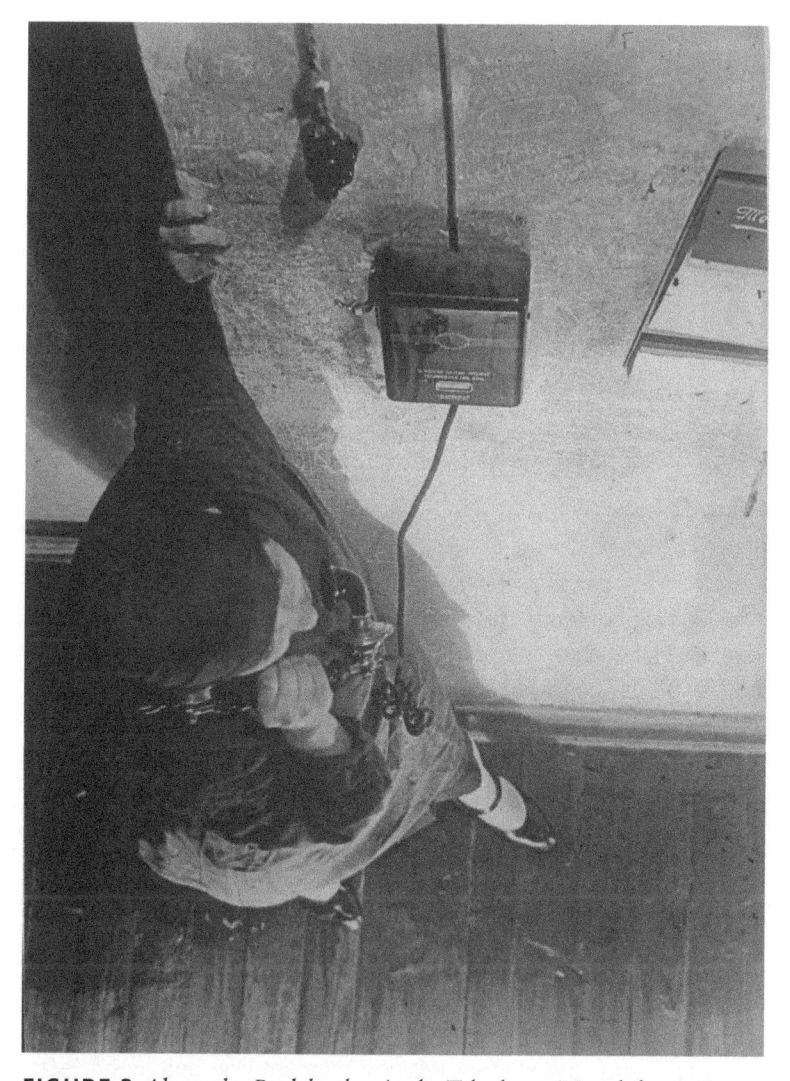

FIGURE 2 Alexander Rodchenko, At the Telephone {Na telefone}. *From a series on the production of a newspaper. 1928.*
Gelatin-silver print, 15 1/2 × 11 1/2". Mr. and Mrs. John Spencer Fund. (56.1970). Location: The Museum of Modern Art, New York, NY, USA. Courtesy VAGA, NY.

and the deaths of millions of young soldiers. At that moment in the twentieth century radical social and economic change was believed possible. The avant-gardes took their project to be that of awakening of the population to the possibility that the world could become something radically different, to the urgency of bringing this about. The experimental turn both toward new media and toward *multimedia art* arose in this context of urgency. It was about not only revitalizing art, but also revitalizing history.

6. And so multimedia art was linked from the first to notions of making art political, that is, vesting it with a political voice. And related, providing a wake-up call to the audience.

The paradox for the avant-gardes was although they despised the bourgeois culture of the museums, collectors, and art markets, that is where they mostly ended up. Their fantasies of designing the future of the world and existing for the masses were undercut by the very experimental character of their work, which was simply too difficult for much of the population to grasp, and barely tolerated by governments. Lenin left the constructivists alone but their buildings were rarely built and they were merely tolerated, not embraced. Ironically the only national leader to embrace the avant-gardes was Mussolini, who believed Italian futurist art reflected his own political aspirations.

After the Second World War the idea of radical social and economic change (on the right or the left) began to weaken as the terror of totalitarianism states on the right and the left could not be swept under the rug. By the 1980s multimedia art turned from utopian politics to *identity politics*, to the politics of recognition and representation, for its political aspirations, in the light of the women's movement, black consciousness, the student left, the Vietnam War and its protests, gay rights politics, and in general the rise in America especially of what is called identity politics. Artists like Cindy Sherman began to fuse performance and photography in a series of film stills. Her series of works mimicked the way Hollywood films, magazine images (this was before the internet), and the image-driven culture of the day stereotyped women. With astonishing sense of *mise-en-scène* she created an entire fictional world of female characters in various poses, all (at that time) in black and white, all featuring herself. There was the young ingenue arriving in the big city, the bad girl from high school, the narcissistic poetess in her salon, smoking a cigarette and being fawned upon, the New Jersey housewife with her shopping thrown or dropped to the ground as her tough of a husband fought with her. Sherman's was a world not only of passive-aggressive women, sneaky men, but also librarians wearing glasses, and women reading while glancing around the bookstore for available men, which was meant to be their real purpose in life. It was a world of young wives or girlfriends, their groceries dropped by the kitchen sink—perhaps because they were assaulted, perhaps out of anger—whose sullen stares at invisible boyfriends, clearly up to no good, recall something between film noir and the New Jersey suburbs (see Figure 3).

If you ask why Cindy Sherman was always there in the photo, as opposed to a proxy or model, the answer would have to be: because

FIGURE 3 *Cindy Sherman*, Untitled Film Still #84, *1978. Gelatin silver print, 8 × 10 inches, (MP# CS–84). Courtesy of the Artist and Metro Pictures, New York.*

I am trying to show that there is no "I" to me when it comes to gender, I am as my roles define me, a fractured series of stereotypes thanks to the media and the male-centered character of American society. And so, the multimedia nature of her work, blending the performance of roles with photography and film, was central to the representational politics of the work.

7. The problematic for art with political aspirations today is two-fold. First to escape the branding, the marketing, the advertising so central to everything from universities to political life, and that dampens the intensity of truth-telling. To bypass these market-driven limitations, limitations that are also part and parcel of the media with its daily drenching of the world in images of disaster cut between commercial breaks. The second problem for political art is to break out of the encomium of the art world that restricts its circulation of work to art world types. To speak to a broader audience beyond the cognoscenti and the converted. These problems, intensity of voice and domain and range of circulation, are very difficult to overcome. One could call them two of the great problems for contemporary culture.

Breakout has in fact been a long-standing problem for art, although the terms of the problem have changed. The avant-gardes wished to break out of the confines of the art world—that circuit of gallery, museum, collector, critic, scholar—to intervene in the world more directly, and with more impact, raising the consciousness of the masses, building the cities of the future. As I said, they mostly failed at this, thanks largely to their hermetic, experimental character which large percentages of the population have failed to understand, disliked, or happily ignored.

Now the idea is not to turn art into a weapon, but a form of address that can reach a broader audience, and a highly jaded one, an audience accustomed to branding and marketing, overwhelmed by a surfeit of images, and highly consumerist.

To see how hard it is to do this, consider the Australian artist and film-maker George Gittoes, winner of the Sydney Peace Prize in 2015 and what he does to achieve even, I think some measure of political voice through his art. His achievement raises by contrast the larger question of the hermetic confines of the art world (in spite of its open texture as a market), of its representational distance from the direct events of the world, of the way it displaces politics, even as it might seek sometimes to acknowledge and engage politics. His trajectory is highly instructive.

Gittoes' art is remarkable because it makes human rights violations palpable to the imagination in a world where their combination of distance and excessive circulation threatens them with constant devaluation. Things that happen a half a world away—whether on the borders of Europe or in the heart of Africa—are things of blunted power, especially when they flood the television in daily fifteen-second visual/sound bites to the point where we hardly notice them (today's torture or bomb wedged between Chevy commercials and Reality TV programs). Susan Sontag warned us twenty years ago that photography has the effect of dampening the force of even the most overwhelming images because of their endlessly repetitive circulation in human societies.[4] Perhaps this archive fever[5] is datable to the stark images from Bergen-Belsen of emaciated, wraith-like human ghosts, but fifty years of overaccumulation of images of horror have turned them into a virtual department store of banalities. It is for this reason that Claude Lanzmann, filming *Shoah*, refused to use any extant photographs of the Holocaust and relied instead on nothing beyond record, survivor, witness, site, and an obsessively theatrical repetition of trains, gates, and stories, thus forcing the viewer to enter into an event whose unyielding power must remain perpetually beyond comprehension. To overcome the deadening effects of images, one must invent an idiom.

Over the course of a long career Gittoes has worked in Afghanistan, Gaza, Chechnya, Rwanda, Somalia, Bosnia, Iraq, South Africa (where I first met him while teaching at a South African university in the late 1990s), and many other places. He sometimes travels with peacekeeping forces or nongovernmental organizations to insure access to disturbational areas of the world. Mostly for the past twenty years he has traveled and worked alone. He is often in real danger. The map of global suffering has been his terrain. Gittoes draws at the scene of devastation, scribbling notes and taking photographs, which he then brings back to his studio in Australia. There he makes huge, staggered oil or acrylic canvases from these materials, exhibiting the entire process. His work thus moves from the position of on-site witness to that of artist-in-studio, and it is only because he starts from the position of witness that the power of his art can unfold as it does. For it presents the viewer with a way of grasping the formless, contingent power of events at their horrifying sources, and retaining that in all that follows. Since the traces of immediacy are retained in his paintings, the work undercuts the comfort zone of autonomous studio productions to shock us, enveloping with something of the immediacy of suffering. We too become witnesses, confronting his victims as he does. So does the distant draw us near. There is a clarity about this that is astonishing, as well as a feat of talent, for anyone who has actually witnessed human trauma knows that it is nearly impossible to capture the power of what one has seen without giving into weak stereotype or formulaic emotion. Events literally fall apart when one tries to represent them.

It is this position of witness, of journalist as well as artist, that partly allows him to break through the comfort zones of the art world, in line with the best war correspondents and other journalists.

Drawing at the scene, speed is crucial. Artists of war must draw fast or paint fast—while the thing burns before the retina. They must commute it into drawing or painting before it turns to ash, fades into the haunting shadows of mourning, becoming spectral. And yet their finished product has to retain this sense of reactivity. It has to look *unfinished*, carry the framelessness of the event itself, of the terrible formlessness of that *now*, while also being finished, well-formed. Gittoes won't paint unless he saw what happened and recorded it, and by the way tried to help whenever possible. And this is crucial to the unique moral urgency of his project, to its combination of journalism and subjectivity, to its capacity to take over from television something of the circulation of information, that he always is there, making drawings right in front of the victims, wandering the aimless trajectory of refugee camps and military operations, scribbling on the sides of drawn pages notes about victim and circumstance.

Gittoes' drawings exist midway between the drawing and the *sketch*. They have the balance, complication, and refinement of drawing while retaining something of the quick, unfinished, spontaneity of the sketch. He executes them on the spot, right in front of the victims, the children in camps, the passersby. The people he draws often stare back at the artist as he works, talk to him, and this relationship of person to person becomes central to the drawing.

More amazing still is that an incessant quality of invention should pertain to each and every drawing. For this is above all what counts: the fact that each drawing seems *invented* on the spot, that no two should be "the same" or "repetitions of the type," as if the singularity of each person, each event, each horror should call for an attention achieved through the invention of a new variation on the idiom, or even a new idiom altogether. Gittoes never rests on the laurels of his style. And this is his way of marking each figure, each gross violation of human rights as a unique, irreducible event in history that happens to a special *someone* and not to a merely anonymous "victim" who quickly disappears into the homogenized vale of human suffering, into the namelessness of terrible things. Gittoes' way of keeping the power of each figure and what happened to them *alive* is to render each as freshly to human consciousness as each person is—or should be—to the world. This is called, from the moral point of view, respect.

A Tutsi preacher stands to recite the Bible, giving those around him an iota of dignity and solace as they are murdered by Hutu extremists during the horror of the Rwandan genocide in 1994 (see Figure 4).

The power of the drawing then links the position of witness to the painting, done back in his studio. And then the painting from that.

Now it seems to me that painting has, for the past twenty years, been in stiff competition with television: regarding the immediacy of the image, the spectacle of presentation, the power of circulation, the juxtaposition of the frame, and in many other ways. Gittoes' project begins from the obvious recognition that the television camera can capture what is happening in the world instantaneously and send it reeling into a thousand television sets without the slightest effort: plastic art will never succeed in gaining this position of power. Between the events of the world and the act of painting there is a time lag built into the creative process which the instantaneousness of the media does not have (the time lag is so short from camera to TV set that we take TV to be "live"). However, plastic art, given the terms of Gittoes' project, can therefore be called on to blend the

FIGURE 4 *George Gittoes,* The Preacher, *1995. Image and rights courtesy of the artist.*

rapid-fire response of the witness with the expressive subjectivity of drawing and painting for which the "time lag" allows.

To reach a larger audience and explore violence in greater depth, Gittoes has for the past twenty years also made documentary and fiction films set in war zones, most recently on the south side of the city of Chicago, a war zone of guns and their brutal effects if there ever was one.

I think Gittoes achieves a political voice not only because of the uniqueness of his project but also because Australia is a country of small population tucked comfortably onto vast tracts of mostly uninhabitable land and he is known as an activist there. This shows how hard anyone in art aspiring to real politics (as opposed to preaching to the converted within the system of exhibition) has to work, and perhaps even how lucky that person has to be in spite of the lifelong talent and toil.

Plastic art is the kind of thing that is very difficult to turn into a political gesture. This is because of the very nature of the medium, which lacks the "voice" to speak didactically in a political way. (In this way video, internet, and voice help in installation, as narrative does in novels and operas.) And also because of the confinement of the global art world, and the tendency of art to become a branded, homogeneous commodity in that market. This turns its political gesture into that of a T-shirt with "Save Africa" written on it. A logo for the consumer. A mere object of taste if you will. And here we have the point of Hegel, not all things are possible at all times, nor in all media. To achieve a political voice and have people listen is difficult, the work of not only innovation but also luck.

Contemporary Art and the Global South

How are the conditions of art and aesthetics associated with globalization magnified or given a special cast when it comes to resource-poor or moderate nations, formerly marginalized thanks to colonialism? This question pertains to a great deal of the world. I focus on South Africa although a number of other places would do just as well. I choose South Africa because I have lived thirty years of my life between the United States and that country, and the first rule of writing is that one should write about what one knows.

In 2017, I published a book, *Aesthetics, Arts and Politics in a Global World*, about the rise of modern art outside of Europe and America and the kind of concepts one needs to properly understand that art.[6] A central theme of that book was the rise of modern art in situations of underdevelopment or what I call, somewhat against normal usage, austerity. For the contrast could not be greater than with the conditions that gave rise to modern art in the Paris of the nineteenth century and in Europe generally. Modern art was born in mid-nineteenth-century Paris in a highly robust art world of galleries, museums, collectors, critics, collectors, a world of bourgeois literacy, and money, in what could be called a rising economy. And its intellectual context was one of European grandiosity at ruling the world and at existing in the thrall of modernity. The Parisian impressionist (for Paris is where it happens first) is enraptured with the spectacle, speed, and fascination of the modern world and seeks to celebrate its every inflection, from the departure of trains to the horse races, to the momentary flush of wind in a woman's yellow parasol as she gazes distractedly at spring flowers while others scurry in and out of the picture, as people do in crowded cities.

Edouard Manet, who invented the modernist stance of critique-in-paint, is keen to critique the commodifying pressure on art central to this market, along with omnipotent and voyeuristic bourgeois absorption that the Parisian brings to it. Central to Manet's concern is the way art became deified thanks to the museum while treated as a mere or near commodity outside of it. The eternalization of art inside the museum proved central to rise in price outside. There is nothing like pricelessness to jack up something's monetary value (which is why diamonds today are marketed as "priceless").

By "austerity" I am not referring to moments of "belt tightening" set by governments at times of economic difficulty or rising inequality, which is the common way of understanding the word "austerity." I mean the absence of robust markets through which in this case art might circulate, be bought, sold and collected, and which in turn gives art a subject (as in Manet).

Then what could it mean for art to arise in twentieth-century conditions where, at least until the globalization of wealth circa the 1980s, there is no robust art world, where the museums are few, collectors fewer, critics rare, the possibilities of exhibition small, and where neocolonial condescension restricted circulation of "non-Western" modern art (as it was then called) from the museums, galleries, and collections of "the West." In the early days of the Indian nation (the late 1940s and early 1950s) when the Progressive Artists Movement formed to create a modern art worthy of that nation, there was little that could be called an art world: few collectors, fewer critics, little public attention, no corporate sponsorship, and no museum of modern art until the National Gallery of Modern Art was established in New Delhi in 1954. As for galleries: to exhibit in Bombay an artist had to hire a room and sit by the door taking money and making sure no one ran off with the paintings. In the absence of an art market, and with few possibilities of circulation, the terms of making art could not be critique of the institutions of art, since there hardly were any. It would have been literally impossible for a Manet to turn his tricks in the world of early-twentieth-century South Africa, or India, or Venezuela, or China because there would have been an insufficiently robust art world to address and criticize.

This lack of a robust art world paradoxically freed the modern artist in such places to work without the pressure of art markets, commodification, and critics, which banished the impressionists to the Salon des Refusés (the room of those refused, 1863). Attaching itself to the nationalism of the incipient nation, or to settler points of view, art was free to roam the local world without the pressure of commodification, not to mention competition. But working without an art world also had its downsides: isolation, the sense of irrelevance, poverty, lack of access to art markets or global circulation, and, most important, national circulation, for without a market to drive the circulation of work and a state committed to its curation, a painting is a tree that falls in the forest when no one hears it.

A painter like Irma Stern, German-Jewish South African, who grew up in the Transvaal and departed for Germany to work with Max Pechstein and Die Brücke before returning to Cape Town as the fires of the First World War were raging in Europe, lived the rest of her life in lonely solitude, mocked as she was by a white settler society largely incapable of appreciating her bold colors and brilliant modeling of the figure, a provincial culture uninterested in her pathways into modern art, her fusion of German expressionist utopian imagery with the cultures of Africa and its green landscapes.

Stern bespoke the pain of isolation in a private visual diary called *Paradise*, composed around 1922 and only much later published. In this pair of images (see Figure 5), the keywords are "Einsam" (alone) and "ohne Liebe" (without love).

Retreating to her home in the Cape Town suburb of Rondebosch, she turned it into a personal incantation of Africa, with huge Zanzibar doors, African sculptures, and her own paintings on the walls. This is not the mere exoticism of the German modernist artists (Pechstein) with whom she had worked in Germany. For them, the late colonial native world was a fantasized escape valve from industrialized and citified modernity, a place wholly imagined, never visited. Stern is

FIGURE 5 *Irma Stern,* Paradise: The Journal and Letters of Irma Stern, 1917–1933, *Pages 31, 32. Courtesy of the Irma Stern Trust/DALRO, Johannesburg/VAGA, New York.*

by contrast *of* the African continent as much as she is of Europe, a settler sitting halfway between, and for her Africa is both an exotic paradise of "Africana" and personal refuge from the unbearable solitude of rough-and-ready Cape Town. It was her way of finding companionship.

Had she remained in Germany it is not unlikely she would be in many European museums today (although she might have perished in a concentration camp, being Jewish). Such is the life of a woman artist who returned home to a kind of internal exile: from the European art world to the South African colony. Fortunately, being white and once married she had enough money to survive in her house, which she turned into a private Africana world. And at the end of her life her paintings became very valuable. (The latest auction information as of June 2018 shows them fetching approximately 450,000 USD depending on the work.)

Now an essential component of modern art arising in a situation of austerity is that it can take on the cast of an *amateur culture*. Lacking the institution of the art academy, the professionalized critic, the gallery, and collector, artists catch as catch can. One, Gerard Sekoto, the great painter of Sophiatown in the 1930s and 1940s, managed to get to Paris where he absorbed the Fauves with their bold, expressive colors and the work of Maurice Utrillo, whose dry street scenes resonated with his feel for the rough, aridness of the Transvaal, and its sharp, oversaturated light, a light that can seem to bleach objects of their color. One can see both elements in his magnificent *Street Scene* of 1942, in which he masterfully depicts the physiognomy of a woman bending into work from a straight back, while a local boy, perhaps a street tough, perhaps a son or neighbor, watches, hands in pockets. Note Sekoto's close attention to the effects of razor-sharp light on the corrugated tin shacks. (Unfortunately, I could find no high-resolution image of this work but if the reader will google the image online, it will come up in low resolution immediately.)

A decade later Sekoto would himself flee the burning fires of Apartheid Sophiatown, which would soon be bulldozed (1955–60), its inhabitants forcibly removed to South West Township, while out of the ashes of this vibrant para-city on the edges of Johannesburg would arise the Apartheid Lazarus of Triomf, a working-class Afrikaans town. Sekoto returned to Paris where he played piano in brothels before going mad. Years later he emigrated to Senegal, which he painted with the pleasure of a man returned to his continent, but never with the closely observing eye and feel for color he brought to his true home, Sophiatown.

Sekoto's fame came only posthumously, along with rise in the prices of his works.

Sekoto's is a Stern story in reverse, each, although for quite different political reasons, ending up in a place of isolation, with little to connect them to the vitality of international art markets, nor even to other artists. These are the stakes of market austerity in a politically charged South Africa and a neocolonial Europe.

By amateurism I do not mean absence of talent; these artists had that in droves. I mean a culture of individuals yet to be properly organized into educational and market institutions, as in the state of science in the eighteenth and early nineteenth centuries where the individual could generate major advances by performing experiments in his own home, or like Benjamin Franklin, by flying kites in thunderstorms, and where scientific societies were not entirely different from explorer's clubs. And I refer to a world of art not unlike that of eighteenth- and early-nineteenth-century scientific practice, where the practitioners were few, leading to the "small sample problem" as the social sciences put it, where there is an insufficient quantity of practitioners to distinguish uniformity of style and purpose from individual idiosyncrasy. These are the days before little science became big science.

To be fair, South Africa was not entirely bereft of art institutions. By 1909 there was the South African Society of Artists, the Fine Arts Association of Cape Town, and, if white, one could study art at university. Black artists could learn their trade only at a small number of places: the Rorke's Drift school for printing established by Swedish missionaries, and the Johannesburg Art Foundation, whose éminence grise, the fine abstract painter Bill Ainslie, taught such master painters as Helen Sebidi, who also studied at FUNDA, a black arts collective founded after the Soweto Uprising of 1976.

In the 1940s and 1950s, the Polly Street Art School was started by white artists determined to provide art education for black painters, run for many years in Samizdat form by the great maker of woodcuts Cecil Skotnes. It was run from an industrial Johannesburg location because the school's mission contravened Apartheid restrictions on where black people could live and study. Many of South Africa's great modern artists learned their trade there, including the masters Dumile Feni and Sydney Kumalo.

And there was another school for black artists which history until recently has blotted out because of its complicity in the Apartheid State. This school, Ndaleni Art School, is the subject of an excellent study by Daniel Magaziner: *The Art of Life*.[7] The school's mission was in accord with South African colonial and also American thinking about how to educate black persons: to train them for a life of manual labor. This goal, if it can be called that, was considered central to the education of black South Africans and widely adopted in their schools before and during the Apartheid period of 1948–90. Manual training included carpentry, basket weaving, the thatching of straw roofs, the making of useful items, and also painting and drawing. Over time, it became clear the things made in such schools were of no market value, and so the emphasis shifted to their aesthetic value, Magaziner shows, paving the way for a genuine school of black art—although not a school on the same ground as white schools, or even the Polly Street Art School. For those art schools aimed to introduce black artists to the trends of modernism, and the broad history of art, in a way that would place them in a position of genuine innovation as modern artists. Apartheid thinking effectively precluded such a kind of training for black people, who were assumed to have no abilities to pass beyond the role of imitative, although well-trained, labor. Defined by and contained by tradition, constitutionally unable to achieve modernist breakthroughs on their own (or any form of modernity except as imitators of Europeans), black artists should rather learn to excel at crafts, with the kind of anthropological use value widely believed to define African culture and capacity.

The school suffered chronic shortages of materials, was ill-funded, but nevertheless trained artists who would go on to do significant work in spite of the limitations of their training.

South African Art Markets and Museums

Contemporary art markets have arisen and are up to a point robust in post-Apartheid South Africa, and they are expanding fast. Two museums of international stature have, for example, opened in the Cape Province in the past year (2017–18): the Zeitz Museum and the Norval Foundation. So, the remarks that follow may soon be out-of-date, which is always the liability about writing on contemporary culture, which may prove one wrong by the time one's book comes out. In this instance it would a happy thing to be superseded by a growing market, since it would be good for art and culture.

At this moment of writing however (2018), the South African art market still remains in a state of insufficiency. By "insufficiency" I mean unevenly and/or incompletely developed markets, leading to an excess of production on the part of artists, that cannot be absorbed by the market. In the present context of South Africa, there are not enough collectors, in spite of corporate engagement. The galleries are top quality but you can count them on two hands (perhaps in a few years this will also change). Museums are spotty, some mounting excellent exhibitions, others unable to open. Local, neighborhood, and city institutions, public murals, and monuments can be wonderful, containing messages of empowerment, reparation, mourning for dispersed communities, monumentalizing struggling heroes, preaching harmony, demanding equality. These are organic to communities and those who take a financial interest in them (sometimes the state or province). They are therefore also haphazard. Art schools are world class but they produce more artists than the market can absorb. This leads to an excess of supply over demand, meaning an inadequately functioning, much less rising, market.

The point has particular force for South Africa, making it a unique place to write about within the wider ambit of the global south. South Africa has been in the position of democratizing at a moment when most of the history of decolonization across Africa and Asia has already taken place, and when globalization has become so robust that the very project of democratic, nonracial nationalism is partly undercut by global opportunities and allegiances and by the sometime brutality of globalization.

The project of nationalism at a late moment in the history of globalization, when the pull of the global is nearly overwhelming, has led to various conundrums for the country. Let me give you a well-known example. After the neoliberal turn of the African National Congress during and immediately following the Kempton talks that led to the writing of the Interim Constitution of 1994, the Final Constitution of 1996, and the Truth and Reconciliation Commission of 1996–2000, the South African government under the leadership of Nelson Mandela signed into power the Growth, Employment and Redistribution Act (GEAR), also in 1996. GEAR mandated redistribution of 20 percent of the assets of white monopoly capital to black ownership, setting the stage for an elite transition with a small percentage of fabulously rich beneficiaries. And it voluntarily took on severe economic restrictions of the kind demanded of debtor nations by the International Monetary Fund, in order to ready South Africa for the massive foreign investment it counted on, given its then elevated moral status under the tutelage of rock star Madiba (Mandela). Such investment was meant to power the economy and solve the problem of unemployment. It never happened. Capital does not invest based on moral value, it invests where labor is cheapest, political climate is stable, and workforce is of proven consistency. The world, in short, went to China, including the South African clothing industry where until the Chinese revitalized it on whatever terms of decency or indecency in northern Natal it atrophied. Over two million jobs were lost thanks to GEAR. And this is the problem of planning *national* revitalization at such a moment of hegemonic globalization.

Thankfully the economic conundrum of globalization did not extend to the writing of the Constitution, which coming late in the day of such national documents was able to cherry-pick the best from Western European Constitutions, Chilean ones, and also from the substantive rights found in Cuba, leading to a document, framed in terms of the dignity of its citizens, whose panoply of rights are among the most comprehensive and humane in the world.

How then do the conditions of the contemporary art world particularly affect an art world like South Africa's, where there is market insufficiency on the one hand and an ongoing demand to acknowledge and participate in decolonization at a late-stage moment of nationalism?

First with a cramped South African market there is more pressure to exhibit and sell internationally, especially in countries with high currencies. This pressures artists, however subtly or unconsciously, to create for the disembodied global market, by relying on branded styles. This attitude of type-casting oneself for the globe, the equivalent of South Africa's GEAR policies in 1996 with their readying the South African economy for foreign markets, can lead to disastrous failure, imitation, second-rate work, *or not* as the case may be. (And each case has to be evaluated on its own merits; this is the first and perhaps the only rule of art criticism.) It is still more lethal if combined with the marginalized outsider's ardent desire for entry into the global emporium nearly at any cost because they can't survive without euros and/or crave international recognition as if it were the only legitimate recognition.

Second, the problem of voice—to whom is one speaking and with what cultural resources—becomes more acute under the pressure to work for an international market, especially for an artist also wedded to addressing South Africa's national, local, and group aspirations at this moment of ongoing democratic transition/decolonization.

One cannot simultaneously make art that relies on extensive local knowledge and art for the international branded market. A thinning of local content is required, which can be a loss or a gain depending on how the material is handled.

Third, when a high-glitz, celebrity, international museum or gallery opens in a situation of market insufficiency there is an excess of demand placed upon it, which it is simply unable to shoulder. An excess of demand is a common condition on South African institutions, especially its universities, which are a flash point for social transformation, an easy target of upheaval and even violence, and which require serious research, engaged and blue sky, without adequate resources and with heavy administrative and teaching burdens. South African universities are stress points for a society where housing, unemployment, inequality, racial typecasting, and township entrepreneurialism are all inadequately addressed. This above all extends to primary education that remains so variable in quality and even safety that the kind and quality of primary school one attends is a direct indicator of future work, income, and class. By the time students who are very badly prepared hit university, it is often too late, leading to failure and resentment.

I have a high-glitz, celebrity museum in mind and I now come to the story of the Zeitz Museum, which opened in September 2017. This public not-for-profit museum was commissioned through a public/private partnership between the Victoria and Albert Waterfront and German businessman Jochen Zeitz. The Waterfront Corporation, already in control of the most visited and lucrative mall in Africa, wished to expand its terrain into the depressed area of old Port between the Waterfront and the CBD, and conceived the idea of a museum. At that moment Jochen Zeitz, who, thanks to his art buyer Marc Coetzee, until May 2018 was director and chief curator of the Museum, amassed a major collection of contemporary art from the African continent. Zeitz did this in virtue of his position as CEO of Puma Clothing.

A partnership then developed between Zeitz, who like all collectors was looking for a high-profile place to exhibit his art in a way that would catapult it into the arena of international attention (visibility) with the side effect of increasing its financial value and avoiding tax, and the Waterfront Corporation, itself a public/private South African consortium. The Waterfront Corporation would build the museum, his name would go on it, and this in exchange for a loan of his art for the period of twenty years (not a donation). The Waterfront Corporation invested over R500 million toward its construction and infrastructure development. Considered by many to be one of the world's leading collections of contemporary art from Africa and its Diaspora, Zeitz's collection includes works by such eminent artists as Chris Ofili, Kudzanai Chiurai, Kehinde Wiley, Glenn Ligon, Marlene Dumas, Wangechi Mutu, and Julie Mehretu (google them all). An astonishing masterpiece by William Kentridge is on loan there but independently, since it is not part of Zeitz's collection.

The Waterfront had been investigating a number of proposals regarding what to do with the historic Grain Silo since it was decommissioned in 2001. According to their CEO, David Green, the decision to transform and renovate the building for the new museum would "breathe life into the Silo district and act as a drawcard to a venture that is non-commercial in nature ... specifically for the enjoyment of all the continent's citizens," while others have noted that the strategic partnership with Zeitz also serves to connect the existing properties of the Waterfronts' owners (Growthpoint Properties and the Government Employees Pension Fund) with the developing financial district in Cape Town's lower CBD.

What the Waterfront Corporation got out of this was enhanced international visibility, a place in the sun of the international art world, an expansion of the vast mall/hotel/restaurant complex that is already an international tourist draw into a major cultural center. It is expected that around the museum a series of galleries will come into place. The piazza to the right of the Zeitz Museum is already full of high-end stereo shops, top law firms, fashion boutiques, and the like. This is high-concept urban renewal for the highly gentrified and largely foreign market.

What about a commitment in an underresourced country beset by vast inequality to the local communities of the Cape? In order to host serious community engagement, a museum must provide three things at a minimum. First, a user-friendly lobby, to invite in people who will likely feel alienated and excluded by the glitz-branded international museum generally whose lobby says: Enter but only if you are in the know and have the dough. Second, it requires an

FIGURE 6 *Thomas Heatherwick Design Studio, Zeitz MOCAA, 2017. View from the front of the building. Photo Cornelius Van Rensburg.*

auditorium where presentations to the public may take place, from schoolchildren to members of communities not usually associated with, nor entirely comfortable in, high-gloss museums. Third, it requires an education department working full-time to arrange a schedule of community meetings. So far, the Zeitz has offered none of these, which can only mean its real focus is on the glitzy, rich Waterfront trade coming from Amsterdam, Paris, Rome, London, and New York, with China added to the mix.

Everything about the design precludes an openness and participatory feel for local peoples unused to the culture of international museums and their art-speak I think. The building does not invite ordinary people into it in any user-friendly way but rather seeks to astonish, shock, and sublime the viewer by means of its Cathedral-sized lobby with a six-story ceiling that resembles something between an unearthly insect's bulging eyes and a concrete filibuster seeking to intervene in the sky (see Figures 6 and 7).

In deference to ordinary people, membership was priced for South African citizens and permanent residents and for Africans across the

FIGURE 7 *Thomas Heatherwick Design Studio, Zeitz MOCAA, 2017. View of Lobby. Photo Cornelius Van Rensburg.*

continent at the cost of a single ticket: ZAR 175 (the equivalent of about USD 12.23). And Wednesday is a free day. Other than that, there has been no gesture toward inclusiveness. Current figures suggest that 40 percent of visitors arrive on the free morning, some of whom are not fancy art types, so perhaps the museum has gained wider interest than one thought among South Africa's various populations.

Moreover, among the unique features of the museum is a large plaque next to the bronzed donor names, listing all the construction workers who were involved in this magnificent enterprise of construction. Who built the pyramids, Bertolt Brecht asks in a famous poem. It was, of course, the slaves and, here, the workers. And so, the building should also be understood as a monument to their labor, which the plaque happily recognizes. And after all this was a Grain Silo, and downstairs below the entrance original machines for the silo are still present, bespeaking a homage to what this building was. Political activist and former Constitutional Court Judge Albie Sachs has rightly called the building a "Cathedral to Labor" (see Figure 8).[8]

On the other hand, the museum has not made it easy for the public to learn about the art they are looking at. Curatorial texts are minimal,

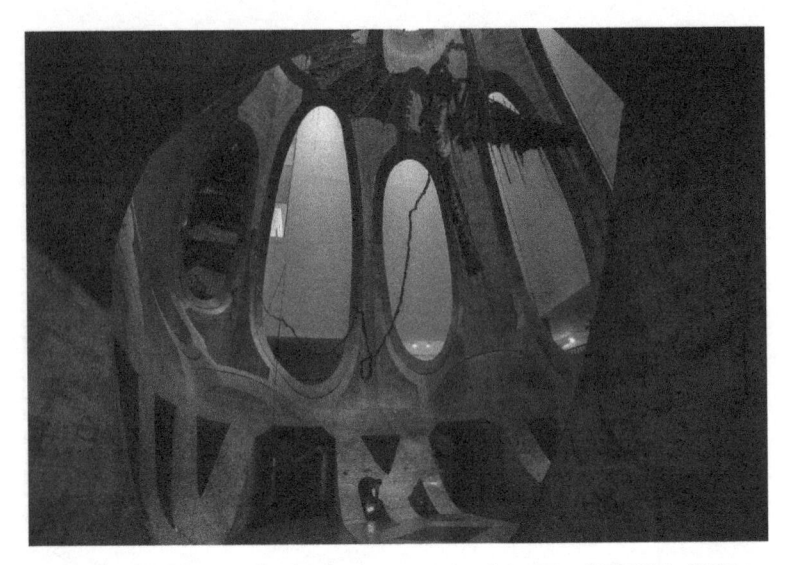

FIGURE 8 *Thomas Heatherwick Design Studio, Zeitz MOCAA, 2017. View of old machines in the basement. Photos Cornelius Van Rensburg.*

with introductions to the opening exhibition "All Things Being Equal" having this degree of terseness: "Numerous questions have been posed around our opening exhibition, the most evocative of these being, 'How will I be represented in the museum?' See for yourself. All things being equal ...."[9]

Not exactly helpful for someone unfamiliar with the complex mechanics of contemporary art.

Some of the museum's texts have curatorial portentousness firepowered by the kind of incomprehensibility all too common in the art world. Others are briefly biographical. There is little continuity.

To return to the story, I now quote from Wikipedia:

The conversion of the Silo building began in 2014 under the direction of London-based architect, Thomas Heatherwick.[4] The museum building was constructed from the conversion of the 57 m tall historic Grain Silo, originally built in 1921 and decommissioned in 2001. The architects, Heatherwick Studio, aimed to conserve and celebrate the original structure's industrial heritage, while simultaneously excavating large open spaces from the 42 densely-packed concrete cylinders from which it is was comprised. Using a variety of concrete-cutting techniques the interior of the building has been carved-out to create a number of galleries and a large central atrium. The remaining concrete shafts have been capped with strengthened glass in order to allow natural light to enter and create a "cathedral-like" interior. From the exterior, the most noticeable change to the original structure will be the addition of pillowed glass glazing panels into the building's upper floors.

Heatherwick is an extremely gifted designer with high visibility on the international radar screen. He is a new and "hot property" internationally.

Once word got out that a major and highly visible international museum was opening in Cape Town every artist wanted to get with the program, and all kinds of shenanigans went on in the process. I myself was approached by a gallery (which I will not name) to buy six photographs for the price of two by a South African photographer on whose work I have written, on condition I would then donate them to Zeitz, so the said photographer could become part of this august and (again, I repeat) internationally visible collection. I declined, mostly because I don't have the cash. Various other artists offered their work gratis. Then there was the case of Roger Ballen, a highly successful and gifted photographer whose work challenges us to deal with difficult images on the verge of pornography and even child exploitation, and works within the style of dreamlike, "art" images, as if apparitions from the unconscious. Now Ballen, a former mining engineer, is also a successful art director for the great post-punk South African rock group Die Antwoord. The point here is that he paid out Rand one million in order to establish the Ballen Gallery for photography in the museum, which is a beneficent thing to have done and allows the museum to exhibit fascinating photographers from across the African continent. Ballen should be applauded for this. Except it came with a proviso. The price of his donation was to allow him to one of his science fiction environments in rooms adjoining the gallery, a horrid work in which all the figurines resemble happy trolls about to devour Little Red Riding Hood. In other words, he paid out one million to get in, which was the price of admission—more or less the same amount as it costs to become a member of Donald Trump's Mar-a-Lago Palm Beach resort.

Now stop to consider this setup. Zeitz has a tax-free collection, which thanks to this museum is catapulted into international visibility, certain to raise its prices. He gets this in exchange for putting no cash into the construction of the museum or more, costly still, its maintenance. *And he gets his name on it.* In the fund-raising world you pay dearly for "naming rights." He "pays" not by donating his collection but merely by offering it on a twenty-year loan (potentially renewable).

As soon as it becomes clear that a direct route to international visibility is extended to South African artists some of whom otherwise exist in a state of partial depravation, a scramble to get their work inside the doors takes place. Artists pay out to become members of this special club, which is on the one hand a paean to contemporary African art and full of interest, while on the other a pit stop for the tourists and art cognoscenti at the edge of Cape Town, a city which already runs on the international tourist trade. And there is little done by way of enhancing local access beyond lowering the prices one day a week and the membership fees.

This setup seems to me the very epitome of a neoliberal partnership between state, province, private wealth, and international art, which is reason to speak critically of it in spite of the fact that it really does add something magnificent to Cape Town and South Africa, a signature museum as glorious as the Guggenheim in New York, the Louvre in Abu Dhabi, a museum that for the duration of its life span may take its place in that rarified, elite world. A visual icon in a world where visibility conveys power, even authority.

Now a huge amount of negativity has been hurled at this museum from within South Africa, and not simply because the national South African sport is neither soccer nor rugby but public winge-ing (complaint). Some of this criticism is captured in my remarks. But some not and I want to turn to it because it is highly instructive. It has been said by multiple artists and critics that the museum lacks *representativeness* across the continent, that it simply reflects the curator's predilections toward decorative and highly ornamented art. This is true. But I think a private/public museum built around a single collector need make no claim to representational equity, indeed the pleasure in private museums across the world is that they are an entrance into a collector's idiosyncratic taste, a personal world created out of the fabric of history not to reflect it but to stand as a testament to individual taste and liberty. This is true of the many private museums of Rome, Paris, Vienna, New York City, and so on. And although the museum does have a public component I don't personally believe it need aim for capacious representation, *as if such a thing were even possible*, given the depth, scope, and variety of the art of a whole continent. Who could presume to stand as the arbiter of representational equity across such a domain? How would "representative" choices be made? The very claim of representation in some kind of inclusive, democratic way is a fantasy of the Enlightenment. And so, I think the furious reaction to Zeitz's partisan policy takes the form of either idle fantasies of total inclusivity or the following complaint: "Here is an internationally visible museum and I am not in it, and for no good reason, because I am just as good as those in it." Which may well be true of the artist making the complaint.

It is here that we return to the condition of market insufficiency, in which there are a paucity of alternatives for those not included in Zeitz, and where Zeitz's curatorial predilections cannot help but feel like exclusion. This is not a matter of identity politics, because the museum has ample art by persons of color, white males, women, young, old, South Africans, Africans from elsewhere on the continent, and the like. It cannot be accused of a failure of *inclusivity* in that crucially democratic way. So, the complaint has to be one of misplaced frustration at an art world in which there are insufficiently robust opportunities, placing an excess of pressure on the Zeitz Museum to compensate the loss. Again, this is the same kind of excessive pressure that is placed on universities and other cultural institutions—and should be understood as such.

The real question then becomes: why the silence from those fully public South African museums which *do* contain something closer to genuinely representative and inclusive collections of South African art (although not the art of the entire continent) because they are collections built over many years. The University of Fort Hare Museum, home both of the ANC archives and of the largest collection of black art in South Africa, is totally dormant and utterly dysfunctional. Curators cannot be retained at the Cape Town National

Gallery (part of the Iziko system of museums) or, conversely, gotten rid of when no longer wanted. The Johannesburg Art Gallery has inadequate presence.

I think there are three reasons for this. First, public museums lack state funding in a mid-resourced country. Second, there has been a failure of leadership in the cultural field by the African National Congress when it comes to the former world of elite Eurocentric culture, namely the museum. The focus, and there is some justice in this, has been on local community culture building in a country where until recently most of the public was barred from public self-representation. Third, the identity politics so central to a post-Apartheid/racialized country make it very difficult for a museum to do the hard but essential job of filtering out work on the basis of quality. There has to be a balance between the justice of inclusiveness, inviting and focusing on formerly excluded/underrepresented persons (of color and also gender) and the commitment to quality. Both for exhibitions of past and of present art. Museums are simply too anxious about doing the wrong thing in a world where political correctness may at any moment rear its head to achieve this balance.

The irony is that it has taken a private institution like the Norval Foundation, opened in April 2018 on the Steenberg Winery estate in the Cape Province and entirely financed by South African real estate developer and art collector Louis Norval, to seriously mount the kind of exhibitions public museums ought to be producing. Norval's opening featured two of the great modern black artists who emerged from the Polly Street School: Sydney Khumalo and Ezrom Legae, and they are continuing on full speed ahead. Perhaps it simply is a matter of cash. Norval Foundation does have the money to mount top exhibitions and public museums don't. But then, South Africa is not poor, although it is corrupt, losing millions through illicit pipelines, and it could offer more if it wished.

The job of the public sector in curating and exhibiting culture has been taken over by the private sector. Or so it seems at the moment anyway.

Norval is doing the work public museums should be doing, and the pressure on Zeitz to deliver the goods remains in part a result of the failure of South Africa's public institutions to step up to the plate. It is partly because of such state failure that the private/public sector is pressured to fulfill a task it cannot and should not be expected to do. This is a story therefore about the insufficiency not merely of art markets but of state-driven culture, and it is the combination of both that leads to unachievable demands on a museum like Zeitz. Contemporary art in South Africa is caught within the tension of such pressures, which can be energizing, or depleting, but they are among the chief aesthetic norms today.

3

Aesthetic Cosmopolitanism

Cosmopolitanism Introduced

In this and the next chapter I will introduce the idea of cosmopolitanism and suggest that it is among the best ways to think about aesthetics in our current, globalized world. Among other things, the cosmopolite will understand the deep links between aesthetics, morals, and politics and the importance of the human imagination in reaching out across the globe to deepen one's own aesthetic, moral, and political understanding and capacity for experience. Cosmopolitanism seeks to expand the self by enlarging its domain of belief, habit, and point of view, allowing one to view one's own culture and society from the perspective of others, in the course of seeking to understand and assimilate their culture and morals. Cosmopolitanism does not seek agreement, but understanding: understanding both of others with whom we are now intertwined thanks to globalization of economy, politics, and culture (including art markets) and of one's own culture and society through comparison and contrast with others. And more than that, synergy. Throughout this discussion I will stress the importance of that kind of imagination called synergy, which finds ways of linking together disparate cultural elements in ways that outrun rules. Since for Immanuel Kant, the great modern philosopher of cosmopolitanism, genius is the ability to create in the absence of rules, synergy is a kind of little genius in all of us, thanks to the imagination.

The idea of cosmopolitanism is as old as the Ancient Greek philosopher Diogenes, who announced himself as a cosmopolite, a citizen of the world, rather than belonging to any city-state. It is also found in the famous remark of the Roman playwright Terence who had a character announce in his play *Heauton Timorumeno*: "Homo sum, humani nihil a me alienum puto," or "I am human, and I think nothing human is alien to me."

The remark seems to imply that even the most foreign of peoples, or those among one's own peoples with the oddest of habits, once understood as human, can with time, effort, and sustained interaction eventually become comprehensible to oneself in the human register they deserve, that one can find one's feet in their language, culture, and society. That one can come to see them as on a par, deep down, with oneself, in spite of differences.

But suppose one cannot find them human, cannot find humanity in them? Suppose they are just too foreign? Then do we throw up our hands with the great philosopher Ludwig Wittgenstein in his *Philosophical Investigations Part II* and say about that distant tribe, "wir können uns nichts zu finden," "we cannot find ourselves [in them]."[1] Are these people therefore not human, because we cannot penetrate their foreignness? What would it mean to call them *of our species* if everything about them is so different that we cannot find them so? Are we then entitled to reduce these beings to slaves?

Recall that colonialism followed from the mercantile exploration of the world by the Spanish and Portuguese seeking trade routes to Asia, and earlier still by the great ships of Venice. The initial encounters between Europeans and natives of the fifteenth century led not to understanding nor, as yet, enslavement or servitude, but initially to the gasp of wonder that such beings could exist on the face of the earth. Were they even peoples? This wonder was also true of the pre-Columbian peoples Cortez encountered. When his conquistadores arrived in Mexico, suited in full armor and on horseback, the pre-Columbian peoples they encountered thought horse and rider were one being, so that if a soldier fell off his horse it meant the being had broken in two. The original settlers in the Jamestown colony of 1613 referred to the native peoples as "naturals," meaning of nature rather than humanity, like children or animals, not yet trained and educated. Again, this was not yet a moment of violence, nor of domination, the desire was often to understand and coexist. But it was a moment in which the appellation "human" was thought uncertain in its application to such peoples, even if they were also thought of as "peoples," which would seem to imply "humans," although that is also unclear.

It was only later, when empire was established and the domination of such strange beings as the naturals became essential to empire, that strategies for deflating their traditions, condescending to their ways, and racially stereotyping them according to rank inferiority took shape, as they did throughout the eighteenth and nineteenth centuries. Only then did the concept of race become a central filter through which native peoples were seen, which made them humans, but of a decidedly lesser order.

One could give them the gift of European enlightenment, baptism, European education in some limited fashion, and the rest, but in the manner of how one gives a gift to a child, when one believes the child can never pay it back, because they were unable to. Nor was it believed the native would ever properly profit from this gift. For the view was (we have seen) Europe offered the colonized the gift of European Christianity and missionary education under the belief that the colonial would always lag behind in his or her capacity to assimilate it, ending up as a second-rate, imitative version of the European. This cultural strategy allowed the European to believe colonialism was organized for the benefit of the colonized, who, if they could never really achieve modernity, were at least being offered the chance, the gift.

With such stereotypes and hierarchies in place, there was little room for more genuine encounter with the peoples of the world, of the kind that would lead to knowledge, deepening of one's imagination of what it is to be human thanks to what was learned from them, while acknowledging how hard it might be to achieve understanding. The dominant ideology of colonialism refused the project of understanding who the native was. The colonial interest was as a norm to restrict knowledge to that required for administrative control. Deeper understanding was a threat, like deeper relations of love or desire. For these might lead to sympathy, fellow feeling, a sense that in spite of everything the colonizer and colonized had more in common than either thought, which would have been a threat to the colonial order of ruler and ruled.

The colonizer feared this without being willing or able to acknowledge it. Just as for the most part he feared or ridiculed or was silently amused by those of his tribe who "went native."

There were, throughout the long history of colonialism, those who did seek deeper understanding of the native, understanding of the kind that would place the native on a similar footing to the European, as happened when Michel de Montaigne penned his famous essay, "Of Cannibals" in 1580,[2] a remarkable essay of reversal. Montaigne challenges the common belief of his time that while the European is civilized, the cannibal is savage, the proof of the cannibal's savagery being that he or she after all eats other humans. Yes, Montaigne says, they do sup on others, point taken. But what is the moral upshot of this, he asks, let's look into it: the cannibal only eats people when hungry, does not kill them for pleasure or profit, is not profligate in his habit. Whereas we in Europe, he goes on, although we do not eat one another, happily devour one another in war, raping, pillaging, killing, and all under the belief that the cause of war justifies this. (When Montaigne lived, war was mostly an activity of pillage, rape, and destruction waged against innocent populations by soldiers who were given the incentive to steal whatever they wished as a kind of military "perk.") We are the profligate ones, not they. So, who is the real "cannibal" Montaigne asks, without quite answering the question, for his purpose is to render the categorical difference between us and them (Europe and the native) *uncertain*, to produce a skeptical result about who is the better, who the worse, and how. The purpose of the essay is to shatter the rigid moral categories that were already developing in Europe around the idea of civilization, categories that were already typecasting the native into a morally inferior position, as a subspecies. To force Europe to reflect on its own "cannibalizing" practices rather than use the other (the native) as an excuse to self-applaud.

But there was a further result his essay intended, which is central to the cosmopolitan project. Montaigne meant to imply that the native is much closer in behavior to us than we think, much more *human* in his practices as we would see it, while we are less exalted (humane) than we believe. This puts us and the native on something like the same moral footing. If not the same footing then at least in the same moral ballpark, which in turn means that the native is less foreign to us than our categories preach.

The brilliance of Montaigne's essay is to establish terms of likeness between them and us, which is a way of proving them less foreign than our disdain and revulsion allow. In order to do this Montaigne has to break up or what will later be called "deconstruct" those categories. And not to say something definitive like: now we realize we are the same. But rather to leave this an open question, how different we are and why. A dose of skepticism about human differences with respect to moral rankings is a good thing, Montaigne would say. And this is the essence of cosmopolitanism. It can only remind me of the line from Georg Cukor's screwball comedy *The Philadelphia Story* (1940), in which Cary Grant, aka Mr. C. K. Dexter Haven (played by the great Cary Grant), tells the woman he will within a day remarry, "The time for making up your mind about people is *never*."

The demands of cosmopolitanism are an antidote to the Enlightenment world of Hume and even Kant, since they refuse the universal standards of morals and of taste, and Kant's famous claim that aesthetic judgment shares with moral judgment the claim, or presumption, to speak in a universal voice, for all persons across the globe, as if one were the exemplar of all humanity, which Kant explicitly believes. Cosmopolitanism says: every people is articulate, every people speaks language, every people has traditions, morals, ways of living and being that are of an order of complexity as to demand years, even generations to grasp. And then at best partially. And in ways that will absolutely disrupt our received hierarchies. In many ways the project of anthropology as a discipline grew out of this belief, refusing the rigid categories of colonialism, which prevented the colonizer from ever humanizing the native, as was his wont.

Montaigne does not throw up his hands and say: every group of people is as good as every other and therefore immune from criticism. He rather says, every people must be taken seriously, to be learned from, to be understood as complex and subtle, and in some ways deep. And to do this we have to learn to stand aside from our own categories (in Montaigne's case categories of civilization and primitivism) enough to also challenge them in the course of coming to know the other. In the course of this project, criticism will inevitably emerge, along with a host of other differences, some of which may remain permanently strange to us. We need not seek agreement.

This is I think the best way to take Terence's remark that nothing human is foreign to me. However foreign the various peoples of the world are, they can all be grasped as human, however difficult and incomplete a project this may be, however much it may force us into self-scrutiny about ourselves and our ways in the light of the encounter. This does not mean we should stop condemning others. Condemnation is a moral necessity, without which the very project of morals collapses. It rather means that although we condemn, we should also seek to understand. In some cases, understanding will mitigate condemnation, in other cases not. Cosmopolitanism says understanding is an attitude that ought to be maintained even where condemnation is sharp. It is a prescriptive position, even a regulative ideal.

It is because of the shifts to one's own categories that will inevitably occur in the hermeneutical encounter that understanding the other may sometimes alienate one from one's own culture. This is a good thing. When one finds one's own ways of being in the world a bit foreign, a bit strange, when one asks, as Nietzsche did, how can Western Europe be like that, one is not merely humbled, one may gain purchase on oneself. This is what Montaigne wishes to show Europe about its own savagery. The savage becomes humanized while we become shocked at ourselves. He is the medium for our own self-revelation. And so, a chief moral reason to take up the cosmopolitan stance is that through the encounter with the other one grows in knowledge about oneself, about one's own culture.

The Idea of Perpetual Peace

Cosmopolitanism has its modern formulation by Immanuel Kant himself. Kant's key text is his essay "To Perpetual Peace: A Philosophical Sketch."[3] In that essay Kant says that the best route to ongoing and stable peace is for citizens to adopt the standpoint of the world, of all humanity. Kant is writing against nationalism which divides people, it's very terms of belonging having the liability to produce a partisan and self-interested standpoint. Kant's idea is that if every person would think of themselves as attached to all humanity rather than first and foremost to a singular nation, group or religion, the road to peace would have, as John Lennon sang it, *a chance*. Indeed, it would be assured because partisan politics would be replaced by a universal sense of moral equality.

Kant's idea of morality is that of acting out of respect for others is acting in the way one would want them to treat oneself. For Kant, and I will go over this terrain in the final chapter of the book, this is to treat all others as ends in themselves. Since all persons should do the same in acting morally, Kant concludes that to act morally is to act in the name of all humanity. Whatever one does, one must will the maxim according to which one acts as a universal law. To act morally is to speak universally, in the name of all peoples.

And this is precisely what Kant means by the cosmopolitan standpoint: the standpoint of all humanity. It is not just that each person should think of herself as the moral guardian of all others, it is that each person should aim to act morally in a way that speaks in the name of all humanity. The moral standpoint simply is, for Kant, the cosmopolitan standpoint.

It is simply untrue to my own experience that every time I judge I aim to judge universally. In this global world of recognized diversity, I hardly know what that would even mean, given my sharp sense of human differences across the African, Asian, and American subcontinents (not to mention Europe, Australia, etc.). As the French philosopher Jean-Paul Sartre says in "Existentialism Is a Humanism" (an essay he strangely disowned later in his life but which is in my opinion among his best writings), I do not judge universally, except in the form of compulsion (to force others to do the same[4]). But I do set an *example* by what I do or feel or experience that becomes part of the world. The example may be exalted, a model of spiritual and emancipatory action: the example Gandhi set. Or it may be horrid, as when killing is gradually normalized within a society, each shoot up of a school or church or workplace making it that much easier for the next one.

Whatever anyone does, the example stands for others who may or may not wish to take it up as their own. This is where sharp differences between people become highlighted, and sometimes intractable. The claim to speak universally is best reframed as a desire that others follow my example, a promise of the value of doing so, a gift to them of a possibility, which others may or may not take up for whatever reasons. Those reasons can be debated but debate also terminates at a certain point and I simply say, with Ludwig Wittgenstein: this is what I do. This is my commitment.

Kant's claim about standing as an exemplar for all humanity is a dogma of the eighteenth century, the century where moral truth is believed rooted in rationality, God, or natural rights universal to all. Yet where the European believes himself entitled to speak for all without listening to their own voices. It is a kind of missionary position this, that of the good servant of the Lord who travels to the colonies under the belief that every person deserves universal baptism and, hence, the shelter and guidance of Christ. Access to universality was given to the native as a gift from the European, who nevertheless doubted the native could get very far with it. And so, the contradiction in the history of human rights. While moral rights, and moral actions, were believed universal, the universal voice was a European one, the native's voice remained unheard.

This is not to junk Kant's formulation of cosmopolitanism. Without any commitment to universality of rights, and also to certain moral duties of respect and acknowledgment that follow, the very possibility of humanitarianism falls apart. And with it the concept of humanity. However contentious, there is a crucial place for universal declarations of human rights, international bodies (the United Nations, the World Court) to enforce them, the human rights-based organizations and philanthropists (Bill and Melinda Gates) mobilized to address problems of health, education, gender equality, racism, migration and refugees, journalists at risk, that are globe-wide, and to do so in the name of human rights and dignity as such.

This is an Enlightenment legacy, even if it took a sea change in the character of law to bring it about. For the Treaty of Westphalia of 1648 establishing the modern nation-state mandated the internal sovereignty of every nation, meaning what happens inside one's country is one's own business, not the business of humanity. The vast landscape of violence, genocide, and extrajudicial killing that was the horror of the first half of the twentieth century with its two world wars led to the need for a new world order and set of international rules that would mandate and facilitate international response to violations of human rights even within national borders, not to mention across global regions, as the Nazis had done, littering Europe and the Soviet Union with corpses. And this in turn required a new and expanded set of moral concepts, those of "crimes against humanity" and of "genocide," formulated by two Jewish European refugees in the terrible days of the Nazi persecution: Hersch Lauterpacht and Rafael Lemkin.[5] The idea behind these concepts was that certain kinds of crime, against civilians at a time of war—crimes against humanity, and of an order that intended to wipe a people off the face of the earth in virtue of their religion, ethnicity, gender, race, sexuality, or other group characteristic—genocide, cannot be contained in the moral and legal language of murder, or even torture, since such crimes addressed a domain and range of people that called for response to their rights as a group. Such crimes were thought offenses to human dignity as such, demanding universal response.

The culture of humanitarianism, arising from the ashes of the world wars of the twentieth century, and empowered by these new concepts, is absolutely committed to the universal voice. This commitment to moral universality empowers its legal and political instruments for addressing crimes against humanity and of genocide, such as the international trial (the Nuremberg Trial following the Second World War), truth commissions, and the World Court. However ambivalently, 150 of the world's nations have signed on to the human rights instruments of the United Nations.

Of course, Realpolitik inevitably intervenes, and sometimes with disastrous consequences. In 1994 Kofi Annan was Secretary General of the United Nations, at a moment when ethnic conflict between Tutsis and Hutus in Rwanda threatened to turn catastrophic. He made a disastrous mistake in withdrawing United Nations peacekeeping troops, leaving only an inadequate skeletal force. Two months later, when it was clear genocide was taking place, he tried to correct his mistake by assembling troops to go in and stop the killing. But no nation would supply the United Nations with troops, and the United Nations is dependent upon the member states for its military force. It has no troops of its own. Over 800,000 people were killed in three months, before the genocide was stopped by Tutsi forces operating from neighboring Burundi. The failure was spectacular.

Perhaps the most successful humanitarian organizations are those unaligned with particular states and not dependent upon those states for authority, funds, and troops. Doctors without Borders, Amnesty International, and the Red Cross are examples.

There is thus considerable truth in Kant's idea that morality should stand above politics as a watchdog, demanding the standpoint of free, equal, and universal human rights, in spite of the practical problems which ensue. This is a cosmopolitan standpoint insofar as it is meant to transcend nationalism, cultural difference, gender, language, and everything else that keeps people apart and supervene over these forms of partisanship. Practical impediments to intervention in the name of humanity as happened during the Rwandan crisis with its failure of United Nations response are precisely what Kant worried about: partisan policies of individual states refusing the humanity of others.

Cosmopolitanism and Human Diversity

So, what is wrong with Kant's essay if there is so much that is right about it?

What Kant could not acknowledge was the full force of human diversity, given his belief that human beings are entitled, when acting morally, to act in the name of all humanity, given the way the colonial/Eurocentric beliefs of the day colored his own lens on it. In this day we can no longer believe ourselves entitled to act in the name of everyone else, because we know well that others will not, in this or that circumstance, find themselves in accord with what we believe is the right thing. They will believe it wrong. This is the fact of human diversity, something our moment of intense globalization teaches well and has to, which means in the interesting moral cases, we have no way of proving to others very different from ourselves that we are right and they are wrong. For they will feel as strongly that they must prove that they are right to us, leading to a moral standoff. We see this every day across our world in divergent attitudes toward women and freedom, economic equality vs. degradation, the role of nations each against the other, and in many other ways.

In this day and age to take oneself morally seriously is to understand that for the hard issues, a serious, committed person could believe differently from what we believe, however fiercely we believe it. Hard ethical issues divide nations and communities in half: in the United States the death penalty, the role of government, the right to bear arms and how far that Second Amendment right should be taken, a woman's right to an abortion, the question of euthanasia, the relationship of tax to inequality, and many other things. I have strong views on all these things, but I also have friends of intelligence and character who disagree and I know they have their reasons. About every one of these issues if we are serious with ourselves we can imagine how a serious person might believe what we absolutely don't believe. And vice versa. Well that is a kind of respect also, a way of saying: I deeply disagree with you, we share different conceptions of life, but I know you are not foreign to me, you are human also.

These conflicts take place between persons who are otherwise very much alike. Which means seeking to understand the positions of others is a mandate both about persons faraway across the globe and about one's next door neighbor whose views on abortion are totally different from my own. Indeed, faraway peoples are now, given the globalization of the past thirty years, far less far away than they once were. Just as we now recognize that our next-door neighbor is much further away from us than we might have thought.

The peoples of the world began to become more alike during colonialism, which made their differences, their disagreements more sharply etched. And the peoples of the world have become dramatically more alike in the past thirty years, given globalization. Globalization means peoples are interconnected through manufacturing, communication, the flattened English of the internet, plane travel and telecommunications. I Skype my wife every day when I am in Ann Arbor and she in Cape Town, and my child also, and we sometimes speak for hours, sharing our lives. Persons around the globe increasingly purchase the same goods when they can afford them, all made in China. They read one another's newspapers when they care to read rather than watch Fox TV, they are absorbed in one another's cultural objects, which are increasingly everybody's objects. Their forms of taste grow closer and closer. They are linked by shared forms of pleasure or discomfort. They are globally positioned in terms of equality or inequality.

Cosmopolitanism is a less brave adventure than it might have been, say, two hundred plus years ago when Kant penned his essay simply because we are more alike as peoples. When persons become more alike (whether they wish to or not) their *differences* appear more sharply, because they have so many terms in common to articulate them. Another way of saying this is that it takes underlying forms of alikeness to even *specify* differences, a point made brilliantly by the philosopher Donald Davidson a generation ago in his essay, "On the Very Idea of a Conceptual Scheme."[6] Davidson points out that the ascription of differences (diversity) between two parties is only coherent if underlying terms shared in common can be found, on the basis of which their differences can be specified. If one group of people believes the world was created by God while another by a big bang their difference can only be spelled out assuming they more or less mean the same thing by "the world" and "life," which is to assume a significant web of beliefs in common between them, about everything from nature to the course of lives lived on this planet, to the perception of stars, to what an event is, and so on. At every point the web may differ from one party to the other but as Davidson reminds us, at every point, there have to be sufficient terms in common to specify the differences. Otherwise the very *idea* of difference becomes purely abstract and speculative, because real differences cannot be specified coherently. In short, the very possibility of disagreement depends on underlying agreement.

This is true of culture as well as morals and beliefs about what modernity calls science, therefore of *aesthetic differences* as much as any other. To say that two parties have deep aesthetic differences is to say something that cuts deep. But you can only say it if you are prepared to specify the common terms between these parties that allow for aesthetic difference to emerge as genuine difference. For A to be different from B there has to be some C both share in common in order for the difference between A and B to be formulated. Aesthetic cosmopolitanism seeks to understand the A, the B but also the C. And so, for example, to say that traditional Chinese opera has profound aesthetic differences from Italian opera is to say something quite believable. But it masks the "C," the features both forms of opera have in common in order that the differences can be formulated. Many of these underlying similarities are so obvious we do not bother to notice them. Both forms are composed, although not in the same kind of way, both involve musical gesture, which is also physiognomic, both have narrative, characters, pomp and circumstance, an audience, an expressive purpose associated with singing or emitting sounds, and much more. This is not insignificant: without these commonalities, we would have no way of saying the Chinese, or the Italians, make what can coherently be called *music*. And if we had no way of saying that, how would they be human?

But if cosmopolitanism is made easier as a stance, given the way people are becoming more alike, it is also an antidote to market-driven likeness, or sameness between people and their consumables. The marketplace has the tendency to steer the production of cultural objects in the direction of their becoming nearly identical. We saw this in the previous chapter. Real and vivid diversity is thus reduced to mere product difference, as if African art were the same as Finnish art in every way except for a frisson of difference that brands the product as having the whiff of Africa, giving people the illusion that by buying into African art they need do no more than buy the normal but with that little touch of color, shape, and whatever else that "brands" the consumable as from the southern continent. This pressure toward product conformity, I earlier said, is to a degree offset by a genuine interest in global diversity also present in the marketplace, at least on the part of some producers and consumers. Cosmopolitanism is therefore demanded by the market not only because we live in a world of genuine diversity but also because our world and its products are becoming so homogenized that the diversity behind them, occluded by the market and its demands, demands recovery. Cosmopolitanism wishes to *encounter* diversity and learn from it, but also to *recover* it. If this is a paradox it is the paradox of globalization in which we live.

And so, the cosmopolitan stance is both occasioned by globalization because it brings diverse peoples into daily and sustained contact across cultural lines, and also because the market threatens to evaporate real diversity, which cosmopolitanism aims to find and acknowledge, even if this hardly means agreeing with it.

Cosmopolitanism Names a Challenge Not a Solution

The finest contemporary book on cosmopolitanism is that of Anthony Appiah, *Cosmopolitanism: Ethics in a World of Strangers*. In that book Appiah begins by articulating his own version of cosmopolitanism:

> there are two strands that intertwine in the notion of cosmopolitanism. One is the idea that we have obligations to others, obligations that stretch beyond those to whom we are related by the ties of kith and kind, or even the more formal ties of shared citizenship. The other is that we take seriously the value not just of human life, but of particular human lives, which means taking an interest in the practices and beliefs that lend them significance. People are different, the cosmopolitan knows, and there is much to learn from our differences. Because there are so many human possibilities worth exploring, we neither expect nor desire that every person or every society should converge on a single mode of life. Whatever our obligations to others (or theirs to us) they often have the right to go their own way. As we'll see, there will be times when these two ideals—universal concern and respect for legitimate difference—clash. There's a sense in which cosmopolitanism is the name not of the solution but of the challenge.[7]

The problem for cosmopolitanism is to reconcile this belief in the productive importance of diversity ("the right to go their own way") with the universal stance that allows me to be a citizen of the world, given that I am no longer licensed by the moral principles of Enlightenment Eurocentrism to speak in the name of all and yet do believe in some version of universal human rights associated with the practice of humanitarianism. A universal stance can no longer be understood as: I speak in the name of everybody. It is more of a humanitarian stance: our world needs to achieve and maintain commitment to certain universal human rights on pain of moral loss. And this given that disagreements about rights will no doubt remain profound.

The diversity of how peoples think of rights is easy to see simply by looking to the Constitutions in play across nations. The US Constitution recognizes civil and political rights, procedural rights to prevent discrimination, the right to a trial by jury, and so on. Its Amendments allow for the rights to freedom of speech, the right to bear arms, the right of women to vote, and more.

But the South African Constitution, beginning from the concept of the dignity of the individual, says, if you believe in human dignity you have to assign each and every citizen of the nation substantive rights: the right to health care, to a job and to a house, this in the name of a country which in 1996, when its Constitution was drafted and accepted as the supreme law of the land, was in the process of transitioning to democracy from a state that had been viciously racist, restricting persons of color from South African citizenship, forcibly removing them to artificially gerrymandered Bantustans in the middle of nowhere, without resources, with little public transport to help them get to work in the cities as menials each and every day, disallowing them freedom to move across the land of South Africa when and where they wanted (since they were not technically South African citizens they had to apply for a pass to travel to cities, could only stay there if working, etc.), criminalizing sexual relations across race. All of which consigned "non-European" persons (as persons of color were called) to massive impoverishment and inequality, a situation whose legacy is felt in the country today. And so, the Constitution is both foundational and reparative: mandating housing, health care, work are rights for all citizens, not mere privileges to be retracted at will.

There is more. Since linguistic diversity is central to South African life, the Constitution also mandates group rights. The idea is that unless your language is preserved you will lose your culture, which will diminish your dignity and freedom of choice. Individual freedom, it was believed, depends in part on the vitality of one's community, one's group. And so, instruction in schools is required by the Constitution in all eleven languages, along with broadcasting over the state media. In practice these mandates are undercut by the fact that everyone knows that to get ahead you have to speak excellent English and so any parent who can afford it sends their child to a school where instruction is in English. These schools are far better resourced than schools where instruction takes place in Zulu or Xhosa. As to the media, since the state lacks funds to broadcast news and sport in all eleven languages in the course of covering a soccer (football) match, the commentary continually switches from English to Afrikaans to Zulu to Setswana, making it incomprehensible to everybody. (Well that is I suppose a form of equality also: incomprehension for all[8].)

The point is that a brief survey of Constitutions will reveal significant differences in the character, breadth, and culture of their conceptions of human rights. These matters can be debated, meaning everyone is I think capable of understanding how the other's constitutional choices came about, and, with serious effort, something of what it would be like to live in these differing moral and political worlds. China does not acknowledge human rights, but a substantive concept of prosperity and well-being for its citizens that focuses on health, housing, work, economy rather than civil and political rights, which are minimal in China. the goal is to bring the people as a whole up from poverty to prosperity. This goal is Confucian. But we can, with serious effort, understand how China is humanitarian in its own way, and where it emphatically isn't.

Three Kinds of Moral Disagreement

Appiah says the challenge of cosmopolitanism is to address three kinds of moral disagreement.

He begins by distinguishing thin moral concepts from thick ones. By a thin moral concept, he means a concept like "good," which everyone shares but interprets differently. In itself the concept, shared universally, is abstract and means little until fleshed out in terms of individual and social belief, attitude, norm, and practice. (This was G. W. F. Hegel's critique of Kant[9].) A thick moral concept, a concept like religious practice or child-rearing, is highly robust, deeply embedded in the ways people do things. It has a great deal of moral content. Every form of child-rearing involves bringing up children in some kind of family or community, and involves care for health, education, discipline, training, some conception of preparing a child to be free, some form of cultural transmission to the child. Child-rearing is also guided by larger social constructs like gender, sometimes—if not often—privileging male children over female.

We all know there is a lot for people to disagree about when it comes to child-rearing, often within the same family (between spouses, across generations, etc.). But disagreement will also depend on underlying similarities against which disagreement is sharpened. All communities believe that child-rearing involves the regular feeding of children, some kind of sustained affection and positive regard for the child, the earning of money to pay for a child's needs, the need to bring a child up to succeed in the world or at least endure it. Disagreements will also be profound: about the role of acceptable violence on the part of parents in the name of "training," the role of education, the issue of knowledge (how much and in what way and at what age a child should learn about sexuality, trauma, etc.). About the role of control in child-rearing vs. the cultivation of freedom. About the kind and character of culture a child should absorb, about what he or she should become, about duties children should be taught toward each other, toward parents, society, and so on. Some forms of child-rearing will be deeply repulsive to others (and vice versa). And yet: even disagreements that fall into the category of repulsion and contempt depend on prior and significant agreement, that is, of the fact that the other party is also *human* and in spite of it all raises a child in ways not entirely different from one's own culture or group.

The first kind of moral disagreement Appiah discusses occurs when one person or group has a thick moral concept and another doesn't. These are some of the most intractable disagreements there are. The idea of an autocratic religious state would be one such example. One society (or some of its members anyway) may have a strong concept that religion should dominate politics and much of the rest of life. Another is constituted in the rejection of religion. This is a huge and usually unresolvable difference, with vast personal, moral, and political implications. It is the kind of example for which even *understanding* the other side is difficult, and for which contempt may be acute. These are the kinds of examples about which one is tempted to say: How could they! How can they! How can I possibly understand them! How can they be human and do this! They are examples in which moral disgust may be fierce. Montaigne's proviso is here of importance. The more one seeks to find traces (perhaps historically) of similar beliefs and attitudes within one's own culture the better one can understand what it is for another to hold the thick concept (authoritarian religion). And we may add, to also appreciate that there is inevitably significant resistance to its grip within the targeted culture. Not simply outside it.

Were such examples the moral norm, cosmopolitanism would be a practical disaster, since these are the deep rifts that we may well believe require battle to resolve rather than the possibility of negotiation, much less agreement. No theory of the world, cosmopolitan or otherwise, can resolve all moral conflicts between diverse peoples. Even the project of understanding comes to a stop somewhere, sometimes.

Fortunately, not all the time, which would be incoherent, given Davidson's reminder that we have to find ourselves in agreement with others about some things, many things in fact, to find ourselves at "war" over a particular moral issue with them and be able to state what it is we find unacceptable.

The second type of moral disagreement across groups is perhaps more common: when groups share thick moral concepts but differ as to how they are to be fleshed out or applied. Appiah's example is that of Ghanaian vs. American forms of good parenting. A commitment to good parenting is pretty much universal but its terms may differ dramatically. Ghanaian parenting involves extended families such that the uncle is as important as the father; American child-rearing is based in the nuclear family, and so on. This kind of moral disagreement is understandable, and perhaps one for which one wants to say, there are good and bad things on both sides. Moreover, America is perhaps a bit more Ghanaian than it thinks, at least in some cases? And vice versa?

Although Appiah does not say this, it is likely that moral disagreements of the first kind become slightly more understandable if they can be connected to disagreements of the second kind. So that the practices of scarifying Xhosa men, circumcising them during adolescence, and sending them out into the wilderness to face the extreme dangers of nature is a practice about which one may be appalled. Young people regularly die during this ritual. In mitigation, and this need not lead to agreement, one needs to understand it, as any anthropologist will tell you, in terms of more broad Xhosa concepts of parenting, masculinity, the need for strength, deep communal bonds (which are in fact reinforced by a time of ritual solitude or apartness from the group), and so on. The South African Constitution, recognizing the importance of diversity, that is, recognizing how important certain practices may be for people that others may find repugnant, reserves a place for customary law, so long as it does not conflict with basic individual rights like the rights to life, liberty, health, and so forth. In the light of this directive the practice may be allowed, but only if individual South Africans of Xhosa descent have the individual right to opt out. This seems a fair compromise between the recognition that people do what they do, they are diverse. And the recognition that human dignity mandates the primacy of their *individual rights* just as it does ours.

Those in favor of banning the practice believe young men of rural Xhosa descent will never have the power or independence to resist their elders and take a decision about undergoing the circumcision ritual. So, there can be no practical question of individual rights to choose in this instance. Circumcision is forced, inevitably coercive. It is a hard issue.

The third kind of moral disagreement is when multiple values are involved in moral choice, which different parties weigh differently. Here I can offer the example of free speech vs. the giving of offense. The First Amendment right of free speech in America is so highly valued and so capacious in its application that unless one runs into a crowded movie theatre and screams "fire," threatens a person with harm, is judged to have spoken in a way that leads to reckless endangerment, one can more or less say anything and get away with it on the grounds of First Amendment rights. In America Nazis can march down the streets of Skokie, Illinois, then home to many Jewish Holocaust survivors, screaming Heil Hitler, and actually be defended by the American Civil Liberties Union on the basis of the First Amendment. This happened in the 1970s. In other words, in America hate speech becomes criminal only if a direct link to violence or its potential can be demonstrated, and the onus is on the accuser to prove this to a judge.

In my own judgment this interpretation of the First Amendment has had a disastrous effect on American politics by allowing the media to run wild with propaganda, untruth, manipulative ideology, fake news.

Perpetrators of fake news can lie to their heart's content and it is very difficult to do anything about it, thanks to the current interpretation of the First Amendment. Recently free speech has been used as an argument in favor of unlimited campaign contribution, even though it is a commonly known fact that excessive contribution puts legislators in the pockets of those giving the cash in a way that subverts public will. The argument, advanced by Justice Kennedy of the Supreme Court (now retired), is that cash contribution is a form of free speech, and therefore its capping violates First Amendment rights.

No such thing would be possible in South Africa, where laws pertaining to free speech are highly constrained by "hate speech" and radio stations have been shut down, people arrested for speaking in racist terms publicly.

Germany, like South Africa, is motivated by a genuine wariness about its own racist past and has little legal or moral tolerance for hate speech, because it knew too well how hate speech in a climate of racism can lead to atrocity. South Africa shares this memory of the past. And so, their approaches to Freedom of Speech are simply different, given the acknowledgment. They weigh free speech against other things like the giving of offense, social solidarity, truth, and freedom from violence and racism differently than America currently does.

These are significant moral and political disagreements that signal different ways of being in the world. Appiah suggests (although this is quite unprovable) that in the majority of cases such disagreements can be understood and registered between diverse peoples, even if no agreement will be forthcoming and humans will agree to disagree, or at least learn to tolerate one another in spite of strong dislike for the position of the other. Meaning the majority of moral disagreements across peoples are of the second and third kind, not the first.

One must add as a complicating factor that societies or groups are seldom uniform in modern life. Whether in America, the United Kingdom, South Africa, or Saudi Arabia one will find all manner of forms of dissent, acknowledged, unacknowledged, in public, in private, secret or shared, invisible or visible. And so, the idea that cosmopolitan is about an us-vs.-them is far from accurate. It is a moral flaw central to the most virulent forms of nationalism and racism: to see the world as a state of perpetual war between us and them. Indeed, this is a basic tenet of fascism: the other, within and without, is always a threat. In fact, the nonuniformity of groups and nations (not to mention families) is essential to both the vitality of modern societies and also to their democratic drift (insofar as they do have democratic drift) because it formulates itself as individual liberty, expressed as dissent.

And so, the key to cosmopolitanism is that one must be able to *talk through such differences, and to do so as openly as possible.* In other words, cosmopolitanism requires a democratic public sphere and is in turn a crucial component of that sphere. Wherever the public sphere is cramped or curtailed by authoritarian regimes, financial capital and lawyers, the media or simply hate, cosmopolitanism, democracy, and finally liberty suffer. China restricts internet access and dissent, America obliterates subtlety of opinion through propagandizing, aggressive news that formulates itself in the form of Reality TV and other forms of Roman gladiatorial entertainment. Russia lives on fake news. Journalists are under threat across the globe.

We will never agree about all issues of rights. Agreement is the ideal. Toleration second best and crucial for the conduct of life. (I don't approve of what you do nor you of me but we can each find the other livable.) The third option is refusal. Here conversation ends leaving us in a state of conflict. We hope war is not necessary. Societies are rarely uniform in their attitudes, and we may still hope for support within dissenting regions of the society with which we have an unresolvable quarrel. In Saudi Arabia there are profound disagreements about what rights women should have, and there is significant ongoing dissent. During the Rwandan genocide moderate Hutus risked their lives by dissenting from the radical stance of the Interahamwe, those radical Hutus responsible for the violence against Tutsis.

This lack of uniformity within societies makes cosmopolitanism possible, since it is rarely us vs. them but rather a pattern of different points of view both within and outside of any society. What also makes the establishment and practice of rights more tractable is the culture of humanitarianism, with countries signing on to the human rights instruments even if ambivalent, as most are when commitment to rights conflicts with internal self-interests. Humanitarianism often fails when most needed: Rwanda. But without it we would be even less well off with respect to rights.

The Aesthetic Analogue

Aesthetic cosmopolitanism similarly names a challenge. At least in some cases we truly want all people to judge as we do, to feel as we do, to be overwhelmed as we do, about Beethoven, Shakespeare, The Ballet Rousse, about opera (Italian and Chinese), about Australian aboriginal art (see below), about whatever art we feel really deeply about, or some of it anyway. But even our neighbors fail to feel as we do, see as we do, desire as we do. This is a good thing, given that a world where everyone judged exactly as I do would be a world not only bored to death with its utter conformity but also one in which my own sense of difference from others, my own independence of judgment, my own feeling that I have an angle on the world that is *mine* would seem to lose its point, since everyone else would judge exactly as I do. Cosmopolitanism, I said, is dedicated to the preservation, as well as acknowledgment, of diversity, while also dedicated to negotiation between different parties about various matters, often without leading to consensus.

And so sometimes I long for universal agreement about things deeply felt by me, believing all others would do well to love them and learn from them as I do, while also acknowledging that others go their own way and must be allowed to do so—as I am allowed by others to do the same. Cosmopolitanism does not relinquish the importance of some universality of judgment. I would love to see a community of taste in which all appreciate the power of Mozart as I do: a universal community. And I sort of feel others are missing something when they fail to care about that angelic composer. Cosmopolitanism understands that to square the aspiration of universality with the recognition, and applause, given to people going their own way is and must be central to aesthetic as well as moral experience. And that this poses a challenge to universality of judgment and of ranking. Sometimes I want human life to be the same, so that I can find self-confirmation in others. While also, in another mood, wishing them the freedom to go their own ways. These attitudes will always be in a certain tension within me, and I think within everyone else who cares about art.

To what extent can one find similar kinds of cases in aesthetics to the moral cases Appiah singles out in his book as relevant to the cosmopolitan challenge? Consider the first case, where one group has a thick moral concept and the other not, making it hard for each to understand the other's way of being in the world. Is there an analogue with aesthetic concepts or practices?

As a first point it is increasingly difficult to find peoples of the world who dramatically lack thick aesthetic concepts held by, say, persons in Europe, India, or China. The globalization of the past thirty years has increasingly interconnected all people in a web of shared beliefs and ways of making and understanding art. In previous books I wrote a great deal about the hegemonic character of modern systems of the arts, which take up isolated groups of carvers from Southern Africa, aboriginal peoples, rural Indian painters in watercolor who had for generations worked entirely and exclusively from their own internally evolving traditions but in the voracious desire for contemporary art markets to find new kinds of saleable products, to discover the new, have over time been assimilated into the global system. It can be disastrous to tradition or it can cause it to remain in place within a now global frame of contemporary art. Artists may choose to refuse the pressures of the art world, remaining in a state of willed isolation so they can continue to work within tradition.

And so, there are aboriginal artists who remain in rural areas and get on with what they have done for millenia. But as often as not their children, or children's children, end up migrating to the big city, attending art school and revisiting their aboriginal past in the form of an ethnicity fused with modernist styles, often for political purposes. Such fusion of old with new, of tradition with modernity, turns lives formerly lived in cultural isolation into lives lived through identity politics.

Now it took some time for those not of aboriginal descent to understand aboriginal art practice. This was not only because until recently aboriginal peoples were treated with humiliation and indifference, sometimes like the South African Khoi and San peoples, shot for the mere sport of it. They were believed unworthy of rights. Once the attitude of violence was overcome, it proved very difficult to understand what aboriginal peoples are doing in paint, because their work is so caught up with community, ritual, and spiritual practice.

For they hold thick aesthetic concepts not shared outside their extraordinary community and certainly not by the contemporary art world in any of its manifestations.

The first point to make is that the painting of aboriginal artists is strikingly beautiful. Done on large, bold canvases (and formerly on bark until canvas and acrylic paint were introduced to them in the 1950s), their paintings are filled with concentric circles, tiny dots in irregular formations, weirdly compelling geometric shapes. The colors are bold and brilliant; the rhythm and tonality dazzling. Almost hallucinogenic. An aboriginal painting is easily misidentified as abstract expressionist art.[10] But that would be a mistake because the art is not abstract but speaks a language of representation unique to this community of persons which arose and lived in total global isolation for millennia until the arrival of the British and their convicts.

And more than that, it is motivated by a spiritual purpose unique to that community. Call that a *thick aesthetic concept* that is not shared by others.

The key to aboriginal art is its spiritual purpose. I know of few cultures that give such social primacy to painting. The painter is a kind of high priest whose purpose is to connect to the world of the ancestors. It is believed that in the recesses of the past there existed the Dreamtime, in which all the beings of the world were greater and more magnified than they are today. Aboriginal religion is animistic: everything is alive and redolent with spiritual value, from snakes and lizards to rocks, plants, and the stars. The entire world pulses with life. During the Dreamtime the ancestors gave birth to the world as it is known today, a world in which everything is alive with spiritual value. The key to painting is that it is one of the ways for time to be obliterated in the hallucination or dreaming of art, so that return to the world of the ancestors may take place in spirit. The point of painting is to return to the Dreamtime and commune with the ancestors. Hence the ecstatic character of the painting.[11]

Aboriginal art will tend to be about this or that ancestor: a rock, a mountain, a snake. And this being will be visible to the trained eye in the hieratic narrative of an aboriginal painting, through the patterns of dots and other forms. Interceding events may also be included: fires, storms, and other things. The paintings are usually done from two points of view: horizontal and vertical. The vertical point of view is that of Google Earth, in which one looks at a narrative or space from above. This is partly the result of the work's being painted on the ground, with the artist above. At the same time a painting will be organized to be viewed horizontally, following its intricate lines like a person walking them. The very concept of a map internal to this work differs dramatically from the modern conception. The modern map is a way of giving representation to the geometry of cities, towns, continents, the world: how they are laid out, distances between them, angles of intersection, bodies of water separating one from the other, and so on. You know it by studying it. When an aboriginal painter paints horizontally it is not to make a *representation* of the world, but to provide a narrative of movement. It is through *movement* that space is known, that the aboriginal person knows the world around them. The geographical eye of the aboriginal painter is not that of a mapmaker, representing static relations of size, location, and distance. Knowledge of space is provided by walking, circulating, knowing a place by doing "walkabout" in it. The lines in an aboriginal work are like of music, or what has been called songlines by Bruce Chatwin in his masterpiece about aboriginal culture, *The Songlines*.[12] They are to be played, and the instrument of performance is the ambulatory body (Figure 9).

For a community of hunters and gatherers this is a way of knowing the world in terms of its contours of circulation: in terms of how one moves around it. Paintings are such "maps of locomotion." This is their dynamic character.

To make walkabout is to visit the ancestors: the mountain, the rock, the place where the snake had lived. Walkabout is communal ritual of merger with the past, the origin myth, the source of spiritual and physical life. It is a spiritual act and in fact highly regulated by the community. Not everyone has been traditionally allowed to paint, any more than every Aztec was allowed to become a priest. Because painting has been so important to the community for so long, as a ritual of return, reunification and sustainability, the community over time has evolved an amazing number of astonishing painters, in the way Viennese musical culture led to an amazing number of magnificent composers and performers in the eighteenth and nineteenth centuries.

There are certain affinities with the Surrealist imagination, which aimed to bring together a perception of reality and the unconscious world of dreaming in what Andre Breton called a convulsive beauty. Surrealism was among the avant-garde movements that came into

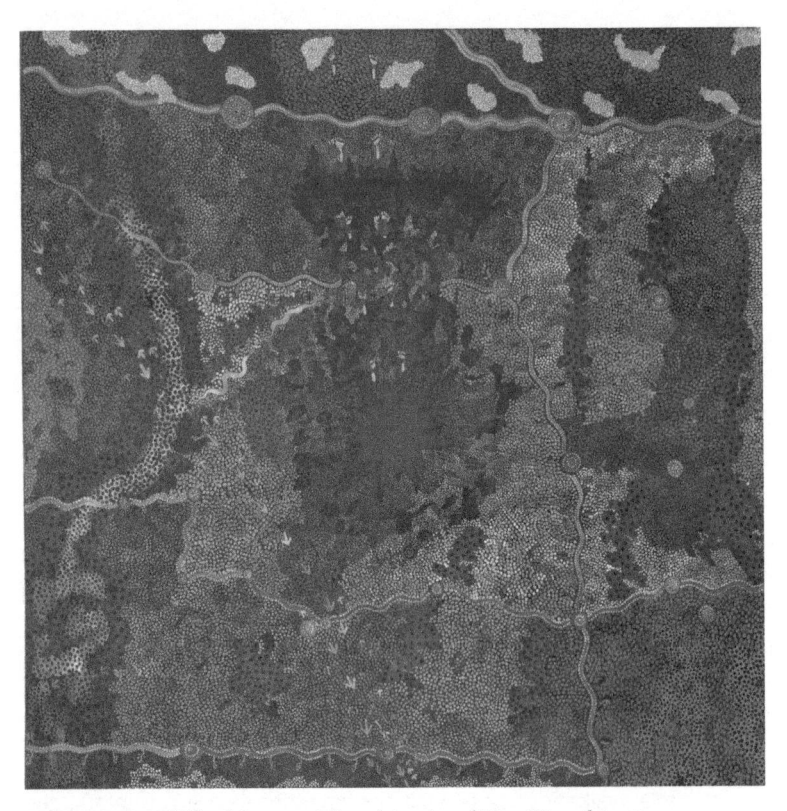

FIGURE 9 Clifford Possum Tjapaltjarri and Tim Tjapaltjarri, Warlugulong, 1976, Gallery of New South Wales, Sydney. *Rights courtesy of Aboriginal Artists Agency Limited.*

existence after the First World War, seeking radical transformation of what these artists saw as a bankrupt society, living off the hypocritical illusion of its civility and rationality when in fact the war had proven (to them anyway) that the system of modern treaties, values, science, and technology that had meant to lead to European progress had instead unleashed global war, violent bombs, poison gas, and the horrors of the trenches, wiping out an entire generation. If that was not demonstration enough that reality is also a dream (meaning a nightmare) then nothing was. And so Breton preached a convulsion of beauty through art that would come straight from the human unconsciousness in the form of an "automatic" pen, hardly controlled by the artist who would turn into a medium for a séance of creation. Freud was very important to the Surrealists, who had learned from him that even the dream has its own interpretative logic, its own script. And so why not write the script of the dream into the medium of the artwork in a way that would take human reality and fuse it with the dream's strange mechanisms.

Failing to find the ecstatic available to them through the channeling of the unconscious directly into the artwork (which they never managed to make happen), certain of the Surrealists ventured out to the "primitive" anthropological world of Haitian "voodoo" ritual, Native American potlatch, and other forms of culturally mesmeric intensity where they hoped they could recover some of the tremulous, dreamlike power they sought for European art, and in a way that would undercut Europe's claims to "civilization and rationality" that they abhorred. This project was quixotic, since collective ritual is a practice which Europe was by the twentieth century only able to capture in politics: in the mad public rallies of fascism and totalitarianism, collective nightmares that they were.

Not every social or cultural practice is possible in modern times which represent a loss, not simply a gain. The surrealists sought inspiration from distant tribes and their rituals because they implicitly understood that ritual is a socially coherent and integrated practice of the kind that largely disappeared from modern Europe and especially from its art. They were not, I think, aware that such practices had disappeared from art only to relocate to Europe's fascist and totalitarian politics.[13]

The ecstatic is not identical to the beautiful of the sublime, those central aesthetic categories of the European eighteenth century. The beautiful is about pleasure taken in symmetry, proportion, and harmony. The sublime about the elevation of spirit when it finds itself overwhelmed by an object felt to be so magnificent that the mind cannot encompass its size, scope, dynamic power, or infinity, bringing up feelings of awe and anxiety, also powerful ideas of greatness of one sort or another. (We will take up the beautiful and the sublime in Chapter 6.) The ecstatic is a state of tremulous merger with something, in this case the world of the ancestors.

So perhaps we do have analogues for the ecstatic in the European *past*: in that Ancient Greek art, for example, whose purpose was to catalyze a Dionysian state of excitement of the kind Plato disliked and Nietzsche welcomed. But this kind of example is long ago and far away from contemporary experiences. Unless my superb student Gabriel Schat is right and young peoples' raves retain something of this wild, ecstatic intensity, encapsulated in the exhortation "Get your freak-on."

The traditional aboriginal artist does not think of themselves as producing "art" in the way that concept has currency in the modern system of the arts. To call their work "art" is to bring its values of craft and expressive power, not to mention cultural and spiritual force, within our own concepts. Doing this is perhaps a way of expanding our own concepts or at least knowing them better in the light of what resides adjacent to them. Aboriginal work has many of the ingredients of what we call art: it is made by the painter's hand, well crafted, powerfully organized in its use of the medium. Its content is superbly fused to its form and its communal values are indubitable. And yet it has been made outside the institutional world we think of as the modern system of the arts, and also apart from the intentions to make art that Michelangelo, Beethoven, Picasso all variously had. Aboriginal work allows us to frame our own notions of art in relation to something adjacent to them: too close not to be sort of thought of as art, too far to be simply included in what we call art without remainder.

It was a technique of the twentieth-century philosopher Ludwig Wittgenstein (1889–1951), both in his writing and teaching, to find and invent examples of items about which it was too simple to say either that it was or was not a number, human being, computer, an object or natural or artificial kind, and the like. Such examples allowed, he believed, for the seeing of what he called the "grammar" of our language games. His way of putting the point was this:

> A main source of our failure to understand is that we do not command a clear view of the use of our words.—Our grammar is lacking in that sort of perspicuity. A perspicuous representation produces just that understanding which consists in "seeing connections." Hence the importance of finding and inventing intermediate cases.[14]

One might say that the encounter with aboriginal art does exactly this, since it is a kind of "intermediate case." It is in that middle ground, that productively gray area, that the cosmopolitanism encounter resides. For by placing our modern concept of art against aboriginal work we learn something of its character and limits we would not otherwise have learned. And something about aboriginal work as well.

And yet we also know we will never quite understand what it is to be a traditional aboriginal person making this work, what it in the end means to them and does for them. We stand respectfully at the edges of their world. Even if it shares many things with ours, this concept (of the art of the Dreamtime) is one we do not have. Not even in the depths of our tradition known as Romanticism, which aims for communion with the past and the dead thanks to art. So, the encounter should also make us a bit humble about the prospects of knowing all that well.

Now traditions seldom stay put in contemporary times; more recently the assimilation of aboriginal peoples into the texture of Australian life has led to a new generation of painters who are trained in these very avant-gardes. Judy Watson, an artist of aboriginal descent, created a series of sculptural installations during the late 1980s about dispossession, intrusion, and land rights, making work which aimed to address the ancestors but also the Australian art world and Australian state politics. Rights claims rather than dreaming became the purpose of this art, which recruited the materials of aboriginal tradition to the purposes of avant-garde installation: that is as a way for her to speak politically about her own ethnicity. Her use of aboriginal techniques was not ritualistic, aiming to connect her ecstatically with the ancestors, but as a way of voicing her ethnic oppression in Australia historically and then, in the late 1980s, when she made these works. Made of powder pigment on plywood and called "the guardians," these works call on the spirit culture of the dead to watch over contemporary aboriginal politics—and do so for a national/international audience rather than speaking purely within the aboriginal community. Her intended audience is the art world and Australian society. She no longer speaks to traditional aboriginal artists, but rather *of* them, and from their force of spirit. These are the spirits or bones of the ancestors in her work.

Her etchings from the late 1990s, "our bones in your collections," "our skin in your collections," "our hair in your collections," recruit aboriginal-style Dreamtime painting to the purpose of speaking to the (dis-)possession of aboriginal peoples by the museum and the archive, where they have historically been "anthropologized." Aboriginal works—not to mention bones—end up in museum collections where they sit in partial discomfort and in a state of silent protest.

Watson's work really does belong in the museum, because it is speaking to Australia as a whole, on behalf of aboriginal peoples (Figure 10).

Her work turns traditional aboriginal practice into the cultural sign for a community now understood as an ethnicity. She is no longer speaking within the circle of aboriginal ritual, which turns into identity politics. Tradition has now been fused with the legacies of the European avant-gardes. At this point aboriginal art becomes not only modernist but also postcolonial, since it addresses the Australian nation and its dispossession of the people whose bones it also collected in its then colonial museums: aboriginals.

Watson's work is one example of a large and variegated field. Many artists continue in the old vein, citing, mapping, and dreaming the ancestors. Others seek to speak aboriginal languages to global audiences—often politically—by melding them with what has been learned from the history of twentieth-century art. The very act of speaking of tradition in the context of a modern nation-state already changes the tradition by revocalizing it (placing it in the national art museum, for example, where it speaks differently). There is no one way a tradition endures or dissipates under such conditions but many. No doubt the global world makes it harder and harder for traditions to remain exempt from its tentacles.

And so, a tradition based in a thick aesthetic concept not shared outside the community morphs when it modernizes, into art making which *does* share thick aesthetic concepts with global art and recasts its tradition in that light.

We now turn to the second of Appiah's types of moral conflict: when persons share a thick concept but work out its terms very differently. I think most key aesthetic concepts are of this kind. The beautiful and the sublime may be found in Chinese landscape painting, in Japanese woodcuts, in Italian Renaissance frescoes, in

FIGURE 10 *Judy Watson*, Our Bones in Your Collections, *1997. Etching and chine colle, 29.4 × 20.5 cm, 30.0 × 21.1 c platemark, 40.0 × 27.2 sheet, Mollie Gowing Acquisition Fund for Contemporary Aboriginal Art, Art Gallery of New South Wales, 1998, rights c/o Artists Rights Society. Licensed by Artists Rights Society (ARS), New York, 2018.*

Ancient Greek sculpture, in music across the world, and so on. With different resonances of course, bringing up different kinds of ideas. The idea brought up by the sublime in Italian Renaissance painting is meant to be that of the sublimity of the Christian story humanized to express the ideal aspirations of Christian peoples. The idea behind the Chinese sublime is that of spiritual balance, a quiet, contemplative life in which people and the natural world are in harmony. It is because the Chinese mountain of Wang Shimin's landscape painting (1592–1680) shares so much aesthetic structure with the Renaissance hill towns that form the background for Leonardo da Vinci (1452–1519), that the power and subtlety of their cultural differences can emerge so perspicuously. (Kindly google them both.)

The role of contemplation is certainly different in Chinese society, both as a moral and spiritual commitment. Yet there are also traces of contemplative beauty in Leonardo's Tuscan hills. Moreover, both works carry the sense of awe for the beauty and refinement of the artistic process itself: awe for paint and what it can do in scribing the human. It took centuries for this depth of likeness to become visible to both cultures, they had to learn each other's languages, habits, to view each other through the lens of likeness rather than stereotypical hierarchy to do it. They had to overcome the barriers of race and empire.

The third kind of example is the one where persons give different weights to various shared concepts, my example being free speech in relation to liberty and the giving of offense. These kinds of examples in aesthetics are the daily fare of the critic. For aesthetic concepts live in this state of friction across artists, movements, ages, peoples. It is the very character of them to solicit this kind of aesthetic, moral, and political argument. How the sublimity of prose is weighted against the demand of social commentary by novels, how formal subtlety is weighted against the value of emotional expression, how avant-garde political practice is weighted against artistic autonomy and its similar values, how taste is weighted against conceptual art (which has little to do with taste and a great deal to do with concepts of art and the world), how tradition is weighted against global absorption, how individual liberty in paint is weighted against community values and messages, how art is weighted in relation to philosophy, morals, or politics. It is within this field of antagonisms and relationships that artists make choices, work, and live. It is about this web of antagonisms and relationships between values that critics and theorists write. Take away this web of differences and you lose the very subject of art.

Hence the need for a cosmopolitan perspective that seeks to understand how various peoples make their choices within this aesthetic, moral, and political field of principles, commitments, and differences and to expand one's own horizons in the light of it. That is the essence of cosmopolitanism: a guiding commitment to the dignity of peoples across the globe, to the idea that we may learn something from everyone (however prosaic and obvious this may sound). Also, a recognition of the basic tension between humanitarian commitments centered around universal human rights and full recognition of human diversity. Of course, the moral and aesthetic situations are not the same, even if morals and aesthetics can intertwine in ways with deep consequence for human lives. It is far easier to live with differences in taste and preference across peoples than with moral and political differences. Intractable disagreement about basic moral and political things usually has far more at stake than in the aesthetic cases. This does not mean that the aspiration for aesthetic bonds of uniformity with others is not a profound human fact. It was part of what motivated Kant's idea of a "sensis communis," a community of taste which would then help shape, he believed, moral agreement.

4

Cultural Property and Aesthetic Synergy

The Question of Cultural Property

A central part of the argument for cosmopolitanism Appiah makes concerns the question of cultural property and related, the "ownership" of culture. Property is normally thought of as material (your house, your garden, your flat screen TV). One can own paintings and sculptures. And there is the issue of copyright. Plays, musical scores, literary works, and even performances are routinely protected under the copyright laws for artists and/or publishers who maintain control over their use. When artists pass away, their estates may continue to control, and charge for, use of their works. Properly understood, the purpose of copyright, trusts, estates, or foundations is not to obstruct dissemination of the work but insure that the artist or publisher or estate is compensated for public use. One could call this stewardship of the work, which means availability for proper use by the public according to an idea of fairness so that the artist/publisher is also given their due. It represents a kind of ownership.

But the idea that entire cultures were owned is an ideology of the colonial past. This idea was essential to the cultural power colonialism exerted over the colonies. Europe believed it owned its culture: the paintings in its museums, its philosophy, literature, science, morals, everything that it believed comprised its heritage. The key link was between heritage and ownership. Heritage was believed to convey right of ownership. Since we the Europeans invented it, discovered it, since it is part of the fabric of our modern nations, part of what makes us superior beings, it is ours. European culture might be offered to the native in the form of a gift: a gift of salvation, education, moral uplift. But this paternalist attitude, so central to colonialism and its missionary work, depended on the idea that Europe had right of ownership. For you cannot give a *gift* of something you don't own.

We have seen in Chapter 1 that heritage conveyed character: only people born and bred within these traditions could be capable of grasping and mastering their power and worth.[1] As I said, the colonizer/owner of Eurocentric culture might then offer his or her culture as a *gift* to native populations: this is the project of missionary work, of the mission school and colonial church. Like sharing food that one owns with the hungry, or one's house with someone who needs a bed for the night, the gift of culture was a form of colonial beneficence. It was a gift that was in origin European, the product of uniquely European agency. Few held the conviction that native could assimilate European culture with a capacity for agency and innovation that the European had. The European produced, the native received. And badly.

I have said in Chapter 1 that this offering of the gift, however well meant by fervent missionaries or enlightened liberals, was really a way of creating dependency, since it arrived with the devaluation of the native's own traditions. The native was then left bereft of her own past, left with the only option of being forced to master the gift Europe offered of its culture, above all its modernity. For the concept of heritage underpinning the modern European nation-state was also understood as a key to the modernity of the nation-state, for its heritages were those of law, knowledge, inquiry, morals, science, and civility. And Europe believed the native would never really succeed at such mastery of European modernity, he or she wasn't up to it. This, I said, meant the native must forever remain a second-rate appendage of the colonizer, a recipient of the colonizer's gift but unable to really make use of it on their own. The whole process was meant to insure a perpetual state of dependency of the native on the colonizer, and the menial place of the native in the colonizer's world.

Things were more complicated in actual missionary practice, with subversions of the ideology happening in the villages of the Tswana and elsewhere, a give-and-take between colonial missionary work and what the colonizer/missionary learned from the native. The result was a set of vibrant, hybrid forms, among them African Christianity with its deep roots in African concepts of Ubuntu (as in the adage, it takes a village to raise a child), forgiveness, spiritual apostolicism, and the like. The great work of Jean and John Comaroff is about this.[2]

European colonialism is now officially over, raising the question of the very appropriateness of the concept of cultural ownership understood in these older terms. Almost all culture circulates in one form or another across the globe today. For example, opera is now part of the South African democracy, with Africanized performances of Italian and Viennese masterpieces by brilliant and powerful black African singers, trained in the art of choir as children, in churches where often arias were sung to the dancing of the choir as part of the joy of communal gathering. Their ears were tuned by choir to perfection, and indeed their languages resonate in amazing concordance with Italian and French, given the use of vowels in Xhosa and Zulu. And so, it was in a way natural that black African voices should emerge as a major contemporary force in opera.

When culture circulates globally the issue becomes one of transplantation. How, and with what degree of power or originality, does a cultural form graft into a new culture? With what degree of innovation and/or excellence, and to what social purpose beyond the mere free play of the imagination does it excite in a new and free population?[3] And how are such matters to be evaluated, and by whom?

Sometimes transplantations fail, the donor rejects the recipient's DNA, the body rebels. Opera grafts well in South Africa. But do not think the transplantation is free of conflict. In an earlier book I wrote about one such conflict around the practice of opera in the new South Africa at great length[4] and will not repeat all that here. But the gist was that among young South Africans a conflict exists about what the terms, if any, of cultural authenticity should be for a newly democratic, decolonizing nation. Some believe opera, because an icon of Eurocentric privilege, colonial gift-giving, and social/economic elitism, is the last thing young born frees, as South Africans born after the end of Apartheid are called, should waste their time performing. In doing so, these young people say, the performers, many of whom are black, are simply repeating European dependency and colonial mimicry in postcolonial times when there is something better they should be doing. Young people of talent should instead be delving back into their own traditions to find and reinvent African township jazz, Zulu gumboot dancing, traditional Christian choirs, ancient instruments, old ways of painting and carving and house design, and so forth—this in the name of empowerment, refusal of the colonial past, return to myths and traditions that guided Africans in the past and will now steer them toward empowerment and identity. And so, a construct for authenticity, for what in cultural production is authentic and what retrograde, should be guiding the society during its journey away from colonialism toward its better self.

Of course, many of these traditions are themselves earlier grafts from European sources, including township jazz and Christian choirs. Not all are. So, is one then going to exclude those that, after generations of assimilation, have become distinctive of South Africa because of their partly foreign origins way back then? Pushed far enough, this means only original or first peoples and their cultures are entitled to the appellation: authentic, a theory of authenticity that is evidently self-defeating for anyone who wishes to embrace the panoply of cultural forms comprising the new South Africa (or anywhere else).

Equally important is that this demand that culture be authentically African rather than rehabilitated from colonial Eurocentrism is a theory of ownership in reverse. It says: Africans are the sole owners and proprietors of their past, and to become again themselves they must steer a course back to what they are, to their heritage. Ambivalence toward formerly Eurocentric forms is one thing; the proposal that they are inherently inauthentic to the new South Africa another. Here heritage (African heritage) conveys a demand: you must conform to it or risk being inauthentic.

Against the demand for authenticity, a demand that has wide resonance in South Africa today among black Africans and in the name of decolonization, is the voice of South African opera composer Sibusiso Njeza:

People tend to think of opera as "not our thing" as South Africans; they think it is for the Italians. Yes, Italians are known for opera, but music and storytelling is part of our history; part of our heritage. If we, as South Africans, are able to tell the stories of our own people in our own languages through music, then why not .... Opera is ours now and we need to advance its appreciation so that people can understand it better.[5]

Njeza is saying that he and other South Africans are free to tell stories in whatever way they feel suits their talent and the social urgencies or best ways of telling personal stories. As the American composer John Cage was fond of repeating from his friend the painter Jasper Johns: Permission granted. But not to do anything you want. What was the point of all that bloodshed, struggle, truth and reconciliation, writing of the South African constitution, work of transitional democracy, however satisfactory or unsatisfactory, if not to allow a new generation to be free to sing whatever they wish in the new South Africa because to them, no one owns anything, everything is up for grabs, everything in culture circulates so as to be used, the question being how well or badly you do it. Freedom is for these young opera singers the freedom to follow their taste and passion. Which shows there is a great deal to be said for the importance of taste and passion for aesthetics, and human life, a theme we shall take up later in this book.

The singers are claiming John Locke's natural right to *liberty* in a global world.

There is another aspect to this conflict in cultural politics. Which is that the young South Africans singing opera also see themselves not merely as South Africans, singing in the name of their country, but equally as *citizens of the world*, rightfully able to adopt any style, sing in any opera house worldwide because they are global citizens. In short, the whole issue of how to balance the value of national attachment with that of global citizenship is at stake in the debate around what is proper, if anything, to South African culture. And whether the very idea of "propriety" any more applies.

The opera singers from South Africa have talent and training and are in demand throughout the opera houses of America and Europe, Australia, and South America. What they do not adequately acknowledge, and what the other side of the argument clings to, is that the global south remains in a state of dependency on the global north culturally, for resources, including employment. So that all too often South African talent, once it has been meticulously home grown, heads abroad, thus conglomerating the resources of the global north at the expense of the global south, and in a way that recapitulates cultural inequality across the globe.

I had a number of things to say in my earlier book about whether the older idea of the "third world" announced at the Bandung Conference of 1955 and its canons of anti-Western third world solidarity might be profitably reactivated just here.[6] So that across the global south nations could band together to enhance cultural opportunity for high-priced cultural activities like operatic performance in a way that would have a better chance of retaining or at least keeping in circulation singers who will otherwise flee to the north, not to mention exhibitions and theatre and other economically impracticable events for moderately resourced nations. But my idea is perhaps a pipe dream.

Heritage and the Return of Objects

In response to colonial claims that culture is owned by persons in virtue of their belonging to a heritage (the European one), the decolonizing imagination of the past half-century has responded by saying: You stole our heritage, we want it back. We have the right to it, please return it now. This is very much a live issue as I write (in 2019). In 2018 Emmanuel Macron, President of France, agreed to return twenty-six sculptures to Benin that had been housed in the Musee du Quai Branly in Paris, which houses more than 90,000 African treasures. These were directly taken from the King of Dahomey during the days of French occupation of what is now West Africa. Macron has vowed to return thousands more.

The reason Appiah is so interesting is the original and highly controversial way he responds to this postcolonial demand. His response has two parts.

First it is inflected by a general attitude toward culture. Appiah believes the best attitude toward culture is that insofar as there are owners of it (of paintings, collections, museums, concert houses, ancient artifacts, sites, ruins, great houses, churches, etc.), these owners think of themselves less as owners and more as cultural *stewards* of what they own for all humanity. Thus, preserving the cosmopolitan idea of being first and foremost a citizen of the world whose culture is also open to the world.

Now the international organization UNESCO (the United Nations Educational, Scientific and Cultural Organization), established in 1945, at the close of the Second World War and at the same moment as the founding of the United Nations, is dedicated to a similar idea. That preservation of culture transcends national boundaries. The Taj Mahal is of global importance to humanity and UNESCO considers it the purview of the organization's money, influence, and expertise to curate. Currently the Taj is under restoration. I happen to know the architect responsible for this task and recoil at the level of responsibility his firm has assumed. Imagine failing, causing the building to fall down! You would have to leave the planet earth and emigrate to Mars with Elon Musk. Good luck with that. If India owns the Taj, it does so in the form of stewardship more than anything else. It would be a cultural crime for India to knock it down and put up a Trump tower in its place. A global cultural crime.

UNESCO restricts its global stewardship to objects and sites of unique importance and also to culture at risk. Both of these devotions can only be called admirable.

But Appiah goes further. He believes the best way to understand all culture is to see it as belonging to all humanity: "We can respond to art that is not ours; indeed, we can fully respond to 'our' art only if we move beyond thinking of it as ours and start to respond to it as art."[7]

What I think Appiah means is that to think of art as an object you own is to diminish the sense of its largesse, a largesse that goes beyond oneself into the horizons of many others. It is to lose the link between art and the binding of humanity, a link discovered, if also overstated, by Kant. There is something to Kant's idea that when one judges something beautiful one speaks as an exemplar for humanity. Art rises above the status of property to the status of a thing bonding people together in deep acknowledgment. To merely cannibalize the experience of art as experience of that which is mine and mine alone is to diminish the aesthetic power of the work, it's very purpose.

However, tell this to an Italian, for whom half the pleasure of Italian opera is the way it is rooted in Italian language, customs, emotional attitudes, dramatics, voice, and for whom the enjoyment is amplified because she knows that everyone across the society, from the cleaners to the taxi drivers to the architects and bankers, has opera in their bones just as she does, even if the taxicab drivers sit in the low-priced seats at the top of La Scala and the lawyers in the private boxes.

Now should the Italian turn into a cultural fascist and say to the African, "this opera by Verdi is mine, not yours, I am superior," that would be racist and also point to an aggressive attitude the Italian probably has when attending performances of Italian opera, an attitude that is, to my lights, aesthetically diminishing. However, there is a place for another Italian, not fascist, to think or say, this music really does reflect me in a way it doesn't reflect everyone else. It is part of the texture of my life, of my national struggle. Verdi was a player in the Risorgimento, the national struggle of 1848, his name became a code for the restoration of Vittorio Emanuele as king of a sovereign Italy. Opera is at the very foundation of the Italian nation-state. And so, the Italian could say or more probably think without saying: Yes, we are delighted you too like our operas but they will never play the role for you they have played for us. They are *ours* in that sense. This is a claim of something less than property and more than mere stewardship, which seems to me central to a great deal of aesthetic experience and cultural politics. Appiah does not mention it.

Having said that, a South African could also retort to the Italian: opera means something to me that it could never mean to you. And then go on to speak about the freedom of voice, the connection which the choirs in which he sang as a youth—choirs which regularly performed Italian arias while dancing—about the giddy sense of coming from a township and ending up on the world's stage. In fact, opera could have unique meanings to all kinds of people, which would be proof of its global importance. This is simply another way of putting Appiah's point that art is bigger than oneself and one's own particular horizons. A certain humility is warranted.

Of greater interest is Appiah's idea that the politics of repatriation are misguided. This is the second part of his view.

It has been a virtual canon of decolonization that objects stolen or purchased at unfair prices during the days of colonialism should be returned to the countries of their origin. South Africa called for the return of the bones of Saartjie Baartman, otherwise known as Sara, a Khoi-San woman who had been taken to England in 1810 and then France and exhibited like a museum piece, sometimes naked, to European science and bourgeois society. Known as the "Hottentot Venus," Sara was curated as an example of African freakdom.[8] Two features of Baartman stood out as indicative of Khoi-San anatomical abnormality, as European medicine construed her and her kind, both having to do with her female parts. She had the humiliation of being exhibited naked, to show these unique anatomical features. Europe, gripped by the racist belief that physiognomic difference is to be scientifically construed as a sign of racial depravity and inferiority, used her to prove and broadcast the theory.

In 2002 her bones were returned to her homeland in South Africa from France, upon request by first State President Nelson Mandela. The act was widely believed to be just. Similarly, the Greeks demand the return of the Elgin marbles from the United Kingdom, India its sculptural treasures, Native Americans their bones from US museums including the Museum of Anthropology at my own institution the University of Michigan, which returned them.

It is a central purpose of philosophy to challenge widely held views that seem obvious. That repatriation is a central instrument of decolonization of unquestioned justice is one such view, making Appiah's challenge philosophically brave.

This is what Appiah has to say:

> But what does it mean, exactly, for something to belong to a people? [His example is Norway] Much of Norway's cultural patrimony was produced before the modern Norwegian state existed .... The Vikings who made the wonderful gold and iron work in the National Museum buildings of Oslo didn't think of themselves as the inhabitants of a single country that ran a thousand miles north from the Oslo fjord to the lands of the Sami reindeer herders. Their identities were tied up, as we learn from the sagas, with lineage and locality. And they would certainly have been astonished to be told that Olaf's gold cup or Thorfinn's sword belonged not to Olaf and Thorfinn and their descendants but to a nation. The Greeks claim the Elgin Marbles, which were made not by Greece—it wasn't a state when they were made—but by Athens, when it

was a city state of a few thousand people. When Nigerians claim a Nok sculpture as part of their patrimony, they are claiming for a nation whose boundaries are less than a century old, the works of a civilization more than two millennia ago, created by a people that no longer exists, and whose descendants we know nothing about. We don't know whether Nok sculptures were commissioned by Kings or commoners; we don't know whether the people who made them and the people who paid for them thought of them as belonging to the kingdom, to a man, to a lineage, to the gods. One thing we know for sure, however is that they didn't make them for Nigeria.[9]

The present state or nation seeking return is a different entity from the people who had objects stolen or bought at ludicrous price way back then. Those people are long gone. One cannot return anything to *them*. Moreover, the nation-state now calling for return did not even exist when theft occurred. There was no state of Greece when the Elgin marbles were taken, so who is the nation-state of Greece to demand return of the marbles to it?

Moreover, the demand for return is misguided, Appiah thinks, because it remains within the framework of ownership rather than stewardship, which would be an attitude more open to having objects anywhere, since they should be wherever they are for *everyone*, which makes it less important where they are located.

These remarks are worthy of debate.

As to the question of the proper beneficiary, the reason why the families of Jews whose paintings were stolen by the Nazis or forced into sale at humiliating prices have a claim to get them back is because they can prove legal descent from the victims. Many paintings and other fine objects have been restituted to their heirs of families from whom the objects were stolen. But this is because international laws of inheritance extend to descendants of families. But without proof of descent claimants have no right to the return of artworks. I cannot simply say to some German Museum I am a Jew and you wronged my people in 1942 so give me a Matisse or Picasso and expect the goods to be delivered. Anyway the "you" who wronged my people (and in what sense are they "my" people anyway?) is mostly long dead. There is then a question about the responsibility of nation-states for acts committed in their pasts: when and where responsibility begins and where it stops. For neither the victim nor the perpetrator remains alive.

A best practice example of repatriation happened recently: the return of Gustav Klimt's Austrian masterpiece, the portrait of Adele Bloch-Bauer, along with four other Klimt paintings, to Maria Altmann in 2006. Altmann sued in virtue of being Adele Bloch-Bauer's niece. The paintings had been seized by the Nazis in 1938 from Altmann's Jewish family. Soon after receiving the artworks, she sold the most famous of them, the portrait of Adele Bloch-Bauer dressed in gold against a golden background, to the Neue Galerie in New York City rather than keeping it shut away from the public in her little cottage in Los Angeles, where she was living in much reduced circumstances from her elegant bourgeois Viennese life. This case was successful because a historical wrong was clearly identified legally, agreed to by both parties (after much wrangling) and redressed, and in turn the plaintiff offered the most important work to a museum, turning it over to the museum-going public rather than hoarding it.

My own parents amassed from the 1960s to the 1990s the largest collection of modern and contemporary art of India of its time. And when they came to thinking about its legacy, they believed strongly the work should be returned to India for the benefit of the Indian public. I played more than a little role in this myself and strongly concurred with them about the idea of donation. Unfortunately, no museum in India was able to insure care of the work at the time, much less its exhibition, and no private corporation stepped up to the plate. So, they ended up donating the collection to the Peabody Essex Museum in Salem, Massachusetts, a jewel of a museum from the days of the great ships and mercantile capitalism of the eighteenth century. Thanks to shipping, the Peabody Essex Museum had amassed a significant collection of rare Asian artifacts. There the work resides, parts of it being continually shown in the "Herwitz Gallery." It was the best choice at the time (the 1990s) for preserving these objects for the public, even if Indians must fly to Boston to see them, making it unaffordable for many to do so.

The case of the modern/contemporary Indian art and the moral issue of its return is of a different cast from that of the return of precolonial and colonial artifacts, because most although not all of the work my parents collected was made during and for the Indian nation. Modern Indian art was deeply allied to the national project, and related, the project of decolonization, something widely true of modern art produced outside of Europe and America at the moment when new nation-states were forming out of former colonies after the Second World War. The birth of the Indian nation in 1947 was the very moment a group of twelve painters formed the Progressive Artists' Movement, dedicated to the creation of a new, modern art worthy of the newly modernizing Indian nation. Their goal was to revivify repressed or dormant traditions while reaching out to Europe to discover what modernism might teach a newly modernizing India. It was through the fusion between reaching out to the past and the assimilation of European modernism that their work was innovative. Thus, there was a particular reason why the modern Indian nation-state should be the beneficiary of this art. It was art largely created in India's name.

So perhaps this example is not generalizable to others like the return of objects from earlier, prenational times to nation-states that did not exist when the work had been made and stolen.

Repatriation is always a matter of contestation, because there are multiple moral claims on cultural artifacts, including those of museums in Europe that have for generations put time and money into their stewardship. These museums, fully open to the public, have made African and other objects grabbed during colonialism available to the world (or at least to anyone able to afford to get to London, Paris, New York, etc.). They have digitized many of them, circulating images across the globe. They have carefully preserved objects that might otherwise have fallen into ruin (we don't know). Museums of Europe and America also have a genuine claim on these objects in terms of their history of curation. And so we are in a situation in which there are a multiplicity of claims, all in some interesting sense legitimate—meaning there is no single form that legitimacy takes.

The cosmopolitan understands this and seeks a negotiation. If returned, the object should be widely exhibited and understood to be kept in preservation by the new nation rather than its blanket property. If not returned it should be acknowledged as in some important sense belonging also elsewhere, the past history of its theft foregrounded rather than kept invisible.

The basic issue is a multiplicity of claims, an excess of rights, the legitimacy of multiple perspectives in the matter of reparation. Appiah says:

> The right way [to think about this] is to take not a national but a cosmopolitan perspective: to ask what system of international rules about objects of this sort will respect the many legitimate human interests at stake.[10]
>
> And,
>
> In the spirit of cosmopolitanism you might wonder whether all the greatest art should be held in trusteeship by nations, made widely available, shared across borders ... There is no good reason however to think that public ownership is the ideal fate of every important art object.[11]

But here is the problem with Appiah's position. The urge for repatriation springs from a deep feeling of injustice. There is a deep feeling of offense in postcolonial nations about the wrongs of the past, even if done to the ancestors of some of their peoples and not to the state as a sovereign entity because it did not exist at the time. There is still the feeling: it happened to us. How to best diagnose this feeling? It helps to understand that one cannot easily distinguish the nation-state from its people, a nation is both: the sovereign apparatus of government and the people as such. This "people" is both a real population of citizens that is countable and a more mythic "people" consisting of those who "belong," are "one" with the state and its imaginary and real commitments. Taken either or both ways, the "people" are not separable from the nation-state, which is incoherent without them. The very concept of a nation in part refers to the state apparatus, and in part to its people. To those who are citizens and those who claim identification with the national project, real and imaginary. Now some and perhaps many of those citizens are going to be actual familial descendants of those from whom the objects were stolen. So, it is not right to say, as Appiah does, that because there was no nation around at the moment of theft that its people have no special claim on stolen artifacts (or those purchased at rip-off prices). Lines of descent to the peoples of the past may not be legally provable, but they are definitely there, and the people know it.

The offense felt by postcolonial states has a certain justice in it. Their ancestors really were (in some broad but believable way) the people from whom these objects were stolen. It is not simply that those of the newly decolonizing nation claim identity with their putative ancestors; they actually were their ancestors. Of course, there may be quarrels within the decolonizing nation about who exactly should be the recipient of a repatriated object, a specific village if it is known that it was from this village that the object was taken, or the state, which may have a better ability to curate and preserve the object safely. But these quarrels are best left to the state and its populations.

This is the more luminous point. The past confers a moral demand or what I would even like to call a moral *right*. And not merely through direct familial lines of descent which could in principle be traced from some of the people who belong to a nation back to their ancestors from whom objects were taken or bought at rip-off prices but also through the complex historical process through which a nation-state was born, thanks to the history of colonial degradation out of which it emerged. Not all scars are felt directly on the body. Some are felt because of history claimed as one's own, history through which one's nation and society emerged. The scar has been transferred from individuals to the nation, but that hardly obliterates it. Nobody objects when nation-states acknowledge responsibility for things done in their past, even if the current inhabitants of the state were not alive when the atrocities were committed, nor the leaders of government, and even if all are appalled by what happened.

National debt is not the same as collective guilt. Collective guilt assigns culpability to a group. Debts assumed from the past do not entail collective guilt today, rather the responsible need to repair damage from the past.

This is closely connected to the issue of settler societies and what they owe. A settler society is always a form of theft: theft of land from original peoples. Its sovereignty is achieved thanks to violence. But over generations the society evolves in its own way, the land is developed, blood is shed for it, giving the settler society its own kind of right or legitimacy. Does it have a debt to its original or first peoples? And of what sort? Consider for a moment the kind of moral debts nations acknowledge in virtue of what they have done in the past. It is because they admit a historical wrong that Australia has declared "National Sorry Day" for its past treatment of Aboriginal peoples, and Germany requires every student in school to visit a concentration camp so they will learn up-front and intimately of the past horror their country committed. Even if soon not a single person will remain alive in Germany from that time. These gestures, and the protective laws behind them, are there to ensure it will not happen again through training, law, and the keeping alive of collective memory.

Which debts remain in place across long stretches of time? One need not be able to answer this question in the abstract or as a whole to be committed to the general principle that *some* moral and political debts remain in place across time for nations, groups, persons. I am not sure that Ghana or South Africa have unquestioned rights—national or on the part of groups within—to claim the return of objects as payment of "debt owed." But I do believe they are *right* in this context. Perhaps this helps. It is a moral good, no, a moral *necessity*, to empower persons wherever and whenever inequality and the politics of domination have left them hurt. Put the other way: if one believes in the dignity of all persons, then to empower them must be a basic moral principle. The claims of *empowerment* are here those of *repatriation*.

Who says that in order for repatriation to be motivated you have to find an original owner? This legal concept refuses the postcolonial claim altogether, which is about empowerment because of the scars of the past, not about finding the precise owners from way back when. Which would be absurd, quixotic. Rather the debate over the past year has focused on the idea that Africa ought to be able to participate in the global curation and circulation of objects which were once its provenance. That is an ongoing global injustice that the majority of African objects should be presented to the world through European museums, leaving Africa all too bereft of the materials to participate in its own curation and presentation of objects from its own past to the world. Everyone seems to agree, as I think they should, that whomever ends up with priceless objects from the past has the duty to preserve and curate them for the world.

I think that is wrong, given the ongoing state of global inequality, hegemony, and imbalance of power, to think that Europe has the ongoing right to retain these objects because it does a good job of preservation and presentation to the world through its museums. This is especially true, as I just said, because to keep Africa from participating in the global curation of what were once its own objects is to retain the current map of global inequality in the cultural realm, wherein most of the resources of the world are presented in Europe and America, just as must of the opera singers trained in South Africa end up in Europe and America.

There should be a "cost sharing" relationship that helps to solve this inequality of resources and of global curation wherein some objects are returned while others are allowed to remain in European museums. It is not a matter of return-all or return-nothing. That polarization represents a failure to take both sides into account. And both sides demand to be acknowledged. Terms of proportionate repatriation (what percentage to return and why) would have to be negotiated, but the negotiation would be well motivated because it would acknowledge that both sides have legitimacy.

That would be real cosmopolitanism in action.

Intellectual Property

One of the ways the imbalance of power between rich and poor is corrected is through recourse to the concept of intellectual property. Appiah objects to the idea of intellectual property[12] as partitioning things from the cosmopolitan flow of them. One assumes he is therefore not in agreement with the World Bank, which invented the idea of intellectual property to protect local peoples from exploitation by multinational corporations and powerful states. The idea is best introduced by example.

The Khoi-San, original peoples of Southern Africa, were hunters and gatherers, roaming across the arid deserts of the Northern Cape for long periods of time with little water or food. These hunters and gatherers discovered that a particular desert plant called hoodia, if ingested, could allow a person to walk for days without being overcome by hunger and, above all, thirst. One can live without food for up to ten days before the signs of malnutrition set in, whereas dehydration happens within two or three days—in the heat of the deserts of the northern Cape—less. Major pharmaceutical corporations, learning about this plant from the few remaining descendants of the Khoi-San, aimed to exploit it into a marketable medicine. They stood to earn billions in profit. What the World Bank understood was that unless the Khoi-San and people like them were given some kind of legal protection, they would stand to be totally exploited by corporate power, gaining nothing while the big pharmaceuticals who relied on their knowledge to discover and exploit herbs like hoodia made billions. And so, the World Bank hit on the idea of intellectual property, which is a way of saying that the Khoi-San have a kind of ownership not of the plant itself (which would be absurd as it grows wild in nature) but of the *knowledge* of it upon which others rely in exploiting it for profit.

Such knowledge is understood on the model of a *patent*, through which an inventor gets legal control over their invention. Others wishing to use it (until it expires) must petition and (normally) pay to do so. Intellectual property conveys a similar kind of ownership. Big pharma must pay, or profit share should they rely on local knowledge in the discovery of new medicines.

Now this idea seems to me of indisputable value. It provides another context different from that of copyright in which the idea of cultural ownership has a crucial place in the international commerce of justice. The moral is this. The question of when ownership of cultural goods (including knowledge) is necessary for justice is a contextual question. Perhaps Appiah understands all of these things, for he says,

> The right way [to think about this] is to take not a national but a cosmopolitan perspective: to ask what system of international rules about objects of this sort will respect the many legitimate human interests at stake. ... In the spirit of cosmopolitanism you might wonder whether all the greatest art should be held in trusteeship by nations, made widely available, shared across borders. ... There is no good reason however to think that public ownership is the ideal fate of every important art object.[13]

Either way, the topic of cultural ownership must be disaggregated into a number of specific contextual issues before just solutions can be negotiated and/or ascertained.

Aesthetics of Synergy

The idea I wish to add to the aesthetics of cosmopolitanism is that of synergy across diverse cultural fields. Synergy is a capacity of the imagination: the ability to fuse disparate things into new and coherent patterns in virtue of their underlying or felt affinities. It is an ability that in its very nature outruns rules. One could call it the alchemy of the mind.

Immanuel Kant would have called this "genius," the ability to make new aesthetic objects in the absence of (or better, in ways that outrun existing) rules.[14] Synergy is the "genius" of the cosmopolitan, working between traditions and across global forms. It is his or her testament to the imagination.

Synergy appropriates, it does not claim ownership of the cultural materials it fuses together and integrates, since it is working betwixt and between various cultural domains. It is a form of cultural play.

Synergy is of the greatest importance because we live amidst a barrage of disparate cultural objects that constantly demand comparison, contrast, and fusion into new things. Without the ability to bring disparate objects into a variety of coherent relationships we would be lost in the global funhouse. Synergy is a basic ability of mind. It is not the same as comparison or contrast because it seeks to bring disparate things together into a new, third thing rather than keeping them apart and "measuring" the one in terms of the other, much less "ranking" them in accord with a standard or hierarchy, something the eighteenth-century philosopher David Hume believed necessary for aesthetic objectivity and truth. We will come to Hume's idea later in this book. My point here is that nothing is more common to the global design, production, and use of cultural commodities in our time than the ability to make new things out of multiple and disparate sources, by discovering and creating affinities. This pertains to modern architecture that fused Japanese principles of modular construction and visual transparency with nineteenth-century technological achievements (the Eiffel Tower); it pertains to music, which today fuses African polyrhythms with tonal scales; it pertains to visual art, whose multimedia platforms are often composed of global constituents; it pertains to the design and making of shoes, dresses, hats, automobiles, and just about everything else. The objects composing our world are largely of global design, demanding the imaginative capacity for synergy. In fact, this capacity is so common we often fail to notice its importance. Philosophy is in this instance a matter of what Ludwig Wittgenstein called assembling reminders for a particular purpose, things so common we don't notice them until they are pointed out to us.[15] I think this is true of synergy.

There are a number of ways in which synergy can be compromised. One is when it reduces cultural forms into mere brands, and yokes them together to make a mega-brand (see Chapter 2). A great deal of postmodern architecture did exactly that, mining the history and variety of design forms for their image value, as if Italian mannerist cladding announced that a building was Italianate in the way a cereal box announces that it is organic and fresh. Another is that synergy across traditions may be complicated by lack of deep comprehension, with the result of offense given to one or more of the traditions, often without meaning to. A third is this: some traditions are not only different but *oppose each other aesthetically*. A taste for Chinese opera may preclude or lessen a taste for the European. The more refined you get in the hearing of rhythmical clang and Chinese sing song, the less you are able to stand the big broad, mellifluous sounds of Verdi. The more you assimilate your ears to Bel Canto tradition the less you can stand (much less appreciate) the scratchiness of the Chinese instruments, their harsh plucking sounds, the long growling fierceness, and sharp, high nasal tones of the Chinese aria. One has to learn the art of eye-and-ear-switching, of turning off the eyes and ears you use when attending Chinese opera and turning on a different set of visual and aural expectations and sensitivities.

An example is called for, about how difficult—and rewarding—it can be to successfully synergize partly oppositional traditions. I turn to the music of composer Bright Sheng. Sheng hails from Shanghai where he first studied music. For seven years during the Chinese Cultural Revolution (1966–77) he was exiled to Tibet where he taught piano and spent his time studying local folk music, never knowing if the cultural revolution would end and he would leave the Tibetan hinterlands. Later he emigrated to the United States and became a student of Leonard Bernstein. The opera he composed much later, in 1997, *The Silver River* with libretto by David Henry Hwang, incorporates both operatic traditions so masterfully that one can no longer believe they are not "made for each other." And yet the pleasure in this success comes directly from their clash, which generates a new kind of music, and visual splendor, including a tapestry or tableaux of dancers. One feels the opera is happening in two distinct time frames, one very slow, almost timeless, and proceeding as in if tableaux. Gestures happen at a different scale than in Western opera, which proceeds much faster dramatically (in terms of the unfolding of story) and musically (in terms of tonal shifts and the relation between orchestra and aria). And yet the opera has significantly Western elements, including a kind of pop/postmodern libretto and a fine sense of music theatre Sheng learned from Bernstein, composer of *West Side Story* and *Candide*. Sheng goes so far as to have one of the characters play a Chinese classical instrument, the pipa, rather than sing, the story is Chinese myth reset as contemporary comedy which progressively becomes less comic, more poignant and more arioso.

The Silver River is a model for the production of art today as it crosses not merely cultural boundaries but media. It is an act of synergy where diverse traditions are fused through innovation. I think the cosmopolitan ear of the aesthete who reaches out across traditions has a similarly imaginative, synergizing nature. When an ear trained on Italian opera reaches out to seriously encounter Chinese opera (and I do not mean hearing it once on a tourist junket, I mean serious encounter over time) it learns the art of dropping some of its training to hear otherwise and the art of reevaluating the musical character of Italian opera in the light of Chinese work. But also, the ear and the mind behind it seek imaginative synergies between them. And does so in the absence of rules, since the relationships between Chinese and Western opera Sheng brings into new arrangement have never been so related before.

Cosmopolitanism is not simply the hermeneutical adventure of learning more about oneself through the encounter with the other. Nor is it simply a way of dropping one tradition to make way for another. It seeks new relationships across significant cultural boundaries. And so global innovation takes place not merely in the composer's studio but in the listener's mind. If the eighteenth century discovered the importance of the imagination for aesthetics, perhaps it is time, in the twenty-first, to discover the importance of synergy.

Let me put this another way. Cosmopolitanism does not seek translation across cultures or diverse traditions or disparate visual forms, first because translation properly pertains not to images and cultural forms but to languages. We do not quite know what it would mean to translate one visual form into another unless the visual form is thought of as a kind of "text," which can be done up to a point but never sufficiently captures what the visual form is doing, what its role is, or power. Second because in spite of overall commonalities difference is too profound (between Chinese and Italian opera, for example) to allow for a mapping of one onto the other except in very general ways. And so, the issue is rather to find new ways to put them together, which change both while preserving something of their original meanings.

And so, rather than translation, *synergy* is called for: new forms of relationship, appropriation, fusion. As it had been with the opera of Bright Sheng. Sheng does not translate Chinese operatic elements into Western ones or vice versa. He fuses them creatively into a new and coherent thing, given his sense of what it is about each that disposes it to be brought into a new arrangement with the other. The key is to synergize in a way that produces something coherent. If one does not want the word "synergy" to be associated with coherence (in the ways Bright Sheng's opera is "coherent" or narratively and stylistically integral) then another word like "creative appropriation" or "integration" ought to be used. I am personally fine with the word "synergy" but it is the work this word is meant to do—in capturing the process of fusing and integrating disparate traditions—that is what I really want to highlight.[16]

5

Meaning, Medium, and History in Art

Hegel's Colonial Vision of Art and History

It was the nineteenth century that took it upon itself to understand and theorize the relation between meaning in art and the medium of its embodiment, generating ideas without which I would be unable to speak to the conditions of art today as I have in the first two chapters. Aesthetics as a philosophical discipline begins in the eighteenth century with the study of taste. But a deeper analysis of meaning, medium, and the role of art in history only comes later, with G. W. F. Hegel (1770–1831), whose work is the *locus classicus* of philosophical inquiry into this basic fit (meaning with medium). In this chapter we will study Hegel's ideas.

We will study the importance of Hegel's idea that art must be understood in the light of its contribution to history. This idea is so deeply engrained in the art world today that one cannot think about contemporary art apart from it. However, Hegel's notion of history was not a notion of global and cosmopolitan history. For this philosopher, writing at the apogee of colonialism, Europe and its nation-states was the only part of the globe capable of producing real history. The rest of the world, meaning the entire colonial world, was and would always remain dormant, mired in its own past traditions, condemned to endlessly replay them in the manner of a broken record. And so, the history of art could not be a cosmopolitan history, it could only be a history that favors Europe as the sole actor on the historical stage.

This bifurcation between Europe, which could enter modern life and create modernity thanks to its capacity for historical invention, and the rest of the world, which remained sedimented in the past, was a strategy for the exercise of colonial power. For it consigned native populations to the passive position of receiving the fruits of European history and culture in the form of a gift. We know, the European said, that you cannot generate political, cultural, and social transformation on your own. But we will give you the fruits of our labors, an entry pass into modernity. Of course, we also know you will never be up to innovation in modern life on your own terms. Rather, you will be consigned to imitate what we have done in perpetuity. You will never be free to create your own path into modernity.

The gift of European modernity, offered to the native with the proviso that he or she would never be capable of freely assimilating it to his or her own purpose, but would rather end up a lackey, a menial, following in the footsteps of the European explorer of the future, was a strategy of disempowerment. It aimed to prevent the native from the project of inventing modernity on his or her own terms, in the light of his or her own traditions. For an independent path to modern life would inevitably mean a break from European rule, a staking of independence, liberty, and, ultimately, new nation-states. And so, the restriction of history to Europe by Hegel and the wider Europe he was of was a form of selective empowerment: self-empowerment at the expense of the native world. Hegel was in this sense a colonial, not a cosmopolitan philosopher.

The nineteenth century witnessed three waves of global culture pouring into Europe and stimulating its art. First the Chinese, second the Japanese, and third, at the end of the century, the African. Each of these forms of global influence proved crucial in generating new art in Europe. Europe was in fact dependent upon the colonial world for its own modern productions. And yet it acknowledged no debt. For the thinking was that these global influences are mere materials, like cotton for the maker of shirts or uncut diamonds for the jeweler. Chinese, Japanese, and African cultural objects were not quite considered fine art in the European sense, because they did not arise from European history and tradition. Instead they were lovely curiosities, beautiful relics, strange remnants from the past, there to be put to European use. The critic Edward Said called this "Orientalism,"[1] a set of strategies to exoticize, and thereby other the art of the world, so as to retain European dominance and authority in the cultural field.

But second, since Hegel refuses a global idea of history he cannot begin to think about the complex interrelations between forms of history, and the cultural objects they produce, in the way the past two chapters have detailed. Once one refuses a global account of art in relation to history, or rather histories in the plural, one cannot take a cosmopolitan position on art and its synergies across borders. The world cannot be a place for discovering new ideas of the self and others in the light of the cosmopolitan encounter because it is already known, the colonial formation of us v. them is already in place, the systems of devaluing them and applauding us are already there as an ideology of dominance, and rule.

And so cosmopolitan aesthetics must begin by criticizing the way Hegel subscribes to an ideology that refuses it, and thanks to his embroilment in colonialism.

Having said that, we can begin to think about what is, nevertheless, of importance in Hegel's writing for thinking about art today.

Hegel and the Medium of Art

For Hegel art is knowledge in embodied form: the form of paint, marble, sound, drama, ceramics. Since it is the purpose of art to provide knowledge of one's time rather than to provide the pleasures of taste, which are significantly sidelined by the nineteenth century in favor of interests in the arts, and since the arts have for Hegel the exalted purpose of acknowledging the deepest aspirations of the age, and to do so in a medium (of paint, marble, sound, etc.) the question becomes for his *Aesthetics*, why *this medium* as opposed to *that medium* in any given instance? What does one medium offer that another cannot—or cannot easily?

Hegel begins from the platitude that not all things are possible in all media of art. If you wish to create a work speaking to the complex nature of international financial markets and their relation to inequality, you probably won't choose a solo flute piece to do it. You might rather make a film, quite possibly a documentary film, write a novel or work of theatre, or perhaps create an art installation with text, video, and images of the degraded factories of Bangladesh where workers are locked in for hours at end to slog at the making of the clothing we happily wear. A flute sonata will not likely have the capacity to articulate ideas as complex and abstract as capital flow, much less inequality. On the other hand, should you wish to celebrate the arrival of spring, the flute may be your ticket with its sharp flutters in the upper registers, recalling the dazzle and tangle of birds, the opening of flowers, the arrival of Dionysian ecstasy.

To know what a medium of art is, according to Hegel, is to know its possibilities. The only way to know the possibilities of a medium is to imagine and invent them, so the history of an art is for Hegel the history of discovery and invention through which artists, in forging new uses of a medium, come over time to know what the medium is, what it is capable of. This includes learning the limits of the medium, what it can do, or cannot do except in the most extraordinary circumstances, and learning this by pushing up against its limits to the breaking point. In our time art has pushed up against the limits of art by wishing to turn art into a kind of philosophy and/or politics.

To take an example, some strands of twentieth-century conceptual art have dedicated their work to detailed and precise reflection on visual culture itself, something which presses the capacity of a purely visual medium to its very limits. For normally visual objects require concepts behind them, words on the page if you will, a textual background in order to "speak" abstractly and precisely about the world. This is why the avant-gardes formulated their experiments in the light of the dictates of the manifesto. The manifesto, a political form adopted by the avant-gardes, sought to articulate the link between visual experimentation (in new media, multimedia, etc.) and political force. To explain why, or convince why, abstraction, montage, radical innovation in new Perspex, glass, steel, photography, sculpture and film, multimedia forms like the productions of the Bauhaus have the firepower to speak in the name of the revolutionary future (on the right or the left). And not only that, raise the consciousness of the viewer so as to ready that person for the historical struggle in the right direction. This aim of intervening in history, of riding its crest like a surfer, requires a text to alert the audience to the purpose of visual experimentation, which without a text behind is insufficiently articulate as a medium to generate political understanding, much less political force, from purely visual innovation. Often written by a poet, the avant-garde manifesto, itself a form of art, is also a visionary image of the utopian future which the utopian/avant-garde work must and will bring about. Art itself, thanks to the manifesto, becomes a beacon of what the future will bring. This is its politics.

It is very difficult for a purely visual medium to "speak abstractly" or of complex ideas and situations without the help of words, which is why theory has, since the days of the avant-gardes, assumed a central role in art-making and criticism.[2] It is not impossible to reflect on art and visual culture in purely visual terms (without a manifesto or clarifying text) but very difficult to do it well. The great genius of this was Marcel Duchamp who famously stated in an interview with Pierre Cabanne that "everything in my art was becoming conceptual," depending on things other than the "retina,"[3] worked for twenty years on a single masterpiece, the installation *Étant donnés: 1° la chute d'eau / 2° le gaz d'éclairage* (*Given: 1 The Waterfall, 2. The Illuminating Gas*). Duchamp's installation is situated behind an old wooden door, with a hole in it for the viewer to spy through, like a voyeur. What the viewer sees through this hole in the door is a young woman, completely naked, curled in what appears to be something between a manger (as in the Christ child) and an abandoned field. Behind her is an artificial scene of nature painted as backdrop (in the Hollywood style). The scene is lit with an internal light source of the kind found in French Baroque painting (Georges de la Tour). This lighting is strident and dramatizing. The scene recalls images of the crime-ridden streets of Victorian London where Jack the Ripper did his nasty, miserable work by gaslight. The young woman may be asleep, she may be dead: murdered. Her genitals are directly exposed to the viewer, who is excited and shocked in the manner of a true peeping Tom. Her hairless sex may be a sign of her innocence (the virgin birth); it may be a sign of her violation, it may be that she is a mere doll tossed into the scene. Duchamp worked for two decades on this elaborate setup, which speaks to everything from Victorian crime novels to the history of painting, from cheap thrillers to Hollywood films to the story of Christianity. Duchamp plays the viewer like a musical instrument by placing him in the position of voyeur, a Norman Bates from Alfred Hitchcock's *Psycho*, staring at Janet Leigh through a hole from his office into Cabin 1. The viewer's unseemly position of voyeur is a direct invitation to the dance until the viewer realizes the woman's genitals appear slashed, horrifying him for his lewd moment of excitement. This vitrine—this act of display—uses simulation (of these scenarios) to address a number of related forms of visual culture coldly and from the outside (watching, looking, excitement, voyeurism, killing) whose legacy remains deep in art and wedded to the contemporary world, but which Duchamp's display treats as a strange and bizarre thing.

The purpose of this takeoff on the nineteenth-century vitrine, in which animals were exhibited in scenes as artificial and stilled as Duchamp's woman, is to examine the entire culture of museology, in which the bodies of women are turned into nudes displayed—that is, splayed—before the voracious, voyeuristic viewer. And by extension to reflect critically on the tradition of the nude in Western art, and its connections to male pleasure at seeing the stilled, pliant woman, and these in relation to Victorian crime scenes, the police, and many kinds of novels, including those of horror. His genius is in the visual details, the way the work sits between classical painting (Georges de la Tour and his use of internal lighting), peep shows, cinema, lurid novels, and deep themes of Western male omnipotence or what has come to be called "phallocentrism." Again, it took him twenty years to do it, which is not simply because he had a reputation—largely self-made—of being a lazy man, preferring chess to work, but also because he was truly a thinker in the medium of art, and thinking comes slowly, demanding rigorous revision and self-interrogation, and endless rewriting of thoughts, which means rearranging of the elements of this visual piece.

To understand a medium of art is partly to grasp what comes easily in it and what only with the greatest difficulty. Anyone can take a photo of the sea on their cell phone and it will probably come out lovely, perhaps beautiful. But try to paint it in the same degree of pixel subtlety: if it can be done at all it takes an accomplished painter. What comes easy in photography is difficult in painting. To know this is to know part of what makes each medium the thing it is, in the case of photography, the role of the machine in recording

FIGURE 11 *Marcel Duchamp*, Étant donnés (Given: 1. The Waterfall, 2. The Illuminating Gas, French: Étant donnés: 1° la chute d'eau / 2° le gaz d'éclairage), *1946–66, Philadelphia Museum courtesy of Association Marcel Duchamp / ADAGP, Paris / Artists Rights Society (ARS), New York 2018.*

reality. In painting the role of the hand, at least until digital technology intervenes.[4] Duchamp accomplished a level of conceptual analysis that is in fact of the greatest difficulty in visual/plastic art, although it is a belief of our time that any artist can draw a line on a wall and with the right language behind it take that line to mean anything they wish, which defeats the purpose of art, turning it into a mere index for linguistic meaning, at which point one should dispense with the line drawn on the wall and simply write the book.[5]

Duchamp took reflection on art nearly as far as it could go in the medium of visual means, at which point perhaps philosophy takes over, a thought central to the aesthetician Arthur Danto's story of twentieth-century art, a story adopted from the pages of Hegel who believed at a certain point in history the world became too complex for art to address, at which point it gave the job over to philosophy.[6]

Why History Matters for Art

Hegel was the first person to ask the question, "Why does history matter for art?" and make the answer the centerpiece of his philosophy. It is commonplace today that art experience may be amplified if one knows something about historical background. One approaches the Taj Mahal and is overwhelmed by its jeweled, crystalline beauty, the way it seems to float, luminous as a bird, as if a single breath could blow it over, it's white jeweled marble glistening in the sun, the recessive beauty of its facade almost apparitional. One may have this experience without knowing anything about the building beyond its ethereal, diamantine beauty. But one may appreciate this building all the more if one learns that Shah Jahan commissioned it in 1632 in memory of his beloved wife Mumtaz, that it is her tomb, making it a temple of love, mourning, and eternal rest. In her tomb it is she who is forever elevated, thanks to the building.

Facts do matter for the experience of art, therefore for taste. This is especially important for twentieth-century modernism. How could one evaluate Duchamp's masterpiece without knowing a great deal about the history of painting, of crime, of Victorian novels, of the lurid pictures and peep shows upon which Duchamp is critically reflecting?

But it is equally true of the Renaissance. Without knowledge of the Christian story, one will be at a loss to understand the meaning of an annunciation painting, or a painting of the virgin being assumed to the heavens, or St. Francis giving up his money to the poor. Without knowing that Renaissance paintings were often created for an illiterate population going to church, who could see the stories they knew so well represented in painting but could not read them in the Bible. Renaissance art is therefore devotional. Without knowing Duchamp's own biography, one will not know he began as a painter only to give it up and in the words of Thierry de Duve, spend the rest of his life meditating on what painting is by creating installations and objects that were not paintings.[7] Knowledge of background often deepens, or qualifies, aesthetic experience.

But Hegel believes there is a far deeper way in which art is situated in history. For this we turn to his masterwork *Aesthetics: Lectures on Fine Art*.[8]

It begins with the notion that art is a product of human activity; and it is properly appreciated as such. Humans make art as a way of accommodating themselves to their world. Art is part of the way humans come to *know* their world, and their place in it with others. In this art is of the same order as religion and philosophy:

> [M]an brings himself before himself by practical activity, since he has the impulse, in whatever is directly given to him, in what is present to him externally, to produce himself and therein equally to recognize himself. This aim he achieves by altering external things whereupon he impresses the seal of his inner being and in which he now finds again his own characteristics. Man does this in order, as a free subject, to strip the external world of its inflexible foreignness and to enjoy in the shape of things only an external realization of himself. Even a child's first impulse involves this practical alternation of external things; a boy throws stones into the river and now marvels at the circles drawn in the water as an effect in which he gains an intuition of something that is his own doing. This need runs through the most diversiform phenomena up to that mode of self-production in external things which is present in the work of art.[9]

Art responds to a universal human need to "lift the inner and outer world into [our] ... spiritual consciousness as an object in which [we] ... recognize again [our] ... own [selves]"[10] and "... in this duplication of [ourselves] ... bringing what is in [us] ... into sight and knowledge"[11] for others.

The key to the human, Hegel believes, is that we seek to find and achieve recognition in what we produce, to stamp ourselves on the world so as to find ourselves within it in ways we can recognize and embrace. And by "we" he means not simply each and every individual human being, but the "we" of a society, a place and time. The goal of human activity (which means of human history) is to achieve mastery over our environment, to create a world for ourselves in which we are free to be free as individuals and as a community. This means removing (overcoming) the alienation of our social as well as natural environment, making both conform to our deepest aspirations. The goal is to build a social world in which we find our deepest aspirations capable of expression. In which there is a sustainable match between our picture of ourselves, the world and others, and the way things are. In order to do this both the world and our own picture or knowledge of it must simultaneously evolve. This is the work of history. What history is.

Hegel understood that many of the concepts and building blocks his age took for granted—ideas like equality, freedom, universal rights, constitutional law, also of the string quartet, the symphony, the sonnet, and of three-point perspective in painting—did not simply spring into the world from nowhere, enter the minds of persons, by "natural right" or lucky accident or innate knowledge. We were not born with them and more than that, we cannot have suddenly arrived at them without sufficient infrastructure and traditions of thought in place. Thought is, like science, a matter of gradual discovery and invention. It builds upon itself, in particular on the mixture of its truths and falsities, of successes and failures that lead to innovation. History had to go through various stages in order for the idea of equality, and of the university right to freedom associated with it, to have even arisen in the minds of human beings, much less been instituted in law and the practices of the state and community. Only at the end of a long history of misfires and gradual improvements can such a profound idea have become even imaginable. Alienation is not overcome all at once but through the entire historical process.

This is the shape of the Hegelian dialectic, crucial for aesthetics as well as religion, philosophy, and politics. History advances progressively through a set series of stages, which at the end of history can be shown by philosophy to have been *necessary* stages in human history rather than mere, perhaps lucky accidents. From stage to stage, human actors cast the world in a particular form—the master–slave, monarchy, religious domination, of various kinds of philosophical and artistic culture, of morals and politics—and finally through these inadequate and self-contradictory forms of social arrangement humans manage to bring about a world of equality, its recognition in law, of the modern state, the forms of philosophy and art both adequate to what they aim to represent, and a social world that makes possible individuality in nonalienated relation to community and the state. Only by trying to make the world one reflective of our interests can we realize we have failed and get a better idea of how to do it through what went wrong. Human action is the piston of human knowledge. By making a world, we come to know better who we are and what we want, by realizing what the limitations of this world are. Progress is historical.

The goal of history is the simultaneous finding of knowledge and the making of the modern world. One cannot have one without the other. For it is through the successive staking of a relation between what we know or how we picture the world and others, and what it is, that generates new history, in turn leading to recognition of mismatch, that is, to alienation, which in turn generates new knowledge and a new shape for the world. Out of this process science, art, and philosophy are born and develop, and the state is built with its universities, courts of law, and so on. Human beings come to know their world by staking themselves in it and making it. Then they come to know themselves better by remaking it. This means remaking everything from the state and the court of law to their own knowledge, art, and science.

Happily, for Hegel the final victory of history, the grasping of its golden snitch in this game of historical wizardry occurred—so he felt certain—right in his lap. This happened with the French Revolution and with the enlightened ideas of Immanuel Kant. It remained for Hegel to explain how the process of history had, stage by stage, led to the point where the modern European nation-state with its proclamations of universal rights and its state apparatus of culture, religion, and philosophy could completely express the aspirations of citizens, now fully formed by the work of those who came before them and slogged through the detritus of history to get to the point where they, meaning Hegel himself, were the happy beneficiaries of a form of social construction (the modern state) which could absolutely and without remainder express their aspirations. At which point they could attain true knowledge of who they really are as individuals, a collective, as citizens.

It was a corollary of Hegel's that when the progressive work of history gets mankind to the point where it absolutely expresses them, mirroring their aspirations in the modern state, history is complete. At which point the history of art is also complete, an idea that the great aesthetician of the second half of the twentieth century Arthur Danto took over from Hegel, merely changing the dates. Art history ended, Danto thought, in 1964, with Andy Warhol of all people bringing it to conclusion, at which point the self-reflective character of art had gone as far as it could go and turned itself over to philosophy, meaning to him. For neither philosopher (Hegel or Danto) does this mean that no more artworks will be made, lives lived, wars fought. History will continue, including art history. But with nothing more to accomplish by way of pushing history forward. Since it has already completed its purpose.

Arthur Danto's Hegelian Twist on the Art World

What Arthur Danto, among the most important aestheticians of the twentieth century, added to Hegel was the central role of the modern art world for the understanding of art. When Hegel wrote the modern art world had yet to emerge in history, arising as it did in Paris mid-nineteenth-century thanks to the remaking of the city, the rise of a middle class wanting to display itself in the trappings of commodities, including art, the system of the gallery, the critic, the increasing importance of the museum and concert hall. The great painter Edouard Manet, whom I referred to in Chapter 2, could not have worked his critical twists in paint without that art world in place, with its tensions between art as yet another commodity to be bought in the shop along with a new dress or hat, and art as a rarefied thing eternalized in the museum. With the art world came the critic, the art theorist, a system of players and producers and consumers who increasingly responded to a modernist culture of innovation with theories of art (for or against), new concepts catalyzing innovation (the avant-garde manifesto, for example), new ways of expanding the horizons for what is possible in this medium or that. Art itself became more and more theoretical, and of necessity, since it was exploring new ways to generate meaning.

In the light of these events, all of which happened after Hegel's time, Danto revised Hegel's formulation, arguing that what defines a work of art, indeed sets the horizon or limits of what it is possible to do at any moment in history in art, is a theory held by a historically evolved art world. The Eureka moment that led to Danto's "after" took place in the Stable Gallery run by Eleanor Ward in 1964, no longer in existence, where he witnessed an exhibition of Warhol's *Brillo Boxes* installation. Reflecting on the comic, surprising, highly provocative exaggeration, Danto began by noting the obvious: Warhol's art objects were to all intents and purposes visually indiscernible from the Brillo Boxes one finds in the supermarket. The boxes comprising the Stable Gallery show were in fact made by Warhol, and comically oversized, but in other exhibitions Warhol simply stacked boxes—or Campbell's soup cans—which he had his assistants purchase at the supermarket. Many at the time said Warhol's exhibition was a case of the emperor's new clothes, and Warhol a sickly charlatan. But others, including Danto, reasoned that there was no sham here; Warhol's Brillo Box was a work of art when exhibited in the gallery, his argument being that Warhol's gesture of exhibiting these boxes invested them with the kind of embodied meaning a work of art requires, since suddenly they became comic/ironic meditations on—and celebrations of—the relationship between product, art, and design in American consumer culture, indeed reflections on the very nature of art.

A number of critics understood that Warhol was pushing against the limits of art in a way that forced abstract reflection on what art was and could be. It was Danto who worked out a detailed account of what Warhol had not merely solicited (questioning about art) but implicitly demonstrated. Since these objects were visually the same when on the supermarket shelves and in the gallery, none of their *visual properties* could play the role of defining them as art when in the gallery. Indeed Danto believed and wrote that no aesthetic/sensuous/passion-driven feature could spell out the difference between a thing's being a mere thing, as opposed to a work of art. Rather, a background set of framing concepts (which Danto glossed as a "theory") shared by an art world needed to be in place, which would, however controversially, allow these objects, under Warhol's prestidigitating gesture, to "speak" as art. Art was like language, a way of addressing the world, and like language it was an abstract set of signs given meaning by a set of beliefs comprising a "theory" by the speakers of that language, here the art world.[12]

In the case of art, it is, Danto reasoned, the cultural background of an art world that puts in place a set of concepts that allow the one thing to be schematized differently from the other, as Duchamp's *Bicycle Wheel* exhibited on a pedestal suddenly becomes a play on the very idea of sculpture. When Duchamp exhibited the *Bicycle Wheel* in 1913 it became a brilliant simulation of sculpture, exciting the tactile values of sculpture (you want to spin it, which is not unlike wanting to touch the soft feminine curves of a Canova marble), it was suddenly infused with anthropomorphism (it became a head, a torso, a body sitting on a pedestal), it was displaced from its mechanical function (you could spin the wheel but it went nowhere), and so on. All of these features of Duchamp's artwork make it exactly that: an artwork that so brilliantly simulates classical sculpture that it places the classics under review or scrutiny. However, Danto reasoned, only in an art world with a certain history and background concepts could viewers see and conceive of the Duchamp work that way: as a meaningful reflection on what sculpture is, delivered through the provocation of an "intruder" (the bicycle wheel). Of course, not all agreed that it was art and Duchamp's work, like Warhol's, has received its share of insult. But only within the context of a modern art world (with its conceptual schemes) could this debate even take place.

Warhol thus exhibited to Danto that art is historically evolving, since at any given time the terms for how meaning is to be embodied (and in what medium) will differ from other historical moments: in the Renaissance the terms would have been iconographic, narrative, representational of the Christian story, and of portraiture and landscape. The Renaissance art world, on Danto's view, could not have conceived of, much less processed, Duchamp's or Warhol's gestures as art.

Here for Danto lies a crucial difference between how a language and a work of art acquire and communicate meaning. A language relies on its signs (a, b, c, d) purely abstractly, as rule-governed conduits for meaning. A work of visual art *embodies* its meaning in its visual twists which are *not mere conduits* but reverberate overall with content. Change any visual feature of a work of art and you will likely change its content. It is through the unpacking of the work's visual characteristics that its meaning is unfolded.

And yet, Danto denies that the work's visual properties play any essential role in defining it as art. This is rather weird. Visual properties may not be sufficient to make something a work, since concepts guiding how visual properties may embody meaning, allowing a work of art to "make a statement," are also required. And these have constraints. Duchamp would not have been able to visually play with the urinal or the bicycle wheel before the twentieth century, our concepts would not have allowed for it or even found it comprehensible. In this regard concepts held by an art world are essential for the definition of art. Danto is right about this and it is a good insight. But neither are concepts sufficient, since they are largely about how visual materials may be used to matter in art: be used to make meaning. Visual properties are equally important in the definition of art, in making art what it is.

Danto's theory of art is therefore a significant departure from Hegel's. For Hegel was committed to the belief that the sensuous (in our case visual) nature of a medium is crucial in constituting the artwork, which pours meaning into sensuous form, merging form and content into a sensuous expression of "the aspirations of the age." Danto by contrast sidelines the visual, and more generally the aesthetic, as if how an object appears, feels, and excites passion were completely irrelevant to what as a norm, if not always, makes it a work of art. Even Duchamp's masterpiece *Étant donnés: 1° la chute d'eau / 2° le gaz d'éclairage* depends utterly on its visual characteristics: it toys with the viewer, turning him/her into a voyeur, in a way that solicits complex reflection on visual culture that the work invites, thanks to its visual design. This visual twist on the viewer is central to the way meaning is generated. And I see no reason to deny its aesthetics are central to what makes the Duchamp into an art, in spite of what Danto says.

Why then does Danto exclude the sensuous and the aesthetic from the definition of art, when it is the relationship between these characteristics and those concepts held by an art world which only together spell out what art is? This is a complex question, but of importance here is that Danto's approach reflects the late-twentieth-century predilection for sidelining sensuous, aesthetic characteristics in thinking about what art is. He is not alone in this. Beauty, sensuousness, the sublime, depth of feeling all tend to be marginalized by art theory and to an extent by contemporary art today. Contemporary art and art theory instead focus on assertion, meaning, conceptual reflection, rhetoric, and politics. But does art today really sideline visual and aesthetic properties in the way it sometimes claims? If you return to what I said (Chapter 2) about Kentridge, the answer has to be, for really important art, not at all. Kentridge's work is visually sensuous (the use of drawing), his effect is poetic and haunting, he is utterly involved in creating work delivering intense aesthetic experience. I want to call him a poet.

To retrieve the importance of sensuous, aesthetic features for the understanding of art, we will have to go one century back in time, to the eighteenth, which will happen in the final two chapters of the book.

Hegel's Idealizing Notion of Art

Now Hegel has a magnificent idea. Art does not merely express the aspirations of the age but attempts to do so in idealized form, reconciling the contradictions. It is therefore utopian. Through sensuous symbols, art provides images not of abstract morality itself (Kant's idea of the beautiful), but an idealized image of a new social order, one of harmony, unity, purposive form in which the alienated fragments and contradictory aspects of the actual historical world at a given time are symbolically unified. In art, place and time find themselves embodied in a way that tries to bring together contradictions and resolve problems. Art is utopian in that it expresses what the world might look like at that time, were it better, and how humans might enjoy it. As such it is a way of bringing to light contradictions, problems, and the aspiration to resolve these.

The reason why at certain times in history certain media predominate is because their particular capacities are uniquely suited, Hegel believes, to the age and its conundrums. His history of aesthetics details this. At the moment of classical Greece Hegel believed sculpture predominated because it uniquely had the capacity to reflect a world lived between human beings and the more idealized gods, sculpture being man transposed into the beautiful material of more exalted beings. It is dubious, I think, that in any single age, insofar as one can isolate an "age" from the flow of history, a single medium predominates. In the classical world tragic drama was I would have thought as essential, and if Friedrich Nietzsche is correct, more important, than sculpture.[13] In our time it might be said that film, television, and the media predominate, making it hard for plastic art to get a voice in. This has political as well as aesthetic consequences because art, in seeking a political voice, inevitably finds itself in competition with the media, and usually loses. One cannot fight the mass power, celebrity, and often false authority of a force as large as media conglomerates.[14] But it might also be said that music is a central art of our time, popular, rock, classical, hip hop, rap, which speaks profoundly to the fault lines of our time, especially around race, and has its own mass appeal thanks in part to digital media. So, it is also unclear that there is one medium that predominates, rather a constellation of such.

It is also dubious that art always plays this exalted role of idealizing an age in a way that presents its aspirations in utopian and reconciled form. But the idea should not be discounted for when art does do this it is of extreme historical importance. An example is needed. Hegel's two volumes are filled with these.

A more contemporary example might do better than one from the pages of Hegel's masterwork. Since I lived in South Africa during the 1990s, at the tumult of transition from apartheid to democracy, let me turn to the art made at that moment of whirlwind. We go back to 1992, one year after the formal end of the apartheid state.

Nelson Mandela has just been released from jail. There is an 'interim government' in power to work out terms of transition, with the National Party, under de Klerk, in the process of hammering out an arrangement with Nelson Mandela, representing the African National Congress (ANC). This is a moment when the delicate negotiations about the new democratic state might at any moment collapse. It is a moment of ongoing violence. The moment will lead, as it happens, to the Interim Constitution of 1994, mandating the first democratic elections of that year (with Mandela elected State President) and the Truth and Reconciliation Committees which began their work in 1996. The final Constitution will be completed in 1996. But no one yet knows this, the air is heady with change and rife with uncertainty.

In this heady moment of the early 1990s the South African art scene seemed to express the yearnings of a people to come into contact with the styles and lives of each other, to hear in each other's art the possibility of connection each with the other, to hear in that art the chord of liberation from the strictures of separation imposed by social life, racial and cultural ideology, and political fact. As the new South Africa gradually lumbered into being, artists seemed to have discovered the fact that they shared—if from highly skewed perspectives—a common landscape and a common history. Such was a moment for the expansion of styles in a host of original ways. An African painter would appropriate Abstract Expressionism, recasting it with the patterns of Ndebele villages, Zulu pots, or the landscape of the bush; a young sculptor whose parents are from England but who grew up in this world of green snakes, red earth, and the sublime violence of nature would find West African forms natural.

In this liminal, mixed place called South Africa, formerly one among the ultimate experiments in Western racist state domination, the postmodern dreams of pluralist toleration and the pan-availability of diverse cultural styles finally came into play—at least in art. I think of that moment in the South African art scene as utopian: utopian in the way that its optimism, its heady indeterminacy, and its exemplification of the capacity of artists to restitute connection between styles and persons, all existed as ideal models for the future of the nation itself. The sense of emergence from a white-hot past liberated a tenebrous desire for the future, and the South African art world was for a brief time fueled by vast quantities of that desire: desire for a better society, desire for a new nation, desire for better terms of agreement between persons, desire for the fun and the natural.

It is only at certain times in the history of nation-states, and usually at the moment of their formations or reformations, that art can experiment, while also expressing new terms of citizenship. Artistic experimentation in South Africa has been profound because it has been a way of experimenting—in the sphere of art—with new and idealized relations between persons who will jointly inhabit a nation. And it is experimentation without a single narrative of national unity, but instead with the genuine dynamics of compatibility. (A popular image of the day was that of the "rainbow nation," of different colors beautifully joined together into the bands of a rainbow after the storm.) The hope was that persons would find themselves sharing styles, they would become more alike, and paradoxically more able to voice, communicate, their differences (see Chapter 5). Which means that art was in this instance a practice which set the utopian terms of national communication by symbolizing diverse populations as more alike and integrated, and difference more communicable and negotiable.

Practices of becoming like the other are in the field of subjectivity a kind of experimental work. Such work is far more difficult to carry out in the social and political fields, and as in the progressive moment in India, art therefore becomes a beacon for what is more difficult to achieve elsewhere. Its energy is fueled, its utopian role made possible, by that. The politics of establishing (reestablishing) the nation require that an actual agreement be forged between vastly different racial, ethnic, linguistic, and geographic groups (the ANC, the National Party, the Inkatha Freedom Party, the Zulu, the Afrikaner, etc.), each with vastly different interests and little internal uniformity. Out of these groups must emerge an agreement to set the foundation of the nation—if the nation is to endure with dignity. Such an agreement is very difficult to achieve since any democratic society will consist of persons with divergent views of the social good and their role in it. So, they must come to agree on basics: what the nation is, where dissent fits into it, what kinds of rights are basic to the dignity of their citizens, and so on. And yet in the early 1990s the ANC and the National Party, struggling to achieve basic terms of government, could not at the outset agree about such basic matters as private property, with the ANC demanding to nationalize the mines. These disagreements became tractable largely thanks to the overwhelming negotiating facility and personal prestige of Nelson Mandela, but the art of the early 1990s couldn't have even known that would happen.

And so, the art occupied the position of an idealized exemplar for what would happen only later in the state and society. And for what remains to happen, and is happening only slowly and unevenly, in the field of human relationships across the color line. This is the Hegelian point: the art produced in idealized form, a gesture which imagined the national aspiration by fulfilling it in a way hardly (so easily) possible in other parts of social life.

It has to be said what art imagined was not widely accessible to South Africans, given the underdeveloped state of the South African art world in the early 1990s, and the fact that art did not really circulate across the color line except in the emancipated circles of that small world. Soon, and more popularly, the media would pick up the same theme, with TV shows picturing relationships between persons across lines of race and class before the fact of them, picturing indeed a multiracial middle class before it arose. Which only shows that TV along with art stood as an exemplar by imagining the resolution of racial "apartness" (apartheid) before it really began to happen in ordinary lives.

This form of imagining in visual art happened through the cross-pollination of styles, as I said, in which each began to reach out to the culture of the other and make it their own. Identities were at that moment ready for change, for a perilous intermingling with those long excluded from one's own self-image and sense of power.

If we return to the question of contemporary art, however, I think the rhetorical gestures of much of that art do not conform to the Hegelian idea of expressing the aspirations of the age in idealized form, that is, in a way that reconciles (symbolically) conflicts internal to that age. In our time, and I refer back to Chapter 2, we do have certain key aspirations, up to a point shared by art world players at any rate, if not the human population as a whole, at least those who are progressive. These revolve around global humanitarian aspirations such as environmentalism and economic justice, and also around certain global inequalities focused on race and gender. I do not think, however, that art takes its job to express these aspirations in idealized, reconciled form. Rather it lambastes, criticizes, aims for acknowledgment of problems and for political response. Art is more a cry, a diagnosis, a gesture of defiance than an image of reconciliation. In this Hegel was utopian or idealistic, in his sense of how art interacts with the social world it is of. Art sometimes aims to present the terms of an age (insofar as there are such common terms to the age) in idealized/reconciled form. Sometimes not. The avant-gardes didn't, nor does Kentridge, nor Cindy Sherman, nor Duchamp, nor, nor, nor.

Different historical moments call for different kinds of responses from art. This leads back to an earlier question. If we ask again, "Why should art have a history?" and "Why should this history matter at all for our appreciation of its beauty and power?" this is Hegel's answer. Art is not mere entertainment, a consumer item for the pleasures of taste, however beautiful. Art is a concrete action in concrete media, which is expressive of the aspirations of the age: this is for Hegel why history is essential to its understanding: because it speaks from history and to history.

Finally, it ought to be noted that the history of culture early to the South African democratic transition perfectly illustrates a *more cosmopolitan use of Hegel*. For South African styles are globally influenced as well as organically arising from evolving local traditions. This is how their differences can be played out in the modern world. They are all modern, the result of a hybrid history of a country (South Africa) whose map has been drawn by Europe, by indigenous peoples, by African ethnicities, by white settlers, and on and on. This map is a cosmopolitan map in miniature, since the effects of the globe have drawn it. And so, to bring aesthetics, in this case those of Hegel, into the cosmopolitan present is a task that can easily be done. And should be.

The End of Art

This until art history is complete. At which point the deep role for art is, both Hegel and Danto believe, over. For art history has at that point completed its purpose. Hegel believed the end of art—not the end of history—landed, I said, comfortably in his lap. With the French Revolution and the writings of Kant on equality history had achieved its ideal state. And so there would be no more need for art to drive history forward by giving voice to the aspirations of the age in utopian form. The historical necessity of art was, with the end of history, finished. This did not mean art would stop being made. People make art like they breathe: because they have to. They make art because they wish to. But art after the end of history is—both Hegel and Danto believe—freed from the burden of making history, urging history toward its propulsive conclusion, so that it may dance to whatever tune or drummer it wishes, freely following its taste and passion. Not the worst scenario in the world.

What art is no longer free to do, both philosophers believe, is to contribute to the making of progressive history, because it is already complete. For Hegel this means *all history*, which ends in the European nation-state, for Hegel its culmination. For Danto, *simply art history*, since for Danto the rest of history (economic, political, social, scientific) continues to happen after the end of art. But once art has accomplished its purpose, which is to come to understand the philosophical conditions of its existence, in other words to come to understand *what it is*, art history is complete, at an end.

Again: by "end" is not meant death or work stoppage. What is meant is the precise philosophical idea that history has a progressive shape, which art has contributed to bringing to fruition. Once this task is completed as Hegel believed it was, there is no longer the possibility for art to play this historical role. Art-making should and will continue, but in the absence of driving history.

What then is lost? The answer can only be a certain seriousness, a certain burden, a certain challenge: to make history happen by embodying its aspirations within a medium. Art after the end of art can no longer do this. It is lighter, perhaps unbearably or sadly so, perhaps joyously like the man or woman recently released from prison.

In order to believe a thesis about the end of art one has to believe history (all of it or more modestly the art historical part of it) has a single progressive shape, a purpose which art seeks to bring about by revealing historical aspiration. Drop this idea that history can be assigned a single philosophical shape and the idea of the end of art falls away. There is no end of art, rather an endless address to whatever history continues to present us with year by year, century by century.[15]

I have said that Hegel believed the goals of history were achieved with the French Revolution and Kant, with the formation of the modern European nation-state and its forms of religion, art and philosophy. Suffice it to say this beautifully naive view has been proven completely wrong by the massive tectonic historical shifts of the events of the nineteenth and twentieth centuries. We are hurtled by history, and not toward any single conclusion but in a constantly spiraling state where the goals and possibilities change with events. So much history has taken place with the emergence of the art world after Hegel's time, not to mention modern, postmodern and contemporary art, the bursts of technology that produced the radio, telephone, TV, internet, and Trump-tweet, the horrors of the world wars and remaking of the map of Europe, thanks to decolonization, the birth of humanitarianism, the cold war, the rise of China, that the idea that history has come to conclusion is today a charming, naive anachronism. The day history ends is the day the universe ceases to exist.

Hegel could believe history came to an end with the European nation-state only because he existed within the ideology of the Treaty of Westphalia of 1648, believing the terms of the modern nation-state therein articulated to exhibit finality, when linked to the progression of thought leading to the institutions of liberty, as the eighteenth century conceived them. Since then, national sovereignty has been profoundly rethought thanks to the need for international law and humanitarianism, also thanks to globalization which links nations in ways they could not have then imagined. Human rights have—I have already said—become immensely more complicated and contested, turning into the strengths and weaknesses of humanitarianism. Hegel shared the colonial ideology, moreover, that the only place history could ever take place was in Europe, because native cultures are mired in the past, incapable of achieving modernity except by imitating the European. Drop all of that and the cosmopolite will say: history is happening everywhere; the question is how to understand and learn from and form new relationships with its many diverse strands.

I take the first two chapters of this book to illustrate just how far history has come, including the history of art, since the days Hegel announced history was complete.

The same applies to Danto's narrative of the end of art. First it is also a Eurocentric narrative, since the modernist art that impels twentieth-century history is entirely European and American. That art history is happening, and in a non-derivative, non-imitative way, in India, China, Latin America, South Africa, and so on, that art history is a family of interrelated events happening globally, is irrelevant to Danto's thesis. Had he paid attention to what is going on in the wider world, instead of thinking of it in the usual neocolonial way as inherently imitative and without importance for his thesis about the end of art, then he would have had a very hard time believing that art has come to a culmination point when new events are constantly happening in, for example, China and Senegal, of interest to the increasingly globalized art world and to art markets.

Danto believed that modern art history was propelled by a single goal. A philosophical one no less. And a philosophical goal set entirely within the framework of Western philosophy. Namely the goal of self-revelation of the philosophical conditions that define art. This idea that the point of an enterprise is to discover the essence of the thing studied is as old as Plato and as recent as, well, Danto. Other philosophical traditions think of philosophy in different terms, such as the Indian tradition which thinks of it as a multiplicity of perspectives taken on a thing. But even within Euro-American art and philosophy Danto had to sideline an extraordinary number of purposes impelling the European and American modern art and the avant-gardes to arise at his idea that modernist art had a sole purpose, which was philosophical self-revelation. He had to sideline the experimentalist aspect of modernism, its avant-garde political goals, its essayistic, individualistic styles, its celebration of liberty and audacity, all of which continue with full force to this day, if in modified form (see Chapters 1 and 2). He had to sideline the evolution of art markets, which I have argued continue to change the very character and culture of art. He had to believe that the inherent reflexivity of modern and avant-garde art was purely or essentially philosophical rather than social, political, or expressive. And he had to interpret Warhol first and foremost as philosopher when he was really, I have argued in many places, a student of the brand, the sign, the celebrity, and star icon, perhaps among the deepest and most American of American artists in his understanding of post-Second World War American culture, especially the role of advertising, branding, and money.[16]

Danto was brilliant, among the most important aestheticians of the twentieth century. As an art critic (for the *Nation Magazine*) he was unique and superlative. But his commitment to a single purpose impelling modern art was a modernist/avant-garde anachronism.

When he formulated his audacious thesis about the end of art in 1964, a phase in the history of art did seem to be ending, a sea change in process. And Danto's idea of the early and heady days of postmodernism in the early 1970s was spot-on. It was indeed a moment when art relaxed from the pressures of abstraction and minimalism, the reign of art criticism imposing on art a reflexive mission, the need for art to make a statement of importance about art. Anything seemed to go in those days. If you wanted to be an abstractionist you could do it, a figurative painter you could do that. If you wanted to collage then go for it. If you wanted to build things then do it. People seemed to breathe a sigh of relief that art had opened up and become fun again after all the pain and torment of the avant-gardes, not to mention their historical settings (a Europe of fascism and totalitarianism). At this moment Danto's idea seemed to hold sway.

But history moved on and even Danto admitted that the heady days of postmodernism had given way in the 1980s to a subversion of integrity by certain painters who draped their work in an illusion of importance augmented by sheer incomprehensibility. This moment when the twenty-nine-year-old, rich and famous, swanned around as a kind of New York celebrity wearing all-black (although most of the artists were white and middle class), was given his retrospective by major museums, and the object of documentary films was the moment when art became wedded to the market at a level hitherto unknown. We got the artist as star, celebrity, or scion of notoriety, an aspect of the art world with us to this day. Danto bemoaned this fraudulence by calling the painting of importance,[17] an American or European painting, usually of vast and bludgeoning size and scope, which sought to *look* important, rather than carrying any deep or genuine message. Indeed, it went around as if in the joke about the child of a deconstructionist and a mafioso who tells everybody: I'll make you an offer you can't understand. For those unfamiliar with

Francis Ford Coppola's magnificent film *The Godfather* of 1972, in it the Corleone family constantly "makes an offer you can't refuse," meaning a threat. Incomprehensibility becomes a kind of threat: take me seriously or else. Art theory, it has to be said, reached similar heights of incomprehensibility at exactly this moment, in part as a way of finding meaning in the morass of "important" paintings of this kind. This defect is also with us to this day.

So apparently art history continued to happen after all, as it did with the rise of multimedia art, providing a purchase on ongoing history and as deeply conversant with more recent history as any avant-garde work was with its time. I have said that this ongoing demand for art to make a statement to its times, a demand both of real significance and integrity and of pretentiousness depending, is a direct legacy of the avant-gardes, which are still very much with us (cf. Chapter 2).

The day art history is really at an "end" is the day human history is finished, meaning the day human beings have perished from the earth. The day history is no longer global, forming systemic patterns across the globe (like financial capitalism) and also local traditions, is the day the globe disappears, and with it, Europe and America since these places have always depended upon the wider world for new ideas and styles (as happened during the nineteenth century), even if such dependency was not acknowledged and indeed was repressed. At the moment contemporary art is deeply embroiled with unfinished history, which is global.

6

Taste in Its Eighteenth-Century Context

Why Taste?

We began this book with the conditions of art in the present, moving on to cosmopolitanism and its pertinence for contemporary times. We then journeyed back to the nineteenth century where the terms for the kind of contemporary analysis I used in the first two chapters were introduced: the connection between art, meaning, medium, and broader historical aspirations. What I added to these analytical terms, suitably freed from Hegel's ideas about the end of history and importantly the restriction of history to Europe, was something more directly derived from Karl Marx than Hegel: the analysis of *market economy* in relation to cultural possibility and cultural demand. I am now going to take us back yet another hundred years to the moment when the discipline of philosophical aesthetics came into being.

The point will be to understand how emancipatory that thinking was at the time. But also, to understand its limitations, thanks to its embroilment in empire, nationalism, and colonialism. This embroilment effectively precluded cosmopolitanism, allowing it to arise in the form of Kant's empty universalism, his "stance of being a citizen of the world," which could only mean Europe (Chapter 3). Grasping these limitations will allow us to find a more cosmopolitan way of relying on the power of eighteenth-century thinking for art today. Call this the rehabilitation of aesthetics in an age of globalization. We will then be free to appreciate and incorporate the power of eighteenth-century aesthetics into today's thinking about art.

The discipline of aesthetics arose in the eighteenth century around questions of taste and judgment. Taste is about pleasure or displeasure taken in this or that object. The exercise of taste is, the eighteenth century believed, a matter of experience. But it is also a *judgment* about what is liked and disliked, preferred or disdained, about what is beautiful or sublime, about quality or its lack thereof. I have not yet addressed the issue of taste in this book although it has been central to aesthetic inquiry since the eighteenth century.

The eighteenth century's philosophical turn to taste and judgment was utterly new to European history. It is not that people did not have their tastes and preferences. I am sure, for example, Plato and Aristotle both did. But they did not consider this worthy of philosophy. Taste was ... personal, not anything worthy of philosophical analysis. Plato and Aristotle were rather concerned with the relationship of poetry to truth and to the moral character of a community. Plato thought poetry (by which he meant the dramatic recitation of stories by performers) wild, anarchic, corrupt. He believed poetry stirred up Dionysian frenzy among those attending the performance. Poetry was therefore a debased form of expression replacing the dignified contemplation of the good, the beautiful, and the true by the rhetorical seduction of the poet, who delivered what we would today call fake news. He wished to bar poetry from the ideal state. Aristotle, by contrast, writing about tragic drama (which he also called poetry) celebrated its capacity to portray life in a way more philosophical than history, therefore more true-to-life than history. For while history, Aristotle believed, merely told what happened, tragic drama unfolded the story of what happened in accord with the laws of probability or necessity—given a larger-than-life, noble character like Oedipus or Creon, but one also cursed with a significant character flaw, the tragic drama showed how that character's flaw must, in a perfect storm of disastrous circumstances, lead to devastation for himself or herself and all around them. The ancient Greeks believed in fate, and should each of our fates dole out the wrong circumstances, we too would end in ruin. The purpose of tragic drama was to acknowledge the insecurity of living in a world where we are every one of us pawns of fate, but don't know whether for good or for disaster. Such existential insecurity can lead a person to stalemate, the inability to take the risk of staking themselves in the world. A person could end up, knowing that fate might destroy them, burying their head in the sand like an ostrich. The point of theatre was to purge the audience of its pity and terror at the fact of being in the world. This process of purgation was meant to be communal. Because each and every person attending the theatre carried the same existential doubt, we all could take comfort from the acknowledgment that it is a condition we share, that it is a basic component of being human to share it. The purpose of tragic drama was to restitute, through this shared bond of recognition, a sense of vitality and moral purpose to the community.

These approaches to the various arts highlighted art's relation to philosophy, truth, and the moral capacity of the community. They had little or nothing to do with taste. The question of preference—whether, for example, an Ancient Greek theatregoer does or should prefer the playwright Sophocles to Euripides or Aeschylus—was for Aristotle personal, not of philosophical interest.

All this changed in the eighteenth century, when the question of taste became the central question of philosophical inquiry and aesthetics was born as a philosophical discipline.

Now why didn't this book open with the eighteenth century and taste and then move on to Hegel and contemporary times, given that the eighteenth century is where aesthetics is born as a discipline? My reason is this. The concepts we have built up about cosmopolitanism and its shedding of universal judgments about culture in favor of the encounter with diversity and of creative synergy across different cultural realms, the concepts we have accrued about meaning, medium, and history and also about market economy turn out to be critical in the understanding and evaluation of why the eighteenth century turned to taste and judgment. For while the turn was in many respects a real advance in philosophy, what dropped out were issues of meaning and also social purpose. The approaches to art already in place with Plato and Aristotle, studying particular media of art (poetry, theatre) in relation to questions of truth, morality, and the effects of art on a community was shunted to one side.

On the other hand, the eighteenth century truly understood, and wished to highlight, the importance of an experience that seems to transcend meaning and cultural purpose, freeing the passions, and imagination, of the aesthete to wholly engage and become absorbed in the pleasure of a sunset, a quartet, a mountaintop, in a way that need not deliver meaning or engage the world beyond the beauty or sublimity of the experience itself. No one goes to the seaside to watch a sunset in order to learn about social welfare or cultural commitment. One goes for the wonder of the experience itself. Ideas may or may not matter. What does matter above all is the deep attunement to the setting sun, which is an emotional and spiritual attunement, like loving. This idea that with taste human beings find themselves engaged in an experience of free pleasure, reflective of their freedom to enjoy, deepening their sense of beauty is an idea which, although subdued in our artworld today, is of paradigm importance for what is distinctive and of value in art. There is something right about the assimilation of the experience of art to the experience of nature, which offers similar rewards. This key idea we may thank the eighteenth century for bringing to the attention of philosophy.

The approach to taste taken by the eighteenth century highlighted individual preference rather than communal demand, pleasure rather than meaning or understanding, and aesthetic experience as an end in itself, as autonomous from the flow of life, rather than aesthetic experience as a social conduit for communal acknowledgment and transformation. There is something deeply right about this. But while the turn to taste was a philosophical advance, and I hope to show why in this chapter, it was also a loss, restricting the range of perspectives one needs to understand the depth and importance of art, and we will need some of the concepts already brought forward in this book to understand why. One will find that the answer involves everything that century was about: from its emerging markets to its proclamations of liberty to its global context of empire and also of nationalism to the emergence of new canons of science and objectivity. To the question, what is it about the context of the eighteenth century that gave rise to the turn to taste in philosophy? One must provide a *global* answer.

This global answer will also be critical in deciphering why the eighteenth century believed judgments of taste are universal, *a claim that our discussion of cosmopolitanism has already rendered untenable, given cultural diversity.* And so, what we have already accomplished in this book will play a significant role in unpacking the eighteenth century's aesthetic turn, for good and for bad.

Taste and Individual Liberty

Focus on taste is a focus on *individual* experience. And the modern emphasis on the individual is in the first instance innovative and emancipatory. The late seventeenth and eighteenth centuries articulate for the first time in history the concept of *natural rights*: what John Locke in his *Second Treatise of Government* of 1689 names the rights to life, liberty, and freedom in the acquisition of estates, by which he means title and property.

This declaration of natural rights, or what Thomas Jefferson following Locke will call "inalienable" rights in the *Declaration of Independence*, refuses the domination of church or monarchy over the individual citizen. Such rights are, Locke says, universal and equal across all persons since they are God-given. Natural rights cannot be taken away by any government or religion, they answer to a higher calling. Indeed, the sole purpose of government, Locke argues, is to foster and protect the individual liberty of its citizens, to protect their rights.

Because human beings are by their very nature free, they have the right to enter into a contract with government. This is Locke's famous contract theory articulated in the *Second Treatise*. The sole purpose of government is to secure and sustain the liberty of the individuals who are its citizens. That is the *only* legitimate purpose of government. In order to protect liberty government may place demands on its citizens in accord with the contract they have signed on to, calling on citizens to go to war against any power that seeks to dominate them, demanding taxation to maintain the business of governance. The government must establish a policing authority to maintain law and order, protecting liberty and property and other arms of the state. Citizens must pay for that.

This is all government is meant to do, it's only proper job. This thin theory of government, that its sole purpose is to protect and occasion individual liberty, is the formative idea behind the American Constitution and, if strictly believed, is now thought of as conservative libertarianism.

Should the citizen fail in his or her duty, the state has the right to exert punishment. Should the government fail in its duty, citizens have the right, indeed the *duty* to revolt, abrogating the contract. Locke claims in his preface to the *Second Treatise* that it was written to justify the "Glorious Revolution" of 1688 when King James II was overthrown by a union of Parliamentarians and William III of Orange-Nassau.

Locke's ideas were radical at the time and served as the basis for the democratic revolution in America (1775–83) and, with equally revolutionary thinking by Voltaire and Rousseau, as the basis of the French Revolution of 1793, some few years after the American one.

It should be said that while Locke argued that natural rights are universal, applying equally to all, in practice he did not believe this. As a man who had been a colonial administrator in the American Carolinas and later in the West Indies, both slaveholding colonies, and who had written *The Fundamental Constitution of the Carolinas* in 1669, with its harsh laws regulating slavery, Locke was compromised by his participation in empire, and one can see him battling—unsuccessfully—with the whole issue of slavery throughout the *Second Treatise*. He abhorred slavery, believing anyone who tries to enslave a man makes war with him by seeking to compel labor from him which by right the man should be free to offer or withhold as he pleases. On the other hand, he reserves a place for slavery in the *Second Treatise*, if an uneasy place, and never renounces the constitution he composed for the slaveholding American south. There is from the first a basic contradiction between Europe's announcement of universal human rights and its colonial empire, which denies rights to the native. The modern history of Europe and America is about the simultaneous and contradictory articulation of universal rights hand in hand with its creation of the modern concepts of race and racial inferiority, with the modern practices of racism.

The new focus on individual liberty in the late seventeenth and eighteenth centuries was also motivated by a consumerist turn. Which is why the political theorist C. B. MacPherson referred to this moment in history as the age of "possessive individualism."[1] Thanks to the extraction of goods from the colonies, European markets vastly expanded, to the point where the social good was conceived by economic and political theorists in England in terms of market prosperity and the acquisition of property. This vision of the centrality of rising markets (economy) for the social good may be found in

Adam Smith and David Ricardo, the most significant economists of the eighteenth century and also in the writings on justice of the great David Hume.

Adam Smith believed the market was guided by "an invisible hand" that directed it toward the good. The eighteenth century invented the trickle-down theory according to which the profits due to the most well-off would over time bring up the entire population since the wealth of the few would be invested in expanding markets, leading to more and better jobs, more advanced public infrastructure, and a better life for all, including a more beneficent attitude toward public welfare for the least well-off. The trickle-down of prosperity from the rich to the less well-off would eventually lead to equality of outcomes and a more equitable distribution of wealth. Of this Smith was certain, especially given what he believed to be the natural sympathy and care for others on the part of those made rich by the market. It would be a combination of the natural economy of markets (trickling-down prosperity) and of the nature of human beings (sympathetic and concerned for others less well-off than themselves) that would generate prosperity for all and a reasonable level of equity across populations.

This rosy picture of capitalism, according to which there is no ultimate impediment to the sharing of wealth as markets expand, was related to a general hunger for consumption. Consumption was for the British rising middle classes the epitome of free choice, the ultimate expression of liberty and prosperity.

In the clubs of London men of means spent their idle hours wining, dining, and taking pleasure in the acquired goods of empire, while reading books, magazines, and journals that suited their taste. Their dress bespoke their class, they reveled in fine cotton, silk, gabardine, and wool. Their taste bespoke their belonging to a world that was their oyster, among the favorite foods of the time. Art, like a good cigar, was an object of high-quality consumption.

In spite of the fantasy that wealth would trickle down to the poor, there remained vast poverty throughout the eighteenth century, and of course the poor were not part of the politics, policy-making, or policing of the state. They were its *objects* of control, struggling to survive in dank, filthy, and dangerous cities or on farms as lowly tenant farmers, at the mercy of the Lord of the Manor. The English poor were systematically shuttled off to the Australian continent where they endured forced labor in unthinkable conditions of filth, isolation, and punishment.[2] Only colonialism proved a way of rising from poverty. A man of the lower classes could brave sailing ships to make his fortune in the colonies, where, as the great South African writer Olive Schreiner put it, the sons and daughters of fitters and turners could enjoy the lifestyle of kings and queens thanks to lording it over the natives just as kings and queens lorded it over they themselves back home. Colonial rule was the poor man's chance at liberty and prosperity.

All of this shows how central the global character of the eighteenth century was for the very thinking that century produced about individual liberty and market prosperity.

And about taste. For taste was considered a paradigm of individual human liberty, iconic of the right to enjoy prosperity. And it was the individual, not the collective, the group, or the wider cosmopolitan world that was celebrated by art, according to the eighteenth century.

Taste, Pleasure, and the Imagination

How did the eighteenth century conceive of taste? Its thoughts about taste may be divided between the writing of David Hume in Scotland and Immanuel Kant in Germany. We will explore these philosophers in the following chapter. In this chapter we will focus on a set of assumptions about taste common to the eighteenth century.

All considered taste the ability to take pleasure in an object or to find that it inspires awe and majestic thoughts. Or alternately to find it unpleasant, ugly, horrifying, distasteful.

All thought of taste as a capacity to feel pleasure or displeasure, awe or revulsion in the context of an object. This feeling of pleasure or displeasure, awe or revulsion was considered by the eighteenth century a *judgment*. One might believe oneself compelled to give reasons for one's judgment, but the judgment of taste was not so much a cognitive decision as the overall *feeling* engendered by an experience: a feeling of pleasure or displeasure, awe or disgust.

In order to have such an experience one had to have the ability to synthesize the parts of an object of taste into what the eighteenth century thought of as an *aesthetic whole*, in the way one does with a beautiful scene from a mountaintop in which the angular rhythm of trees bending toward a village appearing in miniature in the valley below, sheltered by foothills, glowing in slanted light and punctuated white cumulus clouds moving low across the horizon. Or the way one follows a quartet through its modulations to the return of theme and final breadth of cadence, or to grasp the play of chiaroscuro and figure in a Renaissance fine point sketch. All believed the ability to apprehend an object or scene in this way was a matter of grasping its *form*, perhaps in relation to content, message, representational meaning.

To synthesize the parts of an object into an aesthetic whole was, the eighteenth century believed, a matter of sensuous perception and of the imagination. Perhaps the best introduction to thinking about taste can be found in the pages of the British philosopher Edmund Burke, who says in his treatise *A Philosophical Enquiry into the Origin of Our Ideas of the Sublime and the Beautiful* of 1757:

> On the whole, it appears to me, that what is called taste, in its mostly general acceptation, is not a simple idea, but is partly made up of a perception of the primary pleasures of sense, of the secondary pleasures of the imagination, and of the conclusions of the reasoning faculty, concerning the various relations of these, and concerning human passions, manners and actions.[3]

The philosopher Paul Guyer has gone so far as to argue that the main achievement of aesthetics in the eighteenth century was the articulation of a theory of imagination. Joseph Addison, for example, writes in 1712 of the various pleasures of the imagination (in an essay of that title)[4] that include pleasures of grandeur (grand-sounding things) and of novelty (the adventure of the new) as well as of beauty.

Taste expressed individuality in its most specific sense: a person's likes and dislikes, preferences, choices, desires, satisfactions, judgments. It was prized because of a paradigm of individual liberty: liberty understood as freedom of choice and preference. Taste was considered so deeply a stamp of individuality that some reveled in the thought that about matters of taste there is no disputing: *De gustibus non est disputandam*. Each has the right to enjoy what they will. If I prefer tea to coffee that is my business, my right, just as it is your right to prefer late night walks in the garden to sitting indoors, and another's right to prefer the sea to the mountaintop, the city to the rural area. To each his own version of life.

Others like David Hume thought it important to argue for an objective standard of taste according to which disputes around taste might be adjudicated, tastes shown to be better or worse, as morals are. More on that when we turn to Hume's essays.

For Immanuel Kant the exercise of taste is a freedom not merely of choice but of the mind's own imaginative capacities. The experience of the beautiful is a matter of how our faculties of perception, cognition, emotion, imagination become harmonized in the context of a specific object, scene, or event. Taste is truly a *free* play of the imagination. A special kind of moment in which our various faculties align freely and pleasurably. For Kant taste is a reflective judgment: about our own capacities, which we acknowledge within ourselves thanks to the pleasure in their aesthetic harmonization. That this harmonization is free proves all important. Through taste we acknowledge and enjoy our natural right to freedom, by taking pleasure in our freedom of mind. This will be pursued in the next chapter when we turn to Kant's *Critique of Judgment*.

The Beautiful and the Sublime

The eighteenth century focused on two general categories of aesthetic experience, the beautiful and the sublime. The experience of the sublime is quite different in character from that of the beautiful.

The beautiful is thought of as a matter of the pleasure taken in an object in virtue of our perception of its symmetry, proportion, harmony, balance of form. Beauty is always associated with form. Perfection of form, as in the concertos of Mozart with their perfect balance between soloist and orchestra, their pitch of anxious, mournful, longing intensity in proportion to the calm fluency and the brightening of sound. Mozart makes counterpoint and modulation effortless, as if endlessly melodic. This is the beautiful.

According to Burke and Kant, the sublime is the experience of being overwhelmed by the size, power, infinity, or scope of an object. It might be a symphony, a mountaintop, even a mathematical equation. Gazing at the sea as the sun goes down suddenly the green ray appears, faint yet visible, a strange infrared beam of last light stretched horizontally like an abstract form bending toward the horizon. In an instant, the green ray disappears into the enveloping darkness. One is astonished. When the overriding feeling is one of harmonious symmetry and form, the experience will be one of the beautiful. When the experience is one of limitlessness, of light appearing with a jolt then almost instantaneously dying into water and sky, one may be shattered by the transience of things, the vast universe of time. Rage, rage against the dying of the light writes Dylan Thomas, and here one is overwhelmed by the inexplicable strangeness, wonder, and brevity of life, as if life had the radiant brevity of a green ray. One feels one is a brief flash in the vastness of the universe, nothing and everything before size and time. This is the experience of the sublime.

The sublime is that experience in which the mind feels overwhelmed by what it is taking in, flooded by a reality too large, forceful, intense, limitless, infinite, deep, or existentially profound to grasp. Here the mind hits the limits of its ability to cognize, to know the world. One thinks of Kant gazing at the starry heavens above and the moral law within. Such wonderment is what Kant calls the desire of the mind (and its failure) to think beyond the limits of reason, to encompass questions that have no answer, to run up against the sense of a power that seems too great to take in or even explain, an infinity that cannot be grasped except by abstract algorithms.

Kant believed this experience of the fierce and implacable mountaintop, this force of oceans crashing against the shore, this being blown away by the astonishing power, intricacy, and depth of a Beethoven triple fugue, this brief appearance of the green ray, brings up what he called "ideas of reason." These are ideas of such perfection that they have no instance in the world, dwelling only in the mind. Such ideas include that of a perfect moral universe. No doubt the experience of the sublime brought up exactly those ideas in Kant's own mind as he contemplated the starry heavens above and felt the moral law within. But there need not be any clear idea that emerges from the experience of the sublime, merely an image of greatness, a sense of shock at the power of life, a bowing before the strange fact of transience, whatever. The key to the sublime is that it is an experience of awe and anxiety at being overwhelmed, an experience of being uplifted, exalted, as if in the sublime were the grounds of religion, or idolatry, or the pure experience of tremulous, shocking, dynamic life. And so, the sublime is not a property of the object (the green ray) but of our perception of it.

The glorious idea brought forth in the experience of the sublime may consist for some persons only in the glorification of the thing sublimed. The sublime idea brought up by art is, in the first instance, the sublimity of art itself. One cannot believe Beethoven *actually wrote that*, that music has the shocking power it does, that it can be so beautiful, so glorious, so amazing. Music itself is sublimed in the experience of it. Perhaps nothing further, just music and its mysterious, overwhelming power. Or perhaps a great deal more such as thoughts about music as a symbol of humanity, of divinity, progress, or nature. Trains of reflective association deepening the experience of the sublime are as free and freely flowing as the harmonization of the faculties is to the experience of the beautiful. This makes the experience of the sublime as paradigmatic of human freedom of mind and soul as that of the beautiful, hence the eighteenth century's gravitation toward these two central aesthetic types.

The beautiful and the sublime are paired together for another, less remarked reason. Often—although not always—the experience of the beautiful and the sublime arise together and unfold in tandem. A work of art that is profoundly beautiful will likely bring up a sense of awe (that Beethoven could actually do that, that music can have this power). A work of art that is sublime may well also be beautiful, although not always. For there are experiences of the sublime when steely power refuses the comfort of harmoniousness, when a mountain is too severe and intimidating to be beautiful, to allow for the kind of pleasure one feels walking in the gentle regions of the alps when crocuses appear through the last traces of snow, and the slopes are effusively green, the buds on the trees fragrant.

Taste and Autonomy

Central to the eighteenth century's interest in taste is its sense that the experiences of the beautiful and the sublime occur *for their own sake*. Nothing needs to follow from the pleasure of gazing down from the mountaintop, or the sublime absorption in the masterpieces of Bellini and Titian in Venice, apart from satisfaction of the experience itself, and then the pleasure taken again in memory. The pleasure is its own reward; the experience valuable in itself and for itself. This makes taste a paradigmatic experience of human autonomy, the autonomy to enjoy life on one's own terms and for oneself. For the likes of Kant, aesthetic experience is deep because it allows the human mind to revel in its own autonomy, to experience—courtesy of art or nature—what it is to be a thing that *has* autonomy, that may live in itself and for itself.

Art is indeed for the eighteenth century a celebration of individual liberty, similarly thought an end in itself. By exercising individual preference for its own sake (pleasure), the free man could take pleasure in his own liberty. Art was a self-confirmation of the European project of individual rights. While this position was theoretically meant for all men (women were excluded), in fact it pertained to the European bourgeois male only. The working class was too busy surviving to have time for the pursuit of happiness very much, and especially in the field of art, of which they knew little. The colonial subject was not believed capable of freedom, except by aping the European master. So, his experiences were not part of the picture. Again, the anti-cosmopolitanism must be drained from this aesthetic picture to give it more force. For if taste is understood as a global adventure, then its diversity has to be foregrounded, not subdued or repressed. We will come to the implications of this for the aesthetic theory of both Hume and Kant in due course.

Note how far this individualistic notion of a life well lived is from the earlier Greek idea of a community that thrives only as a whole, in the form of a city-state. I may be in and for myself, but I am also for others, without whom I am little or nothing, an empty vessel, alone and alienated. Autonomy was prized in this century of revolutions, announcing liberty for all: freedom from tyranny and freedom to discover, write, and pursue one's life script. The eighteenth century thought of each citizen as a molecular whole, philosophically complete in and for themselves. Rather human life was defined by a web of attachments and a web of engagements in the world, through which one knows and inhabits oneself. And so aesthetic experience, reflecting the belief in, and goal of individual autonomy, had to be thought as similarly in and for itself, autonomous from the wider commerce of the world. Otherwise aesthetic experience would not have the power to symbolically reflect the goal of life: autonomy and liberty.

This sense that taste is an experience enjoyed for its own sake, allowing us to take pleasure in our autonomy, arose along with a newfound belief in the distinction between fine and useful art. Fine art, considered the higher of the two, was understood to be a thing made and treated *apart from any purpose*. Or rather, the more it could stand apart from all purposes (economic, communal, religious), the better. This is what made it "fine art." Mozart and Da Ponte might write *The Marriage of Figaro*, based on a play by Beaumarchais so perfumed and revolutionary in its critique of the upper classes and its picture of how persons deal with inequality that it was banned from the French theatres, which almost happened to the Mozart–Da Ponte version in Vienna. They might create masterpieces in the name of the rising middle class and its fierce dedication to liberty. Their work might have revolutionary messages, aiming in the direction of social change. One might even venture to say that their work was political (although one would then have to answer the question of what one meant by politics). But their work was created entirely for the court and the concert hall, the concert hall being itself an eighteenth-century invention where music could be performed purely for its own sake, for the sake of the experience rather than as part of church liturgy or for some further social purpose like entertainment while people ate, for dancing at a ball or background music written for the royal coronation. In short: the belief that fine art is autonomous from social life arose in the context of the institutional history of the museum and concert hall.

Useful arts were thought to be those created to serve a particular purpose: the need for a house, with furniture, the need to wear clothes, the requirement that people travel in carriages, and so forth. Architecture, design, ceramics, master carpentry, and the like were conceptually distinguished from fine art and considered on a lower, utilitarian plane. This even though the various media of art all blur the distinction between fine and useful art, as, for example, Mozart's own operas do, since they are the paradigm of fine art but also have clear social and even political intent. But they build no house, deliver no religious story to the masses (as Renaissance painting does when painted for the church). Their social purpose is visionary, symbolic, ideational, which was enough for the eighteenth century to disqualify Mozart's operas as having any "use value."

Within the museum objects were curated in terms of the category of fine v. useful. The museum of fine arts, as opposed to the museum of technical, industrial, or useful arts, was thought the house of autonomy for fine art and the place where contemplation of art for its own sake may be given free reign.

The museum seemed to possess a magical capacity to convert every object it acquired into fine art by draining it use value. Many works in museums of fine art were not "fine art" because they had originally been made to participate in the web of social practices like religious ritual, dress, architectural dwelling, and the like. But once wrested from their context, whether the Ancient Greek past or the colonial empire, and given a second life in a European museum, these objects became fine. So transfigured, these things were now, in the museum, shed of their original meanings, empty sites for the experience of contemplation, pleasure, and awe. They then lived second lives as mere *sites*, occasions for viewer exaltation and consumption. Few persons gazing at them were interested in their original meanings and purposes. Little attempt was made to retrieve and acknowledge their original meanings and uses. They became *aesthetic objects*.

The aesthetic autonomy of the object was then purchased *only because of the social and political process through which it was drained of meaning and use*. This had everything to do with the processes of colonial extraction wherein goods were wrested from the colonies to live second lives in vitrines, mute and dormant under glass, for the European middle classes. And so, the wider and global range of cultural objects, each with its own meaning and social value, was evaporated into a series of inert things sitting in a museum for European contemplation and national self-celebration (as patrimony). This effectively prohibited serious cosmopolitan engagement with the diversity of meanings and values these objects from all parts of the globe originally had. It was part of a European ideology of disinterest in the wider world.

The European Past as a Museum

This drainage of meaning extended to Europe's own treatment of its past. The Grand Tour comes into being at exactly this moment. The past, especially its ruins, became aestheticized, the church an object of touristic appreciation. British, German, French, and American people of means, with time on their hands, visit Fingal's cave in Scotland (about which Felix Mendelssohn wrote a symphonic piece). The acolyte on the grand tour is told by Johan Von Goethe in his travel writing that he or she must approach the city of Venice from the Brenta River in order to appreciate its burnished, radiant, disheveled architecture sultry in diamantine light reflected off water. Venice itself had descended from being the greatest maritime power for a thousand years to decadence and the status of a tourist attraction. In fall, the tourist/aesthete was required to visit the Villa d'Este, when the leaves turned russet and a dry, cool breeze from the Alps softened the Italian October warmth. Then on to the Baroque splendors of Rome, the pastoral heat of the Mezzogiorno (south of Rome) and finally boarding boats to Greece and the ruins of the Parthenon and of the theatre at Delphi. Europe, especially southern Europe, had become a museum.

This aestheticization of the past has been beautifully described by Walter Benjamin in his famous essay on mechanical reproducibility, something which began in visual art with the woodcuts, prints, and drawings artists made in the eighteenth century of the sites of the tour so that the tourist might have (before the days of photography) images to bring back home.[5]

The Grand Tour was that form of aesthetic education required of all persons who wished to refine their instincts for beauty and culture and had the money to take a year or more to do it. Young men and women were sent on the tour, the males in groups so that they could sow their wild oats between visits to the cathedral or fountain, the women with chaperones so that they would be insulated both from the wild pleasures restricted to men, and from the men—tourists or locals—who wanted them wild. It was a paradigm of the century of taste, a year's journey made for no purpose other than aesthetic pilgrimage for its own sake. Indeed, the idea that aesthetics was an act of pilgrimage, a secular religion of art and ruins and nature, may be found in the three volumes of the piano music of Franz Liszt, *Années de pèlerinage* or "Years of Pilgrimage," which Liszt partly wrote while at the Villa D'Este and published in 1842. The pilgrimage of his piano music is not to Lourdes, or Santiago de la Compostela but to the grand tour. It is an aesthetic, not religious pilgrimage.

The Grand Tour is already a form of globalization since it follows a route or set of routes across Europe and sometimes into Turkey, Egypt, Morocco, even as far as India. These pathways are not merely travel routes but part of a global economy of tourism, giving rise to hotels, guide books, takeaway prints, a service industry. The entire culture of the Grand Tour was rooted in a *museumized* culture that turned the ruin, the monument from the past, and the colonial object into a beautiful, or strange, but essentially lifeless thing: there only to be seen, contemplated, and enjoyed for their formal beauty and aura of the mysterious—what Benjamin called the aura of things past, haunting the present with their vivid beauty.

One finds the attitude expressed even more clearly when one looks to the British and French artists of the eighteenth century who sketched, drew, and painted in the colonies, then sold their work in England and France so that those who would never travel to Southern Africa or the Indian subcontinent could own and enjoy a piece of empire thanks to the image. These artists inevitably pictured the colony as timeless, inert, drained of meaning, a museum site. Painters like Thomas and William Daniell, William Hodges, Sir Charles D'Oyly and George Chinnery went to India. There they ignored the boundless energies of millions and represented India as if it were nothing but an eccentric cousin of Constable's Wivenhoe Park. They did not merely drain India of its life and vibrancy. But also blended their concept of the picturesque with a kind of pre-Raphaelite romanticism of the ancient a century before the pre-Raphaelites.[6]

They fixated on the ancient-like ambience of India, typified by its decaying temples, eternal pagodas, and half-empty palaces, as images of their own past recaptured.[7] An Anglo-Indian landscape painting might contain animals or Indian laborers in its forefront. These will appear to blend into the landscape, as if they are part of nature rather than culture. The viewer's eye might be led along a road or a winding vista from the painting's foreground (where the figures are relatively small and insignificant) to its background, where in the distance (but occupying a central place in the pictorial composition) will be a hill station, a picturesque valley with ancient Banyan trees, or the fragments of a ruin. Or these figures might appear in the back, part of the endless presence of landscape itself. Temple, waterfall, native in a dhoti are all blended into an image of that which will never change. And so, by rendering India as a static universe, the European could contrast their modernity to the native's endless pastness, confirming beliefs in their modernity and superiority, while also adopting the picture of the colonial world as nothing but a cultural museum, a living incarnation of timelessness, thus eternity, with its own exotic pleasure.[8] There must have been something thrilling in this, not simply disconcerting. The point is an entire world was reduced to the contemplation of it. Aestheticized in short. And this aestheticization served a political as well as aesthetic purpose: to confirm the ideology of empire, that Europe was the sole bearer, as G. W. F. Hegel called it, of history, the only civilization capable of progressive modernity (see Figure 12).

The evacuation of meaning and use from the object, the turning of entire civilizations (India) into vast museums, was part of the larger refusal on the part of Europe to know the colonized. You cannot dominate a people without creating an ideology according to which they deserve it, perhaps even thriving under the yoke of oppression (the myth of the happy slave on the plantation, the cheerful native). You must create a system of false knowledge about the beings you control, work to death and keep in poverty. This false knowledge involved the construction of the idea of race, the work of at least two centuries (the eighteenth and nineteenth) involving science, linguistics, literature, morals, philosophy, and all else. The idea of race was inherently hierarchical, with various strategies to explain the superiority of the European.

False knowledge was matched by the refusal to know the native, meaning an attitude of disinterest toward him/her. Real knowledge of the native was restricted by the colonial authorities to the kind of administrative knowledge one required to control them and exploit them as labor: knowledge of their habits, social behavior, groups, work patterns, and so on. One should not be one-dimensional about this, at the same time all kinds of knowledge of the native arose, sometimes

FIGURE 12 *Thomas Daniell,* Ruins of the Naurattan, Sasaram, Bihar, *1811.*
Oil on canvas, 38 9/16 × 53 5/8 inches (97.9 × 136.2 cm). Courtesy of the Yale Center for British Art, Paul Mellon Collection.

in virtue of the intimacy between colonizer and colonized, missionary and subject,[9] woman and man across colonial borders, other times thanks to sustained scholarship by those persons whom Edward Said called the creators of the Orientalist knowledge system, some of whom, like Max Muller, generated entirely new and vibrant fields of study in the process. But such forays into deeper understanding, however vibrant or qualified, were not the norm of those responsible for the implementation and sustainability of colonial power.

The great Nigerian writer Chinua Achebe made this point centuries later when he wrote scathingly of Josef Conrad's masterpiece, *Heart of Darkness*, a book about the dark atrocities Europe inflicted on the Congo by the Belgians, that even this book, so deconstructive of colonialism, nevertheless perpetuated it by demeaning the Africans into stick figures, hardly worthy as an object of understanding, merely there to surprise the European with what Conrad describes as the African's strange civility.[10]

Achebe's own answer to this colonialist disinterest in the colonial subject is his own masterpiece *Things Fall Apart*,[11] a novel about the degradation of an Igbo village in what is now Nigeria, under British rule. The first part of the book is almost anthropological, showing the terms of village life through the story of the book's main character Okonkwo, as if lecturing a Western audience about what that life was actually like prior to colonialism. In part two British administrators take over rule of village life and things begin to fall apart. Okonkwo, determined to foment resistance, ends up a suicide when no one will follow his lead in revolt and he realizes the old ways will never be recovered. The book ends with the British administrator saying well, the book he is writing on colonial Nigeria ought to have a chapter on Okonkwo's suicide. No, he reconsiders, maybe it's not worth a whole chapter, maybe only a paragraph. Meaning not much. The administrator is mostly interested in knowing how to control these people, not in knowing them. His interest in who they are is merely administrative: If knowing something about them will help control them then that fact is worth knowing. Otherwise they are not worth the effort.

Real knowledge could only have been a threat, since it had to mean humanizing the native, which would have made it harder to exploit them. Again, cosmopolitanism was not possible given this framework of power and ideology.

The Native Object and Modern Art

This practice of depersonalizing the native's cultural objects from their original meaning and prescribing contemplation of them as inert things remained in place well into the twentieth century. One can even see it play out in as great a painter as Pablo Picasso.

Picasso saw and studied the West African masks in what was then the Musée de L'Homme in Paris during the years 1905 and 1906 (these objects are now relocated to the nearby Musée Quai Branly). The painter studied them at the moment he was searching to reinvent painting by vesting it with stability and figural integrity, given that the nineteenth century had flattened the picture plane to the point where painting had become an insubstantial, ghostlike thing. In Picasso's own early work (the Blue and Rose periods of 1901–5) melancholic, emaciated, insubstantial figures populate his dark paintings as if hardly there. Nothing could have been further from the Italian Renaissance, which had established the solidity of the object and figure by inventing perspectival painting that creates an abstract, three-dimensional space almost architectural in its hard form and force in which the figures are set. Wanting to find again this deep and core value to painting of *figural solidity*, but relying on neither drawing nor abstract depth of field, Picasso was seeking a way to establish the solidity of the object and the integrity of the figure.

At this moment the hard and curved geometry of the West African mask appeared to him in the museum as a signpost for the future. The West African mask is hard, curved, and stable without any real depth or dimension. It is a mask and since it is a mask, the eyes are cut open so the person wearing this mask in a ritual can see. Wide, angular eyes were for Picasso the sign of fierce erotic power, basic to his own consciousness as a man, and of the women he desired, then loved, then painted. Moreover, the mask has a complex geometry of multiply intersecting sculptural planes, which is where Picasso was headed in creating, with Braque, cubism.

Perhaps everything he saw in the West African mask really is there, although it is hard to tell where Picasso's insight ended and his inventive genius began, where he found features really in the mask and where he fantasized them for his own purposes. Genius is like that: surveying the world from the point of view of finding materials and forms to suit its own power of invention.

Picasso had absolutely no interest in the role of the mask in West African culture, its ritualistic purpose (for it is hardly worn all the time, only on special/sacred occasions), its role in the culture and society that invented it. For him the African mask was a mere visual form, a stimulus. The stimulus proved essential to his achievement of cubism, with his colleague Braque. Together they turned their pictorial surfaces into webs of interlocking cubes and planes that the viewer himself or herself felt at once to be whole, and to exist in contrapuntal tension, with the various cubes and planes vying for foregrounded centrality. Within the logic of these interlocking cubes and planes the masklike form stood out as a marker of the face, a face at once so stable and so hard, and with such intense eyes that it responded to the possessive gaze of the (male) viewer with a rebuttal as powerful as any death threat. This also required a complete revision of the relations of figure and ground, which was an ongoing experimental task for both painters.

The art historian Leo Steinberg famously described Picasso's masterpiece of 1907, *Le Demoiselles d'Avignon*, as a transaction between the sexually possessive gaze of the viewer and the counter-gaze of the five prostitutes in the picture, all of whom except the two in the middle who are at once standing and lying down, have African masks for faces. The figures in the middle have eyes as wide and fierce as anything in any mask. Steinberg describes the erotics of the encounter between viewer and figures as a combat so deadly that the raw power of sex unfolds with near-fatal consequence.[12] John Richardson in the first volume of his biography of Picasso says that in the Spanish town where Picasso grew up, for a young man to eye a woman directly is for him to court reprisal, as if sex has already transacted through the eye. And for her to gaze back into his eyes is for her to court culpability as if she is no longer a virgin. And so, the mere act of seductive looking is a transgression inviting punishment.[13]

It is for these reasons that Picasso's work is called primitivist, meaning a work unleashing an atavistic power capable of obliterating the veneer that passed for civility in the Europe of his time. This attack on civilization (civility), a theme of modern and avant-garde art, recruits in Picasso's case the stereotypes of African sexual licentiousness widely believed at the late moment of colonialism, to invest the women whose faces are masks with what would have seemed to the viewers of the time ferocious erotic power.

And so, the African mask is not only drained of its original meanings—its use in ritual, its spiritual meanings, its capacity for power. Once it becomes inert in the European museum away from its context of use. It is also invested with stereotypical and racist meanings about African primitivism in contrast to European civility, stereotypes Picasso is implicitly relying upon when he unleashes his violent sexual exchanges in the *Demoiselles*, while also being a crucial catalyst for modern art.

As I said in Chapter 5, Europe, by being disinterested in the native object and using it as mere material for its own artistic experiments, was freed from the debt of acknowledging its own dependency on the wider world it rather sought to subdue and control. Here on the African continent.

FIGURE 13 *Pablo Picasso,* Les Demoiselles d'Avignon, *Paris, June–July 1907.*
Oil on canvas, 8' × 7' 8" (243.9 × 233.7 cm). Acquired through the Lillie P. Bliss Bequest. Courtesy of the Estate of Pablo Picasso / Artists Rights Society (ARS) ... Digital Image courtesy of The Museum of Modern Art. Licensed by SCALA / Art Resource, NY. Location: The Museum of Modern Art, New York, NY, U.S.A.

Taste, Art, and Cosmopolitanism

Aesthetics with its focus on taste is born of the liberal ideals of Europe: the celebration of individualism, of individual liberty, of a belief in human autonomy, and its symbol or icon: aesthetic autonomy. It is also born of a consumerist stance. And it is born thanks to the institutions of the museum and concert hall. All of which depended crucially upon globalization in the form of empire and the institutions of the nation-state, above all the museum.

The museum was one of the central institutions of nationalism and empire. Its political meaning was to confirm the power of the European nation to turn the cultures of the world into its own inert pleasure dome. Do not think this was lost upon the class of persons who visited the museum, or who went on the Grand Tour. The past, the colonial world, raised into things of beauty for the viewer, were also devalued, turned into things passive, no longer possessing their own meaning, their own authority. This made the viewer, the tourist on the Grand Tour, not merely a supplicant but a King or Queen, reigning over the past, over the cultural world, now there entirely for their pleasure and aesthetic edification. The exercise of taste was directly or indirectly an exercise of power.

That the eighteenth century's turn to matters of taste must in part be understood in the light of empire goes a long way toward explaining how the eighteenth century marginalized meaning and use while elevating taste and contemplation. When art becomes understood as a matter of individual pleasure rather than collective or historical experience, much of what matters in art is diluted: social and political consequence, the relation to power, money, science, and its general embroilment in what Ludwig Wittgenstein and the aesthetician Richard Wollheim following him called role of art in "the form of life."[14]

Out of the consumerist stance toward the object of taste, in which the object served the sole purpose of pleasing the viewer, the modern aesthete was born for whom life became a matter of refined and pleasing experiences. This modern decadent is also a by-product of empire.

The turn to taste was a philosophical advance. It was also a retrograde philosophical move which the nineteenth century would seek to correct, as we have seen in the previous chapter.

The question is how to rethink taste in a way that squares the perspective of individual preference with larger questions of meaning, medium, and the work of art's interaction with markets and with history. In one sense nothing could be easier. It is one thing for me to believe a work of art is deeply meaningful, it is another for me to like it. There is a basic distinction between understanding the meaning, and also the importance of something, and being pleased by it. This distinction, when applied to jokes, is the distinction between understanding a joke and laughing at it. You can understand, even appreciate the importance of a joke without finding it funny. You can imagine how others might double over even if you don't.[15] That is a matter of your particular taste. And this distinction, when applied to people, is the distinction between admiring someone and liking them. We all are aware of people of whom we approve at a distance but don't really like, and with whom we would hardly want to go on a two-week cruise. No doubt this is also true of how certain people regard us. Decent, sure, but not to their taste.

Taste extends to every of art's features, to the kind of meaning, medium, and social statement we "prefer" in a work. Some people prize art that revolves around identity politics, others do not. Some are highly tolerant of art that derives meaning from the theory or text behind it, others find this a degradation. For some it is preferred that art speak deeply to its historical time. By this I do not simply mean preferred on the basis of aesthetic principle but preferred in that the person finds such art enjoyable, it gives them pleasure, they *like* it. For others, art is preferred that offers a place of exquisite refuge from the burdens of history, that bends the mind like a kaleidoscopic fun house, art that makes them laugh or gives them the sense of religious transfiguration.

Taste also extends to the choice of *medium*. Some adore dance, or classical theatre, others performance art, still others TV. Within the field of classical music there are those who are mad for opera, others who, while recognizing its powers, are not really captured by them, finding the soprano or tenor voice strident rather than revelatory. Chamber music is more their thing.

At a certain point it becomes difficult to distinguish questions of taste and preference from those of aesthetic evaluation, since as often as not what is liked becomes admired on the basis of aesthetic principle, what is disliked is disliked because of some principled lack. I am not fond of art that claims depths of meaning thanks to some kind of statement or theory tacked on to it. This is a dislike of mine based in the principle that art should have to *earn* the right to make a statement by embodying that statement or theory within its texture and form. I bristle at art that aims to shock for its own sake, that is brash or aggressive for its own sake. (I dislike people for similar reasons.) Others disagree with my taste and my aesthetic principles. A certain degree of respect and toleration are demanded for others, however intense one's own commitments may be. Up to a point one must agree to disagree in aesthetics principles.

Which returns us to the earlier chapters on *cosmopolitanism* because this is precisely the stance given to the cosmopolite (see Chapter 3). I believe the best way to think about taste is from the cosmopolitan perspective where attitudes of respect for diversity balance one's personal and principled aesthetic and moral commitments. Indeed, the very distinction between aesthetic and moral commitments should not be overstated, since aesthetic principles often slide into moral principles, including beliefs about such moral dimensions of art as authenticity, honesty, sympathy, kind of political statement, and the dignity in the picture of human life a work of art offers. The great Kantian philosopher Friedrich Schiller (1759–1805)[16] believed the quality of care one takes in crafting aesthetic form is already a moral commitment, since formal excellence is an example, indeed a symbol, of human integrity. For Schiller aesthetic quality simply is a kind of moral quality.

The cosmopolite embraces intersections between aesthetic and moral commitments, believing culture is a web of preferences, habits, aesthetic forms, and moral truths that overlap in many different ways and sometimes run together. This does not mean the distinction between aesthetics and morals, between taste, aesthetic quality, and moral value is obliterated. We can find—and it is essential to human practice to find—a variety of ways in which aesthetic questions can be distinguished from moral questions. This is especially true of the aesthetics of nature, where joy taken in the green ray of sunset has little or nothing, happily, to do with questions of inequality or what the state owes its citizens. Two people can absolutely disagree about how to address inequality while sharing a love of the moment when the sun disappears into the ocean and the sky darkens. Conversely two others can share the same views about the politics of inequality while differing profoundly about what foods they like or places they prefer to visit. These things are commonplaces. There is no single distinction or relationship between taste, art, and morals but many. Within that multitude, life is negotiated.

An example is always useful and here is a well-known one: Leni Riefenstahl's fascist film *Triumph of the Will*, her 1933 documentary on the Nazi Nuremberg rally of that year. The rally, which took place the year Adolph Hitler came to power in Germany, was a parade of such proportion and so clearly meant to live a second life as film propaganda that when certain parts of the filming didn't come out she restaged those parts of the rally on cinema sound stages to get the image absolutely right. There is no doubt her film is propaganda for the Nazi cause. And yet, the opening shots of Hitler in his plane soaring through the clouds as if suspended weightlessly in the air, the unearthly stillness of the shot, then the precipitous dive of the plane to earth all to the ethereal music of Richard Wagner, has a fluency, beauty, and bravado worthy of Italian Renaissance paintings of the Assumption of the Virgin. It casts Hitler and his cause in the aura of the sublime. And this sublimity to the film image cannot help but force the idea of Hitler's greatness on every viewer, of his unearthly genius, as if he were a leader dropped from the heavens like some Christ. What the sublime does is (we have seen earlier in the chapter) bring up ideas in the viewer of such magnitude that they dwarf the mind, overwhelming it. Here the idea is Hitler set apart as a god, in the process of actualizing the Nazi cause in history. It is a subliming of the future, as in the famous Nazi song: the future belongs to us. And as the marching troops fill the image with their vast implacability the quality of the sublime shifts to what Kant calls the dynamical sublime, a pure fact of limitless, inexorable power. Moreover, the purpose of this film was to generate solidarity and Nazi belonging by creating a context where the population could collectively swoon, and swoon in Nazi togetherness. This subliming of a political agenda, casting it in the mantle of the sublime, is what the Frankfurt School called "the aestheticization of politics."[17] This grandiose sense of the leader actualizing the nation into its glorious future was, the Frankfurt School believed, a central feature of fascist and totalitarian politics, a way of producing a society in which the will of the leader fuses with the action of his people, as if the people were his incarnation writ large.[18] And this by rescripting politics as aesthetically sublime, thanks to art and propaganda.

Since the beauty/sublimity of the opening shots of the film force such ideas about the Nazi cause upon one, thanks to the film narrative (it is Hitler flying to his rally in this plane) the viewer is forced to take up the position of being overwhelmed by "the leader," as Hitler was called in Germany. The feeling is: this man thanks to this film is immune from criticism, his cause one that strains the mind to even comprehend. And so moral and political ideas are central to the experience of taste in this instance, insofar as the sublime character of the opening shots and the later dynamical power in the boot-stepping troops and Mädchen in uniform inherently place the viewer in the position of receptivity to such moral and political ideas.

Do you think you can escape from this Nazi image set forth as sublime when you watch, knowing what the politics of this film are about? Do you think you can separate your aesthetic experience of the film's *form* from what it represents and solicits from you? Just try it sometime. And if you can, just how hard did you have to work to do it?

Aesthetics and morals are deeply interconnected, which is why the cosmopolitan understands that disagreements of taste often depend on underlying disagreements in principle—aesthetic and/or moral.

7

Aesthetic Judgment from a Cosmopolitan Perspective

The Universality of Judgments of Taste

The eighteenth century was polarized around the question of whether there is any measure of objectivity to judgments of taste: whether a standard of taste exists or rather one should resign oneself to, or even celebrate, the "fact" that "about taste there is no disputing," taste being exactly that area of human life where liberty—the ability to follow one's own inclinations for one's own enjoyment—is paramount. *De gustibus non est disputandam:* about taste there is no disputing, so the saying goes. One person likes opera, another (Harpo Marx in *A Night at the Opera*) hurls himself from the rafters when he finds himself in the New York opera house, believing opera to be a highfalutin European pomposity meant for windbags and buffoons and sung in overwrought words by overdressed persons in need of a diet plan. To each his/her own.

Is taste purely a matter of what one likes, with no way of adjudicating disputes between one person's taste and another?

Given that the eighteenth century believed that the judgment of taste is nothing but the pleasure taken in the experience itself, the question became, whose pleasure counts and how on earth would one person's taste be justified as better than another's: superior and worthy of emulation or instruction?

Either judgments of taste have no truth at all, the belief went, with no claim beyond personal preference, or they must be universal in scope, compelling all. There is no middle ground. This stark dichotomy was in part a result of the reigning canons of science and rationality, which understood true propositions to be true universally. But it also expressed that century's view of its own culture: that it was of universal scope and at the top of the global hierarchy. Those who believed taste was universal in scope were aided and abetted in establishing universality by their view that most of the world's judgments didn't count. This colonial idea allowed the European to universalize his judgment apart from the thorny, cosmopolitan issue of diversity and related synergy across different cultural forms. Moreover, taste was an epitome of freedom, a way for free persons to take pleasure in their own liberty. However, the native's putative lack of intelligence, imagination, and ability were believed limitations on his capacity for *free judgment*. As we have seen, the native's place in the world was that of imitative lackey, not imaginative and inventive European. Since taste is a free judgment par excellence, the native's capacity for it was compromised. He couldn't really do it. Since few Europeans cared what an Indian or Chinese person preferred, there was no incentive to discover how subtle their judgments might be. Their point of view was simply not on the same footing as that of the European.

Because the question of judgment was restricted to Europe, cosmopolitan explorations of diversity could not arise. This compromised eighteenth-century aesthetics. However, eighteenth-century aesthetics remains indispensable in spite of the taint, because the questions the eighteenth century did raise, about the legitimation of taste, about the quality and character of aesthetic experience, about the kind of judgment a judgment of taste is, remain of vital importance today. I will come back to this at the end of the chapter.

The greatest philosophers of the eighteenth century, David Hume and Immanuel Kant, both believed judgments of taste have universal scope. They differed as to how. Hume believed judgments of taste were objective, rooted in and justified by fact and therefore universal and unassailable. Kant, by contrast, believed judgments of taste are purely subjective and cannot be justified in terms of any fact in the world. However, he believed the judgment of taste (with respect to beauty and the sublime) claims the status of a universal exemplar. The judge judges in the name of all humanity.

Put Hume and Kant together and one can see that it was a shared assumption or ideology of the eighteenth century that aesthetic judgment, if not merely personal, is *universal*. A challenge to this claim is the very starting point for cosmopolitanism today. Recall what Anthony Appiah said (Chapter 3):

> People are different, the cosmopolitan knows, and there is much to learn from our differences. Because there are so many human possibilities worth exploring, we neither expect nor desire that every person or every society should converge on a single mode of life. Whatever our obligations to others (or theirs to us) they often have the right to go their own way. As we'll see, there will be times when these two ideals—universal concern and respect for legitimate difference—clash. There's a sense in which cosmopolitanism is the name not of the solution but of the challenge.[1]

We may wish to believe our aesthetic judgments are fully justified in terms of fact, or that they properly assume universally prescriptive force, but to believe this without taking the encounter with human diversity seriously is to live in a neocolonial bubble.

David Hume's True Judges

The locus classicus of Hume's writing on taste is his essay "Of the Standard of Taste" of 1757. There his question is whether there is objectivity to judgments of taste, a standard in terms of which the differences in taste between persons can be reconciled into better or worse.

Hume begins that essay by noting "two species of philosophy," both having currency at the time, and together in apparent contradiction. The one species of philosophy is, he says, the popular belief that taste is merely a matter of individual sentiment and so there can be no disputing about it. And the second, often believed by the same people in another part of their brains, the belief that without a way of adjudicating differences in taste into better and worse, their daily practices of art and enjoyment would become incoherent. You may disagree about whether Matisse is as important as Picasso, adducing reasons for or against. Perhaps this is a matter of taste about which there is little of substance to dispute, for it is about a preference for one master as opposed to the other. But if you think my drawings are as good as either of these artists—I am a person blessed with visual perspicacity but who cannot draw to save his life—then either you have an impairment of the eye or you have no feel for drawing whatsoever and you should take up another occupation, perhaps accountancy or dentistry. Or you are my mother—meaning someone ready to inflate my every ability, however limited it actually is.

Without the belief that taste can be divided into better or worse, that taste is capable of education, training, and thereby improvement, there would be no place for art schools, which propose to educate artists by training them in drawing, painting, and design. The point of an art school is that there is *something to learn about art*. The knowledge acquired in art school is a form of training and also of intellectual study and exposure. It is the same for learning music, architecture, or any other art. One is meant to come out of school—any school—better, more skilled, and knowledgeable. Otherwise, what is the point?

And yet there remains an important place in aesthetic experience and judgment for personal preference, come what may. I prefer the figurative splendor and incredible geometry of Picasso, you the repetitive, half abstract rhythmic glory and French color palette of Matisse. You feel hamburgers are the finest thing god has given humanity, I do not. Must every preference be ranked and adjudicated? And if not, then which?

These two species of philosophy, both believed and both reasonable—and not only that, both crucial to aesthetic experience and judgment—are in contradiction when applied across the board and need sorting out. This is Hume's starting point.

Hume's aim is to argue that there is a standard of taste, a way of adjudicating disputes of taste, establishing one as better and the other as worse. The standard can and will allow certain disputes to remain unresolved: not every dispute about taste demands resolution, there is something right about that species of philosophy which says, to each his/her own. He rather wishes to defend the other side: that often, and in crucial circumstances, tastes can and should be ranked into better and worse. His way of arguing this point is by claiming taste is objective. There can be a standard of taste ranking some tastes better and others worse (while leaving some disputes unranked or of equal status) because taste is a matter of detecting and responding to what is *in the object*, and it is the person with finer taste that does the better job at perceiving—and enjoying *what is there*. In this, judgments of taste are not different from judgments about the weather, or how hot it is. Except that taste is far, more, subtle, possessed by the few, while most anyone of sound mind can correctly perceive rain or heat.

Taste is the capacity to detect what is *there in the object in all its subtle parts*. Which is why unlike detecting whether it is raining outside, or if the sun has risen, it takes a subtle form of perception, one not everyone possesses or possesses in the same degree, to make a correct judgment of taste. Indeed, Hume believes only the very few, the most perceptually gifted possess this capacity.

The standard of taste is set by what Hume calls the joint verdict of the true judges. A true judge, Hume says, is so rare that an entire generation may lack one. Now if the standard of taste—of what is better and what worse—is set by the judgments of the true judges, evened out over time from one to the next, then the immediate question is how you identify who this rare being is. After all their rare capacities for that form of perception and pleasure called taste cannot be inspected in the way an eye exam can show that a person's vision is in good working order. Hume's task is therefore to show us that we do in fact have ways to identify the true judge, picking him out from the chaff of imposters, charlatans, and lackeys. And that we deploy this know-how in our aesthetic practices without realizing it. In short, we implicitly know what the criteria of a true judge are, even if we fail to acknowledge to ourselves what our implicit knowledge amounts to. And even if sometimes we do misidentify these persons. It remains for Hume to make the criteria we implicitly rely upon to pick out a true judge explicit, and to demonstrate their plausibility. That is the work of his essay.

First, what kind of judgment is the judgment of taste? Hume's answer is that it is the feeling of pleasure or displeasure with respect to an object. This is the important point, which we will want to find a way to retain in what follows. The true judge need not be intellectual, give reasons for his/her judgment. He/she must simply feel the right things in the context of the right object. This is what is distinctive about the judgment of taste, as opposed to a moral judgment, which Hume believes is a strong impetus to action, or a cognitive judgment, which need not involve either pleasure or the passion to act.

There are five characteristics, Hume tells us, which make a person a true judge: "Strong sense, united to delicate sentiment, improved by practice, perfected by comparison, and cleared of all prejudice, can alone entitle critics to this valuable character; and the joint verdict of such, wherever they are to be found, is the true standard of taste and beauty."[2]

Let us go over these characteristics.

First, the quality of strong sense: the true judge must have a vivid receptivity to the sensuous qualities of art, place, object, person. The person possessing strong sense weeps over the beauty of a sunset, cannot speak after a fine performance of a string quartet, is loath to return down the mountain because she is overwhelmed by the view. That person is so taken with the purple of the stamen, the scent of rosemary in the chicken casserole, the touch of wind in the yellow felt hat of an elderly woman strolling through the green art deco neighborhoods of Los Angeles that he must go home and immediately record his impressions in a diary or poem, essay or blog.

Strong sense, however, may lead to the misperceptions of the excessive enthusiast if not tempered by delicacy of taste, which is, Hume tells us, the ability to notice the subtle parts of a thing. Strong sense is emotional; delicacy of taste perceptual. I shall return to delicacy of taste last, for Hume introduces it by a fascinating, and controversial, example.

The other characteristics are clearer. The true judge must have practiced, since taste, like athletics, demands that one keeps in shape. The great violinist Jascha Heifetz once remarked: "If I don't practice for one day, I notice. If I don't play for two days, the critics notice. If I don't play for three days, the public notices." It is the same with critics of film, or painting, or food, wine, cities, travel. I myself lost touch with the deep study of painting for a number of years and it took some mental effort to get back into it. We all have such experiences of being "out of touch, out of it, out of practice." Practice, or training, is critical to all skilled activities, from surgery to athletics to writing, to being able to notice birds and denote their kind, to an eye for the texture of clothing, to the ability to cook well.

It is the same with the criterion of comparison. Someone whose entire experience of the big city is Ann Arbor, Michigan, will fail to know cities with any authority, until he or she is also acquainted with New York, San Francisco, London, Tokyo, Berlin, San Paolo, Johannesburg, Shanghai, Dubai, Warsaw, Istanbul, Jerusalem, Cairo, and more. Leave out Rome and Jerusalem and this person will fail to understand what it is to have a city that is layered with the archeology of time and past civilizations. Leave out Berlin and the critic of cities will fail to understand what it is to merge city and forest, also to live in a city whose historical scars traverse it like those on a wizened face.

The implication is that since no single person could really know all these cities and more—much less keep practiced and up to date about their changes—everyone's capacity is limited by their experience of comparison. Which is why the joint verdict of the true judges is required. Over time the limitations, excesses, and imperfections of the one judge will be compensated out by the others. This Hume calls the conservation of meaning, that meaning is over time corrected, perfected, evened out, and so ascertained by multiple observers. The same process of conservation and improvement of meaning through multiple judgments, Hume believes, is how any other kind of knowledge is secured, whether knowledge of biology or of human character. It is how epistemological progress takes place, on his view.

Knowledge is generated for Hume by repeated experience, each instance confirming the others. Watch the sun rise once and you cannot yet know it will rise in the morning. It may have been a fluke, or even a miracle. Or you may have misperceived. Watch it rise every morning, and also have your individual experience confirmed by countless others who also see it rise and say so, and the knowledge becomes increasingly secure. In the case of aesthetic judgment, multiple observers (true judges) are required not only to confirm judgment but also because they correct each other's limitations. One judge of cities has never been to Prague, the other fails to know Venice, one does not know Jerusalem, the other Beijing, and so on. Only as a *jury* of a number of judges does the standard of taste get set.

Hume believes this is his reconstruction of what is known in popular wisdom as "the test of time." That over time, we come to the right ideas about how things are. And that only over time are true judgments arrived at and confirmed.[3]

Practice and comparison comprise what Hume thinks of as education. To know an art is to have been trained in it. This is in keeping with eighteenth-century ideas about education. For the eighteenth-century thinker on the British Isles education was largely considered a form of *training*. Training in memorization of the classics by rote, in reciting passages of Shakespeare, in the addition of long sums, in Latin verbs, French grammar, in sport and behavior in church, in when and how to use the soup spoon, in when to break into wit. And so, the Duke of Wellington could exclaim that the Battle of Waterloo was won on the playing fields of Eton.

The fifth criterion—that the true judge be cleared of all prejudice—is also a criterion that no person could completely satisfy without some correction from others. Hume ends his essay by railing against the Catholic Church. It is his way of lambasting the reader with his own prejudices, showing the reader that even he, who writes mellifluously and is a paragon of a reasonable man, he who is setting himself up in this essay as a true judge, cannot be considered cleared of all prejudice. Hume's skepticism about religion in an age when religion still held control over social life was notorious. It prevented him from getting a job at university, which was part of the reason he wrote so many essays like this one on taste: he had to make money. Hume had an ax to grind against religion and was grinding it in this essay. And if he, *le bon David* as he was known in Paris because of his angelic character, could go wild with rant when the right buttons were pressed, then everyone else could. Since no judge can be cleared of all prejudice (that is the implication) it takes the joint verdict of them over time to correct for the misjudgments each will inevitably make based on prejudice.

It is easy to see that much of what Hume says about having good taste is right. One does need to practice, expand one's domain of comparisons, avoid undo prejudice, and be possessed of a certain receptivity to the sensuous qualities of things.

It would be instructive to ask what might happen if the domain of true judges is opened up to the globe from its bourgeois English setting. Can one seriously expect global agreement and correction over time with the goal of consensus: a time-tested standard in the conservative sense? Or would opening the realm of the judges to the wider world inevitably lead to dissent, contradiction, and at best uncertainty? Insofar as this is an empirical question, I think where certain kinds of art are concerned the global judgment is pretty much a matter of universal consensus: about Beethoven, Shakespeare, or Charlie Chaplin for example, who are enshrined across the world. Chaplin was the rave in movie theatres from Buenos Aires to Calcutta as early as 1925, Shakespeare is adapted and performed in Cape Town, Beijing, Moscow, Lahore, and nearly everywhere else, his influence is felt across the arts, Beethoven performed in Kazakhstan and Tokyo as deeply as in New York or Berlin and an icon of freedom in many parts of the world. Most artists are not. They are the object of cosmopolitan disagreement.

The interesting question about even the universally praised worthies is what happens to their work when appropriated across diverse locations. In an earlier book[4] I argued that the appropriation of operatic masterpieces by young South African singers and directors inflects opera with South African racial politics and also singing patterns thanks to the training of many black singers in choir as children. And so, an operatic warhorse turns to the local community where it is performed, speaking both to them and to the world from them. I argued this is a way for performative arts to live. To live through constant change. The career of universally applauded masterpieces is in this sense a cosmopolitan one.

Delicacy of Taste and the Problem of Objectivity

We may now take up Hume's remarks about delicacy of sentiment or taste. It is perhaps the most important characteristic of the true judge. Hume introduces delicacy of taste through the story told by Sancho Panza about his kinsmen. Importantly he misremembers the story from Cervantes' *Don Quixote* in a way that suits his purposes. I quote from his essay:

> It is with good reason, says Sancho to the squire with the great nose, that I pretend to have a judgment in wine; this is a quality hereditary in our family. Two of my kinsmen were once called to give their opinion of a hogshead, which was supposed to be excellent, being old and of a good vintage. One of them tastes it, considers it; and, after mature reflection, pronounces the wine to be good, were it not for a small taste of leather which he perceives in it. The other, after using the same precautions, gives also his verdict in favor of the wine; but with the reserve of a taste of iron .... You cannot imagine how much they were both ridiculed for their judgment. But who laughed in the end? On emptying the hogshead, there was found at the bottom an old key with a leathern thong tied to it.[5]

There are various important points here. First, delicacy of taste is hereditary, a matter of inborn talent, like the ability to draw or to have perfect pitch. You can't teach these things if the person is (like me in drawing) a dud, although you can improve people who have it in whatever degree they do have it through practice and comparison. Second, we now understand that delicacy of taste is the ability to discriminate—in this case literally *taste*—the subtlest portions of a thing, what Hume calls all the subtle parts of the object. Judgments of taste are made on the basis of such fine discriminations. Which means third, that these judgments are abilities to sense and register what is actually *there in the object*, hence their objectivity.

Now objectivity demands some independent means of confirmation, hence the importance of Hume's misremembering the Sancho Panza story in a way that provides exactly this kind of independent confirmation in the producing of that smoking gun, the leathern thong. The leathern thong proves that the kinsmen have delicacy of taste because each tastes some part of its effect on the wine, when others do not.

Finally, neither of Panza's kinsmen get everything right, it takes the 'joint verdict' of both to capture what is wrong with the wine. Judgments about the subtle parts of an object of taste (the wine) are, like all other judgments about the objective world, the product of joint confirmation.

All of this is meant to argue that there is genuine objectivity to judgments of taste, a matter of the ability of those with natural delicacy to perceive in the object of taste what is really there when most of us cannot. And it is meant to argue this by showing we have independent ways of confirming who the true judges are when the smoking gun is produced: by producing the leathern thong. The example is about objectivity (taste detects what is in the object) and about confirmation (we have other ways of confirming perceptual truth). So, when it is raining outside, one way to establish this is to see it through a window. Another to go outside and get wet. Still another by collecting rainwater in a pail, etc. Objectivity requires more than one form of confirmation. And here Hume is arguing this is true of judgments of taste as well. Hence judgments of taste are a form of knowledge.

But how typical is this Sancho Panza example, misremembered from fiction as it is?

Here is the kind of example that would support it. That of a conducting exam the Japanese maestro Seiji Ozawa recounted. In a conducting competition one of the members of the orchestra was told to play a wrong note somewhere in the orchestral selection the young Ozawa was given to conduct. Not a glaring wrong note of the kind most of us could hear; rather a very subtle wrong note. The conductor was meant to hear it and point out which instrument had made it. This was a clear test of delicacy of taste, the ability to make extraordinarily fine discriminations between orchestral sounds and players. The wrong note was the smoking gun. Ozawa won the competition.

But a brilliant ear does not equal brilliant taste although it may be part of what makes taste shine. For taste in music is a matter of envisioning musical balance, shape, pace, intonation, power of expression. These aspects of taste have no smoking gun to prove a person has them. There are people with perfect pitch and terrible musical taste. It happens because they lack the other ingredients required to detect "all the subtle parts of the music." They lack intelligence and imagination.

The true judge is not simply the one who discriminates, as in: the wine tastes of elderberry, concord grape, wildflowers, and a faint aroma of mushroom. A reader of taste must be able to follow through complex narratives, attentive to the creation of character and the interactions between characters, be cognizant of the relationship between quality of prose and narrative line, grasp the implications of narrative for a recounting of the world or an acknowledgment of it, sense why the novel or play is genuinely finished at its end, or alternately understand the compromising character of the work's ending. Are the characters believable? Are they coherently and appropriately worked out? The capacities to be attentive to literary subtlety go far beyond Hume's five characteristics into the talent of the cognitive mind and imagination, the empathy a judge brings to the work, their feel for its power as well as pleasure, their sense of its intellectual, moral, and even political project, of its dialogue with literature, and its vision of language.

For this kind of judgment there can be no smoking gun that will independently confirm the rightness of the judge's decisions. You cannot find a leathern thong or wrong note to grasp that Cervantes' *Don Quixote* is a great work in its fantastical, dreamlike adventures, all the product of stories the mind tells itself in the name of chivalry, that is, the grandeur of life, and this against the decline of the culture of chivalry in the sixteenth century and a nostalgia for its mad dignity. The book is about the complex nature of illusion, closely related to fiction. And about the wonder of story-telling. We live in our fictions, which include the way we tweak, and misremember the past: as Hume does in this very essay to suit his purposes. There is something of Don Quixote in this most reasonable of philosophers, who wants his philosophical outcome to turn out as he believes it ought, grand as that might be. And so, invents it.

How does one recognize and confirm that a true judge is a true judge if there is seldom an issue of the smoking gun, that is, an independent way of confirming the objectivity of his/her judgment?

Hume's difficulty is that he believes taste is objective because delicacy is the probing instrument for truth: for what *is in the object*. But we have no independent way, most of the time, to confirm the objectivity of the judge's judgment apart from this prompt to see the object as he/she does.

I think the only way out of this conundrum is to say, we come to recognize our betters in taste because we also have taste, and only because we also have it. Had we tin ears, we would have no way of recognizing a brilliant judge of music, because we would have no way of grasping the uptake of what that judge says and judges and finding that it reverberates in our own experience. A judge is discovered through their capacity to lead, to better articulate, to acknowledge. To grasp the power of a work (or its limits) before we do, or more deeply, or with more subtlety, and in a way that prompts our own similar experience: this is what makes a person a true judge, at least in this instance. And if it happens regularly over time, gradually we built our trust in this individual and think of her that way. We choose our judges as much as they choose to judge. We find that we are like them, and capable of having our own experiences and judgments refined, expanded, deepened by them. We judge that someone is a better judge by finding that within our community of taste, they count, they lead, and we find it worthwhile to follow. With their prompting we ourselves come to recognize what they perhaps see faster and earlier than us.

This means a true judge is relativized to a community of taste. And this is because their judgment has gone far beyond what is "in" the object into a way of framing it, presenting it. But if all goes well, we respond to the risks they take in responding to a work. Which is all the confirmation of prowess they will ever get.

We know our betters because we are good enough to take the cue they offer us. There is, apart from the exceptional circumstance, no other way to confirm a judge.

Taste is therefore democratized. A critic is not a member of a small elite legislating in virtue of their ability to detect all the parts of an object when we detect few or none. A critic represents us because we choose him or her. The model is not legal (a small coterie of judges with everyone else in the audience watching the trial). It is political, on the model of elected representatives, who can fall out of favor as fast as they are vested with trust.

Taste is a circular and constructivist enterprise. We are led by others because they elevate our taste to their level, and this because we already have taste. This circle constructs communities of taste through training and experience. It is intersubjectively deep, and canonical in its adulation of certain objects, but never immune from the problems of the circle: that some people can't get into it and would instead have other circles in which they fit.

This fact challenges the claim that judgments of taste are objective, at least completely so. Judgments always outrun what can be ordinarily said to be in the object to our imaginative contact with the object and construal of it. The artist makes, and the critic elaborates a narrative, a point of view, a take on the inner gestures of the work and their power. This is not like detecting the taste of salt in the wine, or of leather although that may be part of it; it is like creating a platform for understanding, for seeing and experiencing more deeply. Taste cannot be merely considered objective, in Hume's sense, meaning a way of grasping what is there in the object and only what is there. Indeed, the line between what is in the object and what we bring to it must remain somewhat opaque.

If taste were completely objective, a matter of detecting what is in the object and only that, it would be much less interesting, vital, and diverse than it is. Therein resides its excitement. In the share brought to the object by the person or community engaging it.

So yet again we arrive at the cosmopolitan question. What happens when the community that chooses its judges is globalized into many overlapping communities? The next two sections consider this.

Hume's Elitism

Now if Hume's small coterie of true judges sounds like an entrance exam into an exclusive legal club, the metaphor is not lost on him, for he sees this club as that of the Inns of Court. Hume is conservative, indeed elitist, in a number of ways, one of which is his emphasis on the superiority of the very few over the very many. The other is his modeling of the standard of taste on legal judgment (the joint verdict of the true judges). Just as the law creates an archive of precedent that guides legal decision when it comes to applying the law, so the standard of taste builds up a canon of excellent works, the stuff of old "Western Civilization" classes in the university study of my day: Homer, Aeschylus, Beowulf, Shakespeare, Dickens, Hardy, Thackery, and Forster. These works are in turn confirmed in excellence by subsequent judges, leading to the "dialectic" of the law of taste, in which precedent guides judgment while judgment confirms the aptness of precedent. And so over time, these works take on a special, rarified status, like that of the true judge himself.

I would be the last person in the world to challenge the excellence of any one of these books, nor their importance for humanistic education. But you can see how this works. Over time a set of volumes is set forth as paradigmatic, "true" literature and knowledge, at the expense of all others. Which is why the canon as a concept and a practice was so forcefully and successfully challenged during the culture wars that rocked and rolled the humanities during the period circa 1969–95.

Challenges were made on the basis of exclusion: no women writers, no persons of color, the rest of the world left out, the continuities between the canonized few and many other writers given short shrift because the canon separated those in the club from those prevented from joining. What is important to see is how Hume's position, and that of the conservative canon generally, dovetails with the nationalism of the eighteenth century with its emphasis on heritage. For what is being created by the true judges is British Heritage with a capital "H." The bankable currency of the nation that lends it value and prestige. And what is being relied upon is the failure of the rest of the world to even come into consideration, hence the ideology of empire. Hume's standard of taste is truly an artifact of its time.

To the model of the club I can only respond with the immortal words of Groucho Marx:

"I would never join any club that would have me as a member." Fortunately, in my case no one ever asked me to join anything so I've never had to refuse.

Another defect in the top-down model of judgments of taste is that it completely limits aesthetic experience rather than deepening the role of the free imagination in it. Think about what it is like to restrict aesthetics to "the best," as if nothing else will do. This is not only snobbery, it is a cramping of the vitality of aesthetic experience, as if all art should resemble a wine tasting where seven wines line up and we compare and contrast. I find those evenings when people sit comparing performances of Beethoven, then turn to the comparing of wines, always with the idea that we pick the best and only the best, a torture. They turn my naturally expansive feelings for music (not to mention wine!) into a cold, arrogant position of Paris judging between beautiful women, that paradigm of male superiority. At least Paris had the naturalness to fall head over heels for one of them.

Although the true judge judges by feeling pleasure or displeasure, and sets the standard purely through this aesthetic enjoyment, as if a glorious divvy, whose sheer pleasure in *experience* sets the rule for us to emulate, the whole setup for Hume's essay involves the *obsession with ranking* and this seems to me at the heart of its existential failure to capture the vitality of aesthetic experience. One wants to experience the world with an open mind and an interest in diversity rather than the closed arrogance of hierarchy. You would not want, I hope, to choose a spouse or friend on the basis of ranking persons via characteristics and making a choice between them as if they were bottles of wine, ready at the helm to be disappointed if the wine (the person) does not "hold up." It is not a great way to love or be a friend, I fear. Nor to respond to art and nature in this way.

So: there is a real question to ask about how important ranking is in aesthetic experience, where it is useful, necessary (to education), where it destroys the very openness to sensation and meaning that is at the core of aesthetic experience. Having raised this question, it would be inappropriate to answer it once and for all. For this is in part a matter of personal decision or preference, that is, of taste.

And by "the world," one means the wider cosmopolitan world, not simply the world of British culture. This leads to the question of a standard once global culture is allowed in without colonial condescension (without what Hume calls "prejudice").

The Standard of Taste and the Challenge of Diversity

How can a commitment to a single standard be maintained in the light of global diversity and the recognition of it? What does one do when hierarchy meets a world now understood to contain multiple values, a world characterized by diversity? What does the prospect of a single standard look like once the African is given his due, and the Chinese, and the Tlingit, and everyone else? Can we imagine a single standard comparing their vastly different kinds of objects and tastes? Or, is it rather than each culture has its own standard? Neither seems palatable. The first because we don't know how to hierarchically rank objects as different as opera to jazz, jazz to African drumming, African drumming to Koto music, to Tibetan chanting, and so on, in the huge department store of world culture. For the eighteenth century these vast comparisons, that is, rankings, are an article of faith which the twentieth has challenged. Recent work in Anglo-American aesthetics by Richard Shusterman, Theodore Gracyk, and others in addition to Ted Cohen has elevated popular and other arts to the status of serious objects of taste.[6] An accumulation of writing about Japanese Noh Theater, Chinese Opera, Indian wall carvings, West African folk sculptures, Ndebele house paintings in Southern Africa, Native American ceramics, Amish quilts forms the canonical objects of Hume's standard: Shakespeare, Milton, Renaissance painting, and the like.

Cosmopolitanism insists on the difference between comparison (which requires underlying similarity between cultural objects, see Chapter 3) and ranking. Chinese opera may be compared to Italian opera, but ranked? By whom and for what purposes? And based on what criteria? For the criteria themselves are exactly what is subject to debate across parties! Mr. A sitting in New York City will choose criteria that make Italian opera superior while Mrs. B sitting in Shanghai will choose other criteria that will make Chinese opera superior. Or perhaps the other way around, who knows, or perhaps neither will choose criteria that make one superior to the other. All these alternatives end up being mere "matters of taste and preference," or matters of individual "commitment" to this or that idea of operatic importance about which others may disagree. It CAN be said by experts and concert-goers that this performance of Chinese opera is better than that, just as it can be said that some Italian tenors really are better than others—although here again rankings may be silly or irrelevant or matters of unresolvable debate.

It was only because Hume really believed that Europe was the only continent where serious art worthy of taste arose, and that the only people who could serve as true judges were those men of his class, that the idea of a standard of taste had a prayer of working out. Include the rest of the world and it collapses. Again, we can compare and contrast, it is the issue of ranking that rankles.

We may simply refer back briefly to the problem tackled in Chapter 3 about Chinese and European opera when speaking of ranking across traditions. Some traditions—each highly developed—are not only different but *oppose* each other aesthetically. A taste for Chinese opera may preclude or lessen a taste for the European. The more refined you get in the hearing of rhythmical clang and Chinese singsong, the less you are able to stand the big broad, mellifluous sounds of Verdi. The more you assimilate your ears to Bel Canto tradition the less you can stand (much less appreciate) the scratchiness of the Chinese instruments, their harsh plucking sounds, the long growling fierceness and sharp, high nasal tones of the Chinese aria. How then do we compare tastes in this sphere?

Indeed, one should even avoid talk of this tradition vs. that. Traditions, cultures, heritages appear unified only to the synoptic gaze of colonizer, the tourist, the essentializing theorist. They are not. To know a tradition is to know its arguments, its differences, its breadth of diversity, as well as its underlying similarities and forms of unity. To know, in short, that it isn't exactly "a tradition" at all but rather an overlapping set of evolving cultural projects.

My earlier point from Chapter 3 was that diverse things demand to be appreciated in their play of similarities and differences without being ranked.

The issue of a standard gives way to a multiplicity of standards and points of view, interlocked globally. About some things one can find as the world shrinks thanks to globalization broad consensus: Beethoven, Shakespeare, and Chaplin being three. About many not.

How much use there is to commitment to a standard, or even a multiplicity of such, given diversity, remains an open question. There has to be some role for standards for the reasons Hume argues persuasively at the outset. Without various standards for various kinds of art there could be no coherent role for art training, skill, talent, or education, to the idea that the public discovers the power of a judge and begins to trust that person, to the fact that some people have more refined ears or eyes or ability to taste than others.

And yet even then, there are people who believe standards have little or no role in bringing diverse objects under a single framework of comparative valuation. This is the live-and-let-live idea. An idea that certain people might find congenial to cosmopolitanism, which seeks understanding and synergy rather than ranking, ranking being the ideology of colonialism with its hierarchies.

One such person is my beloved former teacher Ted Cohen.

An Excursus into the Writing of Ted Cohen

Cohen was skeptical of all commitment to standards of taste. He wrote: "If an American has any birthright at all, it is one that releases him from the need to dance to the tunes of others. ... I have not said that baseball is more noble than Spanish painting. I have not said that it is as noble. I have not said anything."[7]

Ted Cohen knew the extraordinary power of Spanish painting, for he had written on it, and yet he asked (as I quoted above), "Is it obvious that the paintings of the Spanish Renaissance are more important, culturally and philosophically, than American baseball?"[8]—a truly philosophical question.

In Cohen's essay "Liking What's Good," he reinforces this refusal to speak in the traditional voice, as he sees it, of philosophical aesthetics, with its canons of taste and excellence:

> By now, whether or not you agree with me, you can see, surely, (1) that I don't believe in any compelling argument to the effect that one thing is (aesthetically) better than another, and (2) that I don't believe it possible to show that it is better to like better things. Where does that leave me? You might say, Nowhere, but I prefer to think that I've been freed to start again, to try to understand what to make of the communities of people who care for the things they care for.[9]

His journey is reformulated into an investigation of what kinds of people care about this or that, what else they care about, and what this might say about them. It might say they are lousy and racist, or that they are uneducated but subtle, or very American, or very French, or very well-dressed, or highly educated, or Trump lovers of the Roseanne Show, or .... But no one is written off. One must criticize without discounting. For each of these groups forms a community of taste. Ted was the kind of writer, Tolstoy being the apex, who refuses to dismiss any character and takes them all seriously, even sympathetically, as Tolstoy did even with Anna's husband Karenin. Ted left the question of who is better or worse, right or wrong undecided and/or qualified. There is something right about this. C. K. Dexter Haven (aka Cary Grant) says in Georg Cukor's film of 1940, *The Philadelphia Story*, "the time for making up your mind about people is never."

I wonder, and I think you should too, about Cohen's question. Why we should like better things? I find that Hume is half right here. We simply do ... up to a point, and that is where standards do have a role. And then up to a point we don't, which is our own liberty: Gustibus non est disputandam. How much and in what way, with what degree of capaciousness or truculence, well, that is for each person to decide for himself. And so, both species of philosophy with which Hume begins his essay are right. Our practices become absurd if we do not acknowledge our commitment to standards. And here I use the plural thanks to global diversity. Standards within traditions and across traditions. And there is a place for the adage that about taste, there is no disputing, because it is a matter of our personal liberty, among our most prized forms of self, also a way in which we form friendships and communities with others that are so important to our happiness.

We up-to-a-point disagree, and should up-to-a-point disagree, both about how much art *can* be ranked across cultures (as within them) and about the whole practice of ranking things at all: how much art (or any other cultural object) *should* be ranked. And how we should respond to such rankings when they can reasonably be made. The role of ranking in aesthetic life is debatable.

This seems to me to be a principle that ought to be fundamental to cosmopolitanism. The skeptical recognition of such uncertainty around the whole question of ranking. Yes, we need it some, no its bad in all kinds of other ways. Bad historically (given the history of hierarchies central to race, colonialism, nationalism, and European heritage). And bad insofar as ranking becomes an obsession restricting the freedom of the imagination and of human empathy in aesthetic practice.

Kant's Subjectivist Approach

We turn to Kant. We have already seen in Chapter 3 that Kant's cosmopolitanism was empty based on an abstract notion of the individual and her rational will, in the light of which she claims to judge for all persons in virtue of their sameness with her. Kant's cosmopolitanism does not address diversity in the concrete. Its importance was rather to refuse the self-interested position of nations or groups in favor of the stance of a "citizen of the world." But the world to which one gave allegiance was one of abstracted, rational beings all of whom judge "the same." This ended up being empty because it avoided Appiah's problem of squaring the urge for universalism with the fact of deep human diversity, demanding a number of strategies for learning from the encounter with others across the globe that do not assimilate them to any abstract universal sameness. With respect to morals, politics, and culture, including art, abstract sameness across the species does not get you very far when what you want to know is how to square societies which believe in the death penalty and those that don't, or Chinese vs. Italian opera.

But the point here is not simply to criticize Kant's cosmopolitanism as insufficient but rather to seek to learn from his aesthetics once they are freed of this fault line. What is there to learn? Let us begin with Kant's distinction, one which Hume does not recognize: the distinction between merely liking something and finding it beautiful. When I say I like something it means it pleases my senses. My liking it is therefore directly bound up with properties of the thing. *I like-a coffee, you like-a tea, I like-a cuppa cuppa coffee* as the 1940s jingle went. What I like is my business, what you like is yours. About mere likes and dislikes there is no disputing. What satisfies me satisfies me—period. I do not speak beyond myself and my inclinations when I state my preferences. This is Kant's view.

Likes are caused by objective properties of the object of taste which interact with my psychological proclivities. And guided by my interests. I have an interest in them because they are pleasing to me, satisfactory in some way. There is no implication that others ought to be similarly pleased.

In the *Critique of Judgment* of 1790[10] Kant begins by distinguishing the judgment that something is beautiful from more prosaic judgments of this kind about what we like. Kant believes when I judge something to be beautiful, there is an "ought" that is central to the judgment. I am saying you ought to find it beautiful too. This extends, we have noted, to all humanity, who ought to similarly judge it beautiful (i.e., take a similarly disinterested pleasure in it). This ought, Kant believes, comes from the way I judge when I find something beautiful.

A bit of explanation is required about what Kant means by "disinterestedness," since it is a concept, however problematic, that figures centrally in the history of aesthetics after Kant.

Kant's idea is stated in this way. When I judge something beautiful I judge *apart from all interests*. This is what Kant calls the first moment of the beautiful. By judging apart from all interests Kant does not mean I am uninterested in the beautiful object or scene in the sense of not being absorbed in it. That would be an absurd thing to say: I am wholly absorbed in the experience of the beautiful, wholly engaged. He rather means that when I judge something to be beautiful, I stand apart from my own individual tastes and preferences and enter into another kind of relationship to the thing judged. My absorption is not conditioned by my tastes and preferences but purely by the way the object or scene occasions a harmonization of my faculties. Since there is nothing specific to me that catalyzes my judgment (neither my individual tastes and preferences nor desires) I can say, although I cannot prove it, that I am judging in a way no different from the way you or anybody else should judge. When we all judge apart from our particular interests, we judge as one. I can therefore stand as an exemplar for all humanity. I can say all humanity ought to find the object beautiful as I do, because all humanity ought to enjoy the same disinterested pleasure with respect to it. This is the second moment of the beautiful.

Because my judgment of the beautiful is disinterested it depends on nothing peculiar to me. I may then be said to judge as an exemplar of all humanity, since everyone else ought to judge the same way, given that they too should judge in a similarly disinterested manner, relying on nothing peculiar to them as I have done. I therefore judge as an exemplar for all humanity when I judge, even if this cannot be proven because my judgment is not based in rules but in pleasure taken of a disinterested sort.

Thus, disinterestedness rules out cultural differences in attitude, emotion, belief, feeling and preference at one fell swoop. The beautiful is what links us all together as rational, abstracted subjects. There can be no question of diversity in this position, it has no place to arise as relevant to the aesthetic judgment of the beautiful. (Although it may arise for ordinary judgments of "what I like.")

What is the pleasure I feel in the disinterested form? Kant refers to it as the harmonization of my faculties, or free play of the imagination when it falls into attunement with cognitive and goal-oriented forms of purposive thinking, is a paradigmatic celebration of my liberty, my freedom of thought and imagination. The beautiful is a way for me to get in touch with, and celebrate, these very capacities. When we take pleasure in the free play of our imaginations, in a way that harmonizes with cognition and sensation, we are taking pleasure in what makes us the free and autonomous persons we are.

Any object that can catalyze this state of disinterested pleasure is worthwhile aesthetically, even if repulsive cognitively or even morally. When one judges that everyone else, all humanity, ought to find the object beautiful as I do, one is really saying: you ought to be able to use such an object as the (mere) occasion for the free harmonization of your faculties of perception, cognition, judgment, and imagination just as I do. And in doing so you will be bonded with all others, who ought to do the same. As it happens not every person will be able to accomplish this flight of disinterested pleasure with respect to every or even most objects. The offering of the "ought" in "you ought to feel as I do" is a hope, a gesture of fellow feeling, a desire to form a *community of taste*, as Kant would put it, of like-minded individuals who can and do take pleasure in the presence of similarly precipitating objects, others like myself for whom mountains will do it, or quartets, or, or, or.

From my childhood I have been drawn to mountains. This comes from half a childhood spent on a Vermont apple farm, where we boys used to climb to the top of the hill behind our old New England clapboard farmhouse with its gray, weather-beaten barn and cherry red carriage house, lugging skis on our shoulders. We would launch ourselves down through the trees, turning hard in the heavy, unpacked snow, our collie dog diving for the tips of our skis as though they were the toes of an unruly animal. In spring we would walk the apple orchards and picnic on a blanket of their white and pink blossoms. There would be morels and partridges and deer. In summer we set off below the farmhouse to cut away at the tangle of blackberry bramble that threatened our lower apple orchards, on occasion discovering an overgrown pasture, now pristine, carpeted in wild flowers, the knurled branches of an oak tree overhanging the river below. We felt we were ancient settlers, discovering an untrammeled continent as if the first to set eyes upon it.

Mountains place me in a community of taste, since many others feel the same. While I know not everyone will be similarly moved, some finding mountains vertiginous, shattering to calm, disturbing in size and irregularity, others simply not caring much one way or another. But as soon as they hit the sea and revel in its warm, velvet blue currents, well, they are where they want to be. It is not simply that these persons will like/enjoy the sea, the warmth of it on one's body, the roughness of sand and taste of salt, the elemental sun above. It is that they will also find the sea beautiful.

Different objects will do it for different people, even if the judgment is meant to be not about the object—the mountain or sea—but purely about the self and its activity of play, catalyzed by these things.

When I approach a mountain now it inevitably rings with the poetry of remembrance. And this inevitably conditions my sense of its poignancy. I cannot separate my capacity to feel the sublime, and the beautiful, when mountains are at stake, from their resonance with my own past. I therefore cannot imagine standing apart from all my "interests" when I judge a mountain beautiful. For *personal qualities of memory*, desire, the resonance of the past, of happiness are central to the quality and character of my judgment. I shall assume these are among the things Kant meant by "interests." So, my judgment cannot be called "disinterested." Not totally anyway and not in any flat-footed way.

If the writer Marcel Proust is correct, the traces of one's past are everywhere central in aesthetic experience. We relive what we have long ago lived in living anew. And this recapturing of the past is central to our sense of the power of experience. Near the end of Proust's six-volume novel, *In Search of Lost Time*, Proust's protagonist Marcel approaches the mansion of old friends after a long stay in a sanatorium and the experiences of the First World War have left him isolated, in contemplation of his death and depleted by the tatters of time. He trips on uneven pavements near the mansion and becomes overwhelmed by memory. The pavements recall to him his experiences of Venice in the past, a place he loved, a flood of memory enhanced when inside the palace of the Guermantes he dips a madeleine (tea cookie) into tea, which then leads him to recall, or to find, called forth in his memory's chamber, the beauty of his childhood in Combray, Normandy, where the family summered. Marcel (channeling Proust) then writes:

> [the] cause I began to divine as I compared these diverse happy impressions [of Venice, the madeleine, Combray etc.], diverse yet with this in common, that I experienced them at the present moment and at the same time in the context of a distant moment, so that the past was made to encroach on the present and I was made to doubt whether I was in the one or the other. The truth surely was that the being within me which had enjoyed these impressions had enjoyed them because they had in them something that was common to a day long past and to the present, because in some way they were extra-temporal, and this being made its appearance only when, through one of these identifications of the present with the past, it was likely to find itself in the one and only medium in which it could exist and enjoy the essence of things, that is to say: outside time.[11]

Proust credits this train of associations, linked to present experience (of tripping on the pavements outside his friends' mansion) as temporarily banishing the demoralizing sense of death, of lost experiences, lost people, lost life, lost time.

My own sense of the free play of my imagination seems to me similarly suffused with memory, memory fused with present experience in a way that deepens the aesthetic element. I find no way of eliminating memory from my experiences or anyone else's. The mountain is the very content of my judgment, the pivot unleashing memory of the past which fuses with my sense of it. So, I can neither imagine aesthetic experience apart from memory nor apart from the object (the mountain). I don't think aesthetic experience is ever merely reflective, a way of using an object in the manner of a blank screen to achieve a harmonization of the faculties, allowing one to take pleasure in oneself as a person. It is the object (the mountain) which occasions, guides, and is the content of aesthetic experience, however reflective it may also be.

Put another way: aesthetic experience is always *personal*, whatever else it is. And this means object-directed. For there is no second-order reflection on oneself, no taking pleasure in one's own capacities for judgment, without *something to judge*. It is that in which we are interested. There is no purely disinterested judgment about anything.

And so no way to avoid the issue of diversity in favor of an abstracted universalism.

Kantian Formalism

How can Kant believe a judgment of the beautiful is about the subject herself rather than the object of her appreciation? Kant's answer is formalist. The third moment of the beautiful specifies that the experience of the beautiful is an experience of "purposiveness without purpose." In the experience of the beautiful our imagination shapes an object into a play of sensuous elements, each of which is there in order to contribute toward the achievement of an overall end. We find in the object a sense of organization in which all the parts seem to conspire toward that end, treating it as if it *had* such an end. Herein resides the pleasure, the sense of perfection, the feeling that everything is there in the work for a reason. And yet no real purpose is associated with that end, just the *feeling* of unity.

This is an idea best introduced by examples. What are we absorbed when we find a peony beautiful? We are absorbed in how the peony seems to droop like a heavy, erotic, perfumed bulb, made of paper-thin strands of pink color, also the way it seems to open like two cupped hands. A peony is anthropomorphic, sensual, scented, luxurious.

When we abstract from our particular interests in these things this is the sense of its form. However, the peony does not actually have that form. Form is our projection onto it. The result of the way our faculties harmonize around the peony, providing pleasure.

Music is the clearest example. Music seems to "move" through various changes toward completion, although no actual movement has ever taken place unless the orchestra gets up and changes seats or something. This is purposiveness—the sense of motion—without purpose—no actual movement, except in the ears. A fine work of music is one in which nothing seems extraneous to this overall purpose, this overall sense of purposiveness. The great Mozart is told "your piece is very good, but ... there are too many notes" by the Archduke of Vienna in Peter Schaffer's marvelous play *Amadeus*. "Which notes would you like me to leave out?" he asks, knowing the answer is, none may be left out, all are necessary to the sense of flow, buildup, resolution that makes his music perfect. It is not for nothing that Walter Pater, following the formalism inaugurated by Kant, announced that all arts aspire to the condition of music. In music meaning can be minimal and form overwhelming. From the opening beat of a composition to its conclusion we follow the introduction of theme, melody, harmonic rhythm, counterpoint and so forth, their intensification through modulation, variation, fugue or whatever until final resolution. It is this arc of movement that matters.

The music theorist Leonard Meyer first described this process as one of music's amassing expectations which are successively unresolved and reformulated, only to be finally brought to satisfaction.[12] The sonata form introduces materials which lead away from the tonic and intensify, after having been stated, through the principles of variation and modulation, finally at the end returning but this time in a way that seeks final resolve rather than movement away. Cadence, that moment in tonal form where a phrase leads to the fifth degree so that return to the first (the tonic chord) feels like a satisfying resolution of musical tension, is essential to the form. Rhythmic implication, phrase structure, contrapuntal intensification are all about deepening, and resolution, of implications.

When is music "worked through" successfully? *When we feel it so.* Meyer later replaced his concept of expectation with that of musical implications which are supposed to be "in the music."[13] But the earlier idea was Kantian.

Form, Kant believes, is *not a property of an object* (the way color or figure or mass or density is), but a mysterious synergy between it and our imaginative minds. How much apprehension of form is objective, how much subjective, is another of the questions of aesthetics for which no satisfactory theory has been offered.

Kant goes too far in thinking form entirely a property of our imaginations and not at all in the object: it is in an alchemical synergy between the two when music is made. What the great poet Baudelaire calls "correspondences" between the object and our minds. This is an idea taken up by the philosopher Richard Wollheim.[14] The willow tree with its long, thin leaves, bending toward the ground gives us the sense it is sad, bowled over by life, as if the leaves were our own tears. This is a kind of alchemy, or synergy, between what is in the object and what we project onto it, in virtue of our apprehension of its shape, color, leaves, and branches. The object after all has to have *some place* in catalyzing the experience of the beautiful, it cannot merely be a nothing. Kant cannot adequately explain what its causal role is in the experience of the beautiful. Although much of what he says about form is highly apt.

And yet Kant happily embraces this conundrum about the object. Whereas Hume wished to ground judgments of taste entirely in *causal properties of the object*, making taste a totally objective judgment, Kant believes the opposite. The judgment of the beautiful, being disinterested, is not strictly speaking a judgment about the object of taste at all. It is a purely subjective judgment, a judgment occasioned by the object but not about it. If the object is a mere placeholder for the subject's harmonization of the faculties around the experience and project of form onto it, then a work of art becomes totally opaque as to why it carries for so many the power it does. Clearly when my faculties harmonize they harmonize through synergy with the dynamic properties of the work. My judgment is about Beethoven's symphony, not about myself, or better, it is about both in a peculiar alchemy between mind and work.

Neither Hume nor Kant can be quite right. And the question of what properties of an object contribute to aesthetic experience and what our imaginations contribute is not one easily solved, since it depends on what one believes a property of an object is and is not. About this, philosophers have always disagreed. Baudelaire's famous idea is that it is the fit between our emotions and imaginations and the physiognomy of the object that allows us to project sadness onto the weeping branches of the willow, spiritual despair and the desire for sanctification onto the thin drooping faces of early Renaissance Sienese painting, emotional heaviness and a familiarity with earth in the mud-like swirling impasto of Van Gogh's paint. Again Baudelaire: "Nature is a temple," he writes, in which there is synergy or correspondence between what is in our minds and what is in the world. Taste is therefore neither purely objective (about detecting what is in the object and only doing that) nor is it purely subjective (a set of judgments purely about the subject as if the object were incidental).

There is more to be said about formalism. The problem with formalism is always the difficulty of adequately distinguishing *formal from nonformal features* of a medium. Chamber music, abstract art: these are the most persuasive examples. But even in the symphonic repertory masterpiece after masterpiece has been made which challenges the distinction between formal and nonformal features, persuading that it is the synergy of these (however they have been defined) which counts for the art. On any formalist theory of music, words become marginal to that medium. Musical form is a matter of phrasing, harmony, rhythm, pitch, voice-leading, timbre, cadence, repetition, variation, and so on. And yet: in the Beethoven Ninth Symphony, final movement, the famous drinking song of joy ("Freude, Schoene Gotterfunkeln Tochter aus Celesium") first appears in the cello section, which sings it alone. There is no doubt they are singing a song, one cannot hear it otherwise. But until the chorus takes up the melody with Schiller's drinking song we do not know whether there will be words (except that a choir is on stage if we are at a live performance). Retrospectively we realize that the cello section has been longing to sing words, as if the instinct for the word has been in the music all along. This is critical to the integration of orchestral and choral elements in this movement, hence to its form. For the cellos are invested with the glory of these words, and sound and word seem to become one. As soon as a feature is branded "nonformal" and consigned to a marginal status within a medium of art, one can usually find a major example in which that nonformal feature blends into the construction of form in a most central way.

In Richard Moran's fine phrase, formalism is a utopian position in aesthetics.[15] Like all utopian ideas, it responds to a deep desire in human experience to retreat from the world of meaning to an encomium of beauty and pleasure, wholly and entirely autonomous from all else, in and for itself, as the eighteenth century would put it. This side to aesthetic experience should not be discounted, simply qualified. No work entirely disappears into pure form, and yet the sense of absorption in a work to the point where all else seems to drop out is crucial for the value of art, and it is moreover a value that links art with the aesthetics of nature: for the beautiful sunset or mountaintop also seems to cause us to leave the world, however momentarily.

Kant's Universalizing Humanism

The fourth moment of the beautiful is Kant's attempt to connect aesthetics to morals. Because the judgment of taste is disinterested, universal, and formal, because it is a reflective judgment about our own free harmonization of our faculties, it is our way of taking symbolic pleasure in ourselves. The fourth moment of the beautiful adds more. In taking pleasure in our internal representations of aesthetic objects as ends in themselves, that is, as entities of the imagination in which all the parts conspire to an end, we are symbolically taking pleasure in our ability to treat others, and ourselves, similarly as ends. That is, we are taking pleasure in our capacity to treat all humanity as *moral ends*.

Kant says that the beautiful is the symbol of the morally good. That is the fourth moment of the beautiful. When we treat form as purposiveness without purpose, as an end, we are symbolically getting in touch with our capacity to treat people that way. Perhaps. Although for some music is precisely an escape from people. While for others, a confirmation of superiority over them. I think of Reinhard Heydrich. From a musical family he played piano and was undoubtedly moved by Beethoven. After which he would go out to commit crimes against humanity. This chief architect of the Final Solution certainly did not believe all humanity was included in his judgment of the beautiful, only those he considered human rather than viral, namely the Aryan race.

Kant could say, these are degradations of the judgment of the beautiful. But I am simply unconvinced that the beautiful has this fourth moment: that the beautiful must in essence and always symbolize the morally good. It is a fine idea, a *sublime* idea. But like all sublime ideas (see the previous chapter) it is the product of the imagination of one philosopher in a humanist age.

A word about Kant's moral philosophy may help at least to lay out the elegance of his idea. Kant derives his moral philosophy from what he calls the "Judeo-Christian tradition." Which is, Kant believes, the guiding moral tradition of Western civilization. The first rule of morals, according to this tradition, Kant believes, is the golden rule: Do unto others as you would have them do unto you. From this commandment never to act toward another in a way you would not want them to act toward you, Kant derives the categorical imperative. Moral action, as opposed to action based in mere inclination (interest), is guided by this rule: act so that you never treat another as a means only, always treat other people as ends—taking into account their needs, interests, desires, personhood. For this is how you would want them to treat you. Do not enslave them unless you would want them to do it to you, nor subjugate women unless you would be happy being their underling, nor discriminate against others unless you would believe it all right for them to discriminate against you.

This is to act, Kant says in the *Foundations of the Metaphysics of Morals* of 1785 and in the *Critique of Practical Reason* of 1788,[16] out of respect for others. In turn they are morally instructed to act in the same way: out of respect for me and my person. The first formulation of what he calls the categorical imperative therefore is: never treat others (or yourself) as a means only. Always act with respect, treating persons as ends in themselves.

Since this principle applies universally, Kant then seeks to capture it in a second formulation, that of the categorical imperative: act so that you could will the maxim under which you act in the form of a universal law. A maxim is something which every person should follow because it is a way of achieving what we all should morally do: respect others. And from this he derives the third version: act so as to act in the name of all humanity. Stand as an exemplar of all.

These formulations are powerful and principled ways in which moral equality is articulated. Everyone should be treated equally (as a subject of the moral law, a person whose ends must be respected) and should act equally to treat everyone else the same way. This does not mean everyone should do exactly the same thing to be moral as everyone else, which would be patently absurd. I want to be a doctor, you want to be a lawyer. What we share is the moral principle that neither of us should act in a way that rips people off, uses them for one's personal gain, cheats the system, and so on. For this is treating others as means only. We make different choices, both guided by the same principle which applies equally and defines our equality with one another.

Since the categorical imperative applies equally and universally, to all persons, it defines moral rights and obligations. Except that it is well known that Kant, writing in his early period, believed whites superior to black persons and went so far as to question whether black persons have a rational will. It is debated within philosophy whether his early racism stuck with him through his later work on cosmopolitanism.[17] Either way, what Kant does not do is raise the question of alternative moral traditions to the Judeo-Christian one on the basis of which he erected his moral theory—and by the way it is not clear there *is* a unified tradition of this kind. I am interested in his lack of interest in alternative moral traditions. In Southern Africa the concept of Ubuntu mandates that every person be treated with dignity because the entire village is needed for the welfare of even a single individual in it. This communalist perspective mandates care, support, help, love, empathy, and goods for all. And rather than saying that everyone should will their maxim universally by following the golden rule, it says everyone should remain wedded to the moral project of the village. Ubuntu is as fine a moral idea as anything the West ever came up with, and very much opposed to the ideology of Europe which begins from the cult of the individual and proceeds to philosophize morals in the light of an individual subject's capacity for moral judgment thanks to her rational will. Kant could know nothing of the moral complexity of alternative cultures because he was part of a colonial world disinterested in knowing anything about the natives they ruled. Knowledge was power and the only kind of knowledge Europe really wanted about its native subjects was that which could be used to control them. I exaggerate, there were exceptions, but disinterest was the norm. This places Kant in the context of the limitations of his time.

Today it is a *cosmopolitan task* to consider different kinds of moral cultures, with the aim of discovering the strengths and limitations of each, and seeking that understanding possibilities for the heightening of one's own moral self and that of one's communities. And to question the universality of judgment in the light of this.

Now the categorical imperative is meant to respect the autonomy of each person, facilitating them in their life plans (their ends, what they want to be, become, plan, do, etc.). Autonomy is not simply, as Kant says, negatively conceived, as a state in which institutions or persons haven't imprisoned you within their walls or according to their wills. Autonomy is also positive. The ability to will one's own life according to one's own terms. Autonomy follows directly from the right to liberty. Since it is the condition for the exercise of liberty that one is autonomous from (the state, church, etc.), and one is autonomous in the positive sense of self-governance (devising and following one's script within moral limits).

It is easy to see how Kant believes he has preserved this philosophical structure in the *Third Critique*. Aesthetic experience takes place apart from all interests like moral experience or what he calls "practical reason." Aesthetic experience is therefore autonomous from life, an experience entirely for its own sake. The judgment of the beautiful is a reflective judgment, about the self, a way of celebrating the person's autonomy. And the moral demands that come with this to treat others as one is free to live oneself: autonomously, according to one's own script.

Here is the third moment of the beautiful. The experience of the beautiful is one in which the aesthetic object seems to have purposiveness but without any real purpose beyond itself. It seems to be integrated as if to achieve an end. This again is clearest in music, where a coherent musical work seems to "move" through time in a way that finally leads to its "end," its resolution, as if everything in the work were directed to this goal. The sense that a work of art is so integrated and directed to an "end" makes, Kant thinks, the work a perfect symbol of moral action, which seeks to respect the "ends" of humanity (of each and every person). When we take pleasure in the final cadence of a work of music we are taking pleasure, he thinks, in the "ends" of humanity, meaning humanity as an end in itself.

The experience of the beautiful is thus a reflective judgment in which we take pleasure in our moral capacity through the symbol of art. This is the fourth moment of the beautiful.

A beautiful, sublime idea. But aesthetic judgment remains an empty formalism when it is based on a concept of *disinterestedness*, which Kant has to do in order to retain the connection between individual aesthetic judgment and intersubjective universality, with the aesthetic judge standing as exemplar to all others, who ought to judge as she does. Once aesthetic judgment returns from the abstraction of disinterested judgment, once the fully embodied person is understood to be the aesthetic judge, then that person's ethnicity, race, history, beliefs, emotions, desires, community, history, and class may and usually do come into it. At which point the question of the diversity must arise. This is the cosmopolitan question and we are back in Chapter 3.

A point from Jean-Paul Sartre. One should doubt Kant's claim that the judgment of the beautiful is made in the name of all humanity, placing oneself in the position of humanity's exemplar. And not simply because my particular set of interests place me in the diversity of the human species rather than an abstracted exemplar for all who are supposed to be the same because they are also abstracted from their particular makeup. But also, because it is often untrue to my experience of judgment that every time I judge I even aim to judge universally. This was discussed in Chapter 3 with respect to Jean-Paul Sartre's "Existentialism Is a Humanism" where the importance of setting a moral example arose, rather than the claim to speak in the name of all humanity.[18]

Setting a moral example in a world of different peoples is making *a cosmopolitan gesture to them*, asking them to reach out and embrace one's own way of doing things. They may be disposed not to follow one's example, at which point the challenge of ethics and aesthetics arises in a way that we have seen in Chapter 3. Kant's claim about standing as an exemplar for all humanity is a dogma of the eighteenth century, the century where the European claims to speak for all. And in Kant's philosophy speaks abstractly, apart from most of who he is. It is a kind of missionary position, that of the good servant of the Lord who travels to the colonies under the belief that every person deserves universal baptism and, hence, the shelter and guidance of Christ.

When the claim to speaking universally is dropped, cosmopolitanism arises as the best picture of aesthetic judgment in a global world.

The Importance of Eighteenth-Century Aesthetics Today

In ending I want to return to the question I raised at the beginning of this chapter. Why bother to study Hume and Kant when the frameworks they rely on are datable to eighteenth-century hierarchy and/or abstract universalism both of which disallow the question of taste in relation to the wide scope of human diversity?

What makes it worthwhile to study eighteenth-century aesthetics is that its recognition of the autonomy of art and the power of aesthetic experience remains indispensable. The eighteenth century discovered the importance of exalted pleasure for philosophy, pleasure taken in an object for the sake of the experience itself. Its emphasis on experience rather than representation, autonomy rather than connectedness, beauty, and the sublime rather than political rhetoric are important correctives to current art practice and thinking about art. The eighteenth-century insight about the transcendent, nonintellectual pleasure in aesthetic experience remains indispensable. Art is not simply about truth. It is not simply about markets. It is not simply a way of "making a statement," nor simply a political gesture, an act of group solidarity in the avant-garde sense. Art is also about engendering a peculiar and at best a marvelous experience. Art is what Alexander Nehamas calls a promise of happiness.[19] Even if also an act of dissent, even a weapon in the struggle for emancipation.

It is how these aspects of art fuse together that matters.

The eighteenth century was surely right that art requires sufficient autonomy from the rest of life to create and work its charms. The kind of autonomy one is also privileged to have when one wanders to the seaside to watch a sunset. One can't do that if stuck in a prison cell, or unable to move, or if the traffic is so bad that the noise drowns out one's concentration, or if pollution prevents one seeing anything more than dirty chemicals in the sky. This although autonomy is always also a utopian dream. No work is "completely" autonomous from the flow of life any more than a person is. One needs a reasonable notion of autonomy. One that also allows for the basic forms of transaction between art and life, and also people and society. Autonomy is, as Kant famously said, also to be understood positively, as the right and ability to pursue one's own path of self-realization, and art, like love, plays a huge role in this project so central to human life. In this taste is indeed a paradigm of autonomy, allowing persons to pursue the things that they enjoy and find exalting for their own sake.

Then we are left with a paradox. Art has to be sufficiently autonomous from life to work its magic, while also delivering meaning and message. Art is both a religion and an instrument. Art seems to engage us in a way that passes beyond meaning into a trance of beauty, sublimity, and pleasure. It feels transcendent, like the sunset does when we are utterly captivated by it. And yet this experience is always also one that delivers meaning and has social use, sometimes profoundly so. The power of aesthetic experience can be set to work for social and political goals (good or evil), it is how these aspects of art conspire that matters: that makes art what it is. I don't think one can provide a theory specifying how the one aspect of art (its transcendent side) links to the other aspect (its meaning-giving and sociopolitical driven side). Rather, one must give a case-by-case story of how these aspects come together in Renaissance art, in baroque music, in classical dance, in jazz, in the avant-gardes, and so on. This is the story of art. I don't think, after three hundred years of trying, philosophy can succeed in providing a general theory of aesthetic experience.

And so, this book does not seek to resolve the paradox but embraces it as central to aesthetic experience and to the nature of art. Which is why the student of aesthetics must study all centuries of philosophical writing—from the eighteenth to the twenty-first. It took philosophy three centuries to grasp the tensions through which art lives.

Notes

1 INTRODUCTION TO GLOBALIZATION

1. David Harvey, *The Condition of Postmodernity: An Inquiry into the Origins of Cultural* Change (Blackwell: Boston and Oxford, 1989).
2. Joseph Stiglitz, *Globalization and Inequality Revisited: Anti-Globalization in the Era of Trump* (W. W. Norton: New York, 2017).
3. Benedict Anderson, *Imagined Communities* (Cornell University Press: Cornell and London, 1983).
4. Fredric Nietzsche, "On the Uses and Disadvantages of History for Life," *Untimely Meditations*, trans. R. J. Hollingdale, ed. Daniel Breazeale (Cambridge University Press: Cambridge and London, 1997), pp. 57–124.

2 THE GLOBAL ART WORLD TODAY: PROSPECTS AND PROBLEMS

1. Arthur Danto, *The Transfiguration of the Commonplace* (Harvard University Press: Cambridge and London, 1981).
2. Rosalind Krauss, *A Voyage on the North Sea: Art in the Age of the Post-Medium Condition* (Thames and Hudson: London, 1974).
3. Daniel Herwitz, *Making Theory/Constructing Art* (University of Chicago Press: Chicago and London, 1993).
4. Susan Sontag, *On Photography* (Farrar, Straus and Giroux: New York, 1977).
5. Cf. Jacques Derrida, *Archive Fever*, trans. Eric Prenowitz (University of Chicago Press: Chicago and London, 1996).
6. Daniel Herwitz, *Aesthetics, Arts and Politics in a Global World* (Bloomsbury: London, 2017).
7. Daniel Magaziner, *The Art of Life* (Swallow Press: Ohio, 2016).
8. Albie Sachs, Private Conversation, May 2018.
9. Zeitz MOCAA, Curatorial text introducing the exhibition, *All Things Being Equal*, recorded by the author on June 18, 2018.

3 AESTHETIC COSMOPOLITANISM

1. Ludwig Wittgenstein, *Philosophical Investigations*, trans. Elizabeth Anscombe (Macmillan: New York, 1953).
2. Michel de Montaigne, "Of Cannibals," in *Complete Essays of Michel de Montaigne*, trans. Donald Frame (Stanford University Press: Stanford and London, 1958).
3. Immanuel Kant, *To Perpetual Peace: A Philosophical Sketch* (Hackett, 2003).
4. Jean-Paul Sartre, "Existentialism Is a Humanism," in *Existentialism from Dostoyevsky to Sartre*, ed. Walter Kaufmann (Meridian Books: New York, 1956).
5. Cf. Phillipe Sands, *East West Street* (Vintage Books: New York, 2017).
6. Donald Davidson, "On the Very Idea of a Conceptual Scheme," in *Essays on Actions and Events* (Clarendon Press: Oxford, 1980).
7. Anthony Appiah, *Cosmopolitanism: Ethics in a World of Strangers* (Henry Holt: New York, 2006), p. xv.
8. The idea that human freedom and dignity require in some instances, and especially for beleaguered minority groups, special group rights, because members of the group require group recognition and identification in order to feel respected and free to be themselves can be found in the philosophical writings of Charles Taylor. His example is the French Canadian Québécois, and the fact that out of deference to them special rights are accorded in French Canada, including the requirement that education takes place in French. I cannot go into the complexities of this particular example here, but urge the reader to turn to his work, and to Anthony Appiah's critique of it. Cf. Charles Taylor, with responses by Amy Gutmann, K. Anthony Appiah, Jurgen Habermas, Steven C. Rockefeller, Michael Walzer and Susan Wolf, *Multiculturalism: Examining the Politics of Recognition*, ed. Amy Gutmann (Princeton University Press: Princeton and London, 1994).
9. G. W. F. Hegel, *The Philosophy of Right*, trans. T. M. Knox (Oxford University Press: Oxford and London, 1952).
10. See my *Aesthetics, Arts and Politics in a Global World* for an extended discussion of this. Daniel Herwitz, *Aesthetics, Arts and Politics in a Global World* (Bloomsbury: London, 2017), Chapter 5.
11. For a good discussion of aboriginal art, see: Howard Morphy, *Aboriginal Art* (Phaidon: London, 1998).
12. Bruce Chatwin, *The Songlines* (Penguin: New York, 1988).

13 Cf. Aby Warburg, *Images from the Region of the Pueblo Indians of North America*, trans. with an Interpretative Essay by Michael Steinberg (Cornell University Press: Cornell and London, 1995).
14 Ludwig Wittgenstein, *Philosophical Investigations*, trans. Elizabeth Anscombe (Macmillan: New York, 1953), section 122.

4 CULTURAL PROPERTY AND AESTHETIC SYNERGY

1 Cf. my *Heritage, Culture and Politics in the Postcolony* (Columbia Press: New York and London, 2012).
2 See the work of Jean and John Comaroff, *Of Revelation and Revolution: Christianity, Colonialism, and Consciousness in South Africa* (University of Chicago Press: Chicago and London, 1991), and *Of Revelation and Revolution: The Dialectics of Modernity on a South African Frontier* (University of Chicago Press: Chicago and London, 1997).
3 Cf. Herwitz, *Aesthetics, Arts and Politics in a Global World* (Bloomsbury: London, 2017), chapter 6.
4 Herwitz, *Aesthetics, Arts and Politics in a Global World*, chapter 6.
5 Sibusiso Njeza, *The CapeTowner*, November 20, 2015, p. 4.
6 Herwitz, *Aesthetics, Arts and Politics in a Global World*, chapter 6.
7 Appiah, *Cosmopolitanism*, p. 135.
8 Sander Gilman, *Difference and Pathology* (Cornell University Press: Cornell and London, 1985).
9 Appiah, *Cosmopolitanism*, p. 119.
10 Ibid., p. xv.
11 Ibid.
12 Appiah, *Cosmopolitanism*, pp. 129–30.
13 Ibid., p. 127.
14 Immanuel Kant, *Critique of Judgment*, trans. J. H. Bernard (Haffner Press: New York, 1951), pp. 46–7.
15 Ludwig Wittgenstein, *Philosophical Investigations*, trans. Elizabeth Anscombe (Macmillan: New York, 1958), p. 127.
16 I am indebted to discussion with Akeel Bilgrami here.

5 MEANING, MEDIUM, AND HISTORY IN ART

1 Edward Said, *Orientalism* (Pantheon: New York, 1978).

2 Cf. Daniel Herwitz, *Making Theory/Constructing Art: On the Authority of the Avant-Gardes* (University of Chicago Press: Chicago and London, 1993).
3 Pierre Cabanne, *Dialogues with Marcel Duchamp*, trans. Ron Padgett (Thames and Hudson: London, 1971).
4 Cf. Ted Cohen, "What's Special about Photography," in *Serious Larks*, ed. Daniel Herwitz (University of Chicago Press: Chicago and London, 2018).
5 Cf. Herwitz, *Making Theory/Constructing Art*.
6 Arthur Danto, *The Philosophical Disenfranchisement of Art* (Columbia: New York, 1986).
7 Cf. Thierry de Duve, *Kant after Duchamp* (MIT Press: Cambridge and London, 1996).
8 G. W. F. Hegel, *Aesthetics: Lectures on Fine Art*, trans. T. M. Knox (Clarendon Press: Oxford, 1975), p. 31.
9 Hegel, *Aesthetics: Lectures on Fine Art*, p. 31.
10 Ibid.
11 Ibid., p. 32.
12 For a discussion of what Danto means by a "theory," see Herwitz, *Making Theory/Constructing Art*, chapters 6–8.
13 Fredric Nietzsche, *The Birth of Tragedy*, trans. Douglas Smith (Oxford University Press: Oxford and London, 2000).
14 For a discussion of the problem of politics for art in our time, see my chapter on Australian artist George Gittoes in Herwitz, *Aesthetics, Arts and Politics in a Global World* (Bloomsbury: London, 2017), chapter 8.
15 I have written about the philosophical stakes for believing any thesis about the end of art, with emphasis on Danto's ideas, at greater length in my essay "The Beginning of the End: Danto on Postmodernism," in *Danto and His Critics*, ed. Mark Rollins (Blackwell: Oxford, 1993), pp. 142–58.
16 Cf. Herwitz, *The Star as Icon* (Columbia Press: New York and London, 2008), chapter 2.
17 Arthur Danto, *Encounters and Reflections* (Noonday Press: New York, 1997), p. 306.

6 TASTE IN ITS EIGHTEENTH-CENTURY CONTEXT

1. C. B. MacPherson, *The Political Theory of Possessive Individualism: Hobbes to Locke* (Oxford University Press: London and New York, 1964).
2. Robert Hughes, *The Fatal Shore* (Knopf: New York, 1986).
3. Burke Loc 388 Kindle Collected works.
4. Paul Guyer, "The Origin of Modern Aesthetics: 1711–1735," in *The Blackwell Guide to Aesthetics*, ed. Peter Kivy (Blackwell: Oxford, 2004), pp. 32–5.
5. Walter Benjamin, *The Work of Art in the Age of Its Technological Reproducibility, and Other Writings on Media*, ed. Michael Jennings, Brigid Doherty, and Thomas Levin, trans. Edmund Jephcott (Belknap: Cambridge, 2008).
6. Cf. Pratapaditya Pal and Vidya Dehejia, *From Merchants to Emperors: British Artists and India, 1757–1930* (Cornell University Press: Ithaca and London, 1986).
7. Bernard Cohn, *Colonialism and Its Forms of Knowledge: The British in India* (Princeton University Press: Princeton, 1996).
8. Cf. Edward Said, *Orientalism* (Pantheon: New York, 1978).
9. Cf. Jean and John Comaroff, *Of Revelation and Revolution Volume 1: Christianity, Colonialism, and Consciousness in South Africa* (University of Chicago Press: Chicago and London, 1991).
10. Chinhua Achebe, "An Image of Africa: Racism in Conrad's 'Heart of Darkness'," *Massachusetts Review*, vol. 18, 1977, pp. 1783–94.
11. Chinhua Achebe, *Things Fall Apart* (Anchor: New York, 1994).
12. Leo Steinberg, "The Philosophical Brothel," *October*, no. 44, Spring 1988, 7–74.
13. John Richardson, *A Life of Picasso, Volume I* (Random House: New York, 1991).
14. Cf. Richard Wollheim, *Art and Its Objects* (Cambridge University Press: Cambridge and London, 1968).
15. Cf. Ted Cohen, *Serious Larks*, ed. Daniel Herwitz (University of Chicago Press: Chicago and London, 2017), chapter 10.
16. Friedrich Schiller, *On the Aesthetic Education of Man: In a Series of Letters*; edited and translated with an introduction by Elizabeth M. Wilkinson and L. A. Willoughby (Clarendon Press: New York and Oxford, 1982).
17. Cf. Russell Berman, *Modern Culture and Critical Theory: Art, Politics and the Legacy of the Frankfurt School* (Madison: Wisconsin, 1989).

18 Cf. Hannah Arendt, "Authority in the Twentieth Century," in *Thinking Without a Bannister: Essays in Understanding, 1953–1975*, edited with an introduction by Jerome Kohn (Schocken Books: New York, 2018).

7 AESTHETIC JUDGMENT FROM A COSMOPOLITAN PERSPECTIVE

1 Anthony Appiah, *Cosmopolitanism: Ethics in a World of Strangers* (Henry Holt: New York, 2006), p. xv.
2 David Hume, "Of the Standard of Taste," from *Selected Essays*, ed. Stephen Copley and Andrew Edgar (Clarendon Press: Oxford and London, 1998), p. 147.
3 For more on the test of time, see Anthony Savile, *The Test of Time: An Essay in Philosophical Aesthetics* (Oxford University Press: Oxford and Toronto, 1982).
4 Daniel Herwitz, *Aesthetics, Arts and Politics in a Global World* (Bloomsbury: London, 2017), chapter 6.
5 David Hume, "Of the Standard of Taste," from *Selected Essays*, ed. Stephen Copley and Andrew Edgar (Clarendon Press: Oxford and London, 1998), p. 141.
6 See selections by both of these philosophers in David Goldblatt and Lee Brown, *Aesthetics: A Reader in Philosophy of the Arts* (Prentice Hall: New Jersey, 1997).
7 Ted Cohen, "Objects of Appreciation," in *Serious Larks*, edited with an introduction by Daniel Herwitz (University of Chicago Press: Chicago and London, 2018), p. 117.
8 Cohen, "Objects of Appreciation," p. 117.
9 Ted Cohen, "Liking What's Good, Why Should We?" in Cohen, *Serious Larks*, edited with an introduction by Daniel Herwitz (University of Chicago Press: Chicago and London, 2018), pp. 161–2.
10 Immanuel Kant, *Critique of Judgment*, trans. J. H. Bernard (Haffner Press: New York, 1951).
11 Marcel Proust, *In Search of Lost Time, Volume VI*, trans. Terence Kilmartin revised by Joanna Kilmartin (The Modern Library: New York, 1993), p. 262.
12 Leonard, Meyer, *Emotion and Meaning in Music* (University of Chicago Press: Chicago and London, 1974).
13 Leonard, Meyer, *Music, the Arts, and Ideas* (University of Chicago Press: Chicago and London, 1994).

14 Charles Baudelaire, "The Painter of Modern Life," in *The Painter of Modern Life and Other Essays*, trans. and ed. Jonathan Mayne (Phaidon Press: New York, 1964) and Richard Wollheim, *Art and Its Objects* (Cambridge University Press: Cambridge and London, 1968).

15 Richard Moran, "Formalism and the Appearance of Nature," in *Michael Fried and Philosophy*, ed. Mathew Abbott (Routledge: New York, 2018), pp. 117–28.

16 Immanuel Kant, *Foundations of the Metaphysics of Morals*, translated with an introduction by Louis White Beck (University of Chicago Press: Chicago and London, 1950); and Immanuel Kant, *Critique of Practical Reason*, translated with an introduction by Louis White Beck (Liberal Arts: New York, 1956).

17 Cf. Pauline Kleingeld, "Kant's Second Thoughts on Race." *The Philosophical Quarterly*, vol. 57, no. 229, October 2007, pp. 573–92.

18 Jean-Paul Sartre, "Existentialism Is a Humanism," in *Existentialism from Dostoyevsky to Sartre*, ed. Walter Kaufmann (Meridian Books: New York, 1956).

19 Alexander Nehamas, *Only a Promise of Happiness: The Place of Beauty in a World of Art* (Princeton University Press: Princeton and London, 2007).

Bibliography and Suggestions for Further Reading

Achebe, Chinhua, "An Image of Africa: Racism in Conrad's 'Heart of Darkness'," *Massachusetts Review*, vol. 18, 1977.
Achebe, Chinhua, *Things Fall Apart* (Anchor: New York, 1994).
Addison, Joseph, *Delphi Collection of the Complete Works of Joseph Addison* (Kindle Books).
Anderson, Benedict, *Imagined Communities* (Verso: London, 2006).
Appiah, Anthony, *Cosmopolitanism: Ethics in a World of Strangers* (Henry Holt: New York, 2006).
Appiah, Anthony, *In My Father's House* (Princeton University Press: Princeton and Oxford, 1992).
Arendt, Hannah, "Authority in the Twentieth Century," in *Thinking without a Bannister: Essays in Understanding, 1953–1975*, edited with an introduction by Jerome Kohn (Schocken Books: New York, 2018).
Aristotle, *Poetics*, trans. Halliwell, Stephen with introduction (Duckworth: London, 1998).
Baudelaire, Charles, "The Painter of Modern Life," in *The Painter of Modern Life and Other Essays*, trans. and ed. Jonathan Mayne (Phaidon Press: New York, 1964).
Berman, Russell, *Modern Culture and Critical Theory: Art, Politics and the Legacy of the Frankfurt School* (Madison: Wisconsin, 1989).
Bilgrami, Akeel, *Secularism, Identity and Enchantment* (Harvard Press: Cambridge and London, 2014).
Bourguignon, François, trans. Thomas Scott-Railton, *The Globalization of Inequality* (Princeton University Press: Princeton and Oxford, 2015).
Burke, Edmund, *A Philosophical Enquiry into the Origin of Our Ideas of the Sublime and the Beautiful* (Kindle Books, 1757).
Cabanne, Pierre, *Dialogues with Marcel Duchamp*, trans. Ron Padgett (Thames and Hudson: London, 1971).
Castillo, Bernal Diaz, *The Conquest of New Spain*, trans. John Ingram Lockhart (Enhanced Media: Digital Publication, 2017).

Cavell, Stanley, *Disowning Knowledge* (Cambridge University Press: Cambridge and New York, 1987).
Cavell, Stanley, *Must We Mean What We Say?* (Harvard University Press: Cambridge and London, 1969).
Chatterjee, Partha, *Nationalist Thought and the Colonial World* (Princeton: 1985).
Chatwin, Bruce, *The Songlines* (Penguin: New York, 1988).
Clark, T. J., *The Painting of Modern Life* (Princeton University Press: Princeton and Oxford, 1984).
Cohen, Ted, *Serious Larks: The Philosophy of Ted Cohen*, edited with an introduction by Daniel Herwitz (University of Chicago Press: Chicago and London, 2018).
Cohn, Bernard, *Colonialism and Its Forms of Knowledge: The British in India* (Princeton University Press: Princeton, 1996).
Collingwood, R. G., *The Principles of Art* (Oxford University Press: Oxford, 1958).
Conrad, Josef, *Heart of Darkness* (Amazon Kindle Classic).
Danto, Arthur, *After the End of Art, Contemporary Art and the Pale of History* (Princeton University Press: Princeton, 1997), p. 165.
Danto, Arthur, *Beyond the Brillo Box* (Farrar, Straus, Giroux: New York, 1992).
Danto, Arthur, *The Philosophical Disenfranchisement of Art* (Columbia: New York, 1986).
Danto, Arthur, *The Transfiguration of the Commonplace* (Harvard University Press: Cambridge and London, 1981).
Davidson, Donald, "On the Very Idea of a Conceptual Scheme," in *Essays on Actions and Events* (Clarendon Press: Oxford, 1980).
de Duve, Thierry, *Kant after Duchamp* (MIT Press: Cambridge and London, 1996).
de Montaigne, Michel, "Of Cannibals," in *Complete Essays of Michel de Montaigne*, trans. Donald Frame (Stanford University Press: Stanford and London, 1958).
Derrida, Jacques, *Acts of Literature*, trans. Derek Attridge (Routledge: New York, 1992).
Derrida, Jacques, *The Truth in Painting*, trans. Geoff Bennington and Ian McCleod (University of Chicago Press: Chicago and London, 1987).
Dewey, John, *Art as Experience* (Paragon Books: New York, 1959).
Eriksen, Thomas Hylland, *Globalization: The Key Concepts* (Bloomsbury: London, 2014).
Fanon, Frantz, "On National Culture," in *Colonial and Postcolonial Theory: A Reader*, ed. Patrick Williams and Ian Chrisman (Columbia University Press: New York, 1994).
Foucault, Michel, *This Is Not a Pipe*, trans. James Harkness (Quantum: New York, 1983).

Fry, Roger, *Vision and Design* (Meridian Books: New York, 1960).
Gilman, Sander, *Difference and Pathology* (Cornell University Press: Cornell and London, 1985).
Gittoes, George, *Blood Mystic* (Macmillan: Australia, 2017).
Goldblatt, David and Brown, Lee, *Aesthetics: A Reader in Philosophy of the Arts* (Prentice Hall: New Jersey, 1997).
Gutmann, Amy and Taylor, Charles, *Multiculturalism: Examining the Politics of Recognition* (Princeton University Press: Princeton and London, 1994).
Guyer, Paul, "The Origin of Modern Aesthetics: 1711–1735," in *The Blackwell Guide to Aesthetics*, ed. Peter Kivy (Blackwell: Oxford, 2004), pp. 32–5.
Guyer, Paul, *A History of Modern Aesthetics, Volumes 1–3* (Cambridge University Press: Cambridge and London, 2014).
Guyer, Paul, *Kant and the Claims of Taste* (Cambridge University Press: New York, 1997).
Hanslick, Eduard, *On the Musically Beautiful*, trans. Geoffrey Payzant (Hackett: Indianapolis, IN, 1986).
Harvey, David, *The Condition of Postmodernity: An Inquiry into the Origins of Cultural Change* (Blackwell: Boston and Oxford, 1989).
Hegel, G. W. F., *Aesthetics: Lectures on Fine Art*, trans. T. M. Knox (Clarendon Press: Oxford, 1975).
Hegel, G. W. F., *The Philosophy of Right*, trans. T. M. Knox (Oxford University Press: Oxford and London, 1952).
Herwitz, Daniel, "The Beginning of the End: Danto on Postmodernism," in *Danto and His Critics*, ed. Mark Rollins (Blackwell: Oxford, 1993).
Herwitz, Daniel, *Aesthetics, Arts and Politics in a Global World* (Bloomsbury: London, 2017).
Herwitz, Daniel, *Heritage, Culture and Politics in the Postcolony* (Columbia University Press: New York, 2012).
Herwitz, Daniel, *Making Theory/Constructing Art: On the Authority of the Avant-Gardes* (University of Chicago Press: Chicago and London, 1993).
Herwitz, Daniel, *The Star as Icon* (Columbia Press: New York and London, 2008).
Herwitz, Daniel and Varshney, Ashutosh, *Midnight's Diaspora: Encounters with Salman Rushdie* (University of Michigan Press: Ann Arbor and London, 2008).
Hobsbawm, Eric, *The Age of Empire, 1875–1914* (Vintage: New York, 1989).
Hughes, Robert, *The Fatal Shore* (Knopf: New York, 1986).
Hume, David, "Of the Standard of Taste," "Of Tragedy," and "Of the Delicacy of Taste and Passion" from *Selected Essays*, ed.

Stephen Copley and Andrew Edgar (Clarendon Press: Oxford and London, 1998).
Hume, David, *Treatise of Human Nature*, ed. David and Mary Norton (Oxford University Press: Oxford and London, 2002), p. 316.
Jean and Comaroff, John, *Of Revelation and Revolution Volume 1: Christianity, Colonialism, and Consciousness in South Africa* (University of Chicago Press: Chicago and London, 1991).
Judin, Hilton and Vladislavic, Ivan, *Blank: Art, Apartheid and after* (RAI: Rotterdam, 1999).
Kant, Immanuel, *Critique of Practical Reason*, translated with an introduction by Louis White Beck (Liberal Arts: New York, 1956).
Kant, Immanuel, *Foundations of the Metaphysics of Morals*, translated with an introduction by Louis White Beck (University of Chicago Press: Chicago and London, 1950).
Kant, Immanuel, *Political Writings* (Cambridge University Press: Cambridge, 1991).
Kant, Immanuel, *To Perpetual Peace: A Philosophical Sketch* (Hackett, 2003).
Kant, Immanuel, *Critique of Judgment*, trans. J. H. Bernard (Haffner Press: New York, 1951).
Kivy, Peter, ed., *The Blackwell Guide to Aesthetics* (Blackwell: Oxford, 2004), especially essays by Dickie, Sclafani and Roblin; *Aesthetics* (St Martin's Press: London, 1989).
Kivy, Peter, *The Seventh Sense* (Burt Franklin: New York, 1976).
Kleingeld, Pauline, "Kant's Second Thoughts on Race," *The Philosophical Quarterly*, vol. 57, no. 229, October 2007, pp. 573–92.
Krauss, Rosalind, *A Voyage on the North Sea: Art in the Age of the Post-Medium Condition* (Thames and Hudson: London, 1974).
Krauss, Rosalind, *The Originality of the Avant-Garde and Other Modernist Myths* (MIT Press: Cambridge and London, 1985).
Kristov-Bargakiev, Carolyn, *William Kentridge* (Société des Expositions du Palais des Beaux-Arts: Bruxelles, 1998).
La Caze, Marguerite, "At the Intersection: Kant, Derrida, and the Relation between Ethics and Politics," *Political Theory*, vol. 35, no. 6, 2007, pp. 781–805.
Lambropoulos, Vassilis, *The Tragic Idea* (Duckworth: London, 2006).
Larsen, Svend Erik, *Literature and the Experience of Globalization* (Bloomsbury: London, 2017).
Locke, John, *Second Treatise of Government* (Digireads.com, 2017).
Lyotard, Jean-Francois, *Philosophy, Politics and the Sublime*, trans. Hugh Silverman (Routledge: Oxford, 2016).
MacPherson, C. B., *The Political Theory of Possessive Individualism: From Hobbes to Locke* (Clarendon Press, 1962).

Manganyi, N. C., *Gerard Sekoto, "I am an African": A Biography* (Wits Press: Johannesburg, 2004).
Martin, Meredith, *Diamonds, Guns and War* (Public Affairs: New York, 2014).
Marx, Karl, *Economic and Philosophical Manuscripts of 1844*, trans. Martin Milligan (Prometheus: New York, 1988).
Meyer, Leonard, *Emotion and Meaning in Music* (University of Chicago Press: Chicago and London, 1974).
Meyer, Leonard, *Music, The Arts and Ideas* (University of Chicago Press: Chicago and London, 1994).
Moran, Richard, "Formalism and the Appearance of Nature," in *Michael Fried and Philosophy*, ed. Mathew Abbott (Routledge: New York, 2018). pp. 117–28.
Morphy, Howard, *Aboriginal Art* (Phaidon: London, 1998).
Mudimbe, V. Y., *The Invention of Africa* (Indiana University Press: Bloomington and London, 1988).
Nehamas, Alexander, *Only a Promise of Happiness: The Place of Beauty in a World of Art* (Princeton University Press: Princeton and London, 2007).
Nietzsche, Fredric, "On the Uses and Disadvantages of History for Life," *Untimely Meditations*, trans. R. J. Hollingdale, ed. Daniel Breazeale (Cambridge University Press: Cambridge and London, 1997).
Nietzsche, Fredric, *The Birth of Tragedy*, trans. Douglas Smith (Oxford University Press: Oxford and London, 2000).
Njeza, Sibusiso, *The CapeTowner*, November 20, 2015.
Oneal, John R. and Russett, Bruce, *The Kantian Peace: The Pacific Benefits of Democracy, Interdependence, and International Organizations, 1885–1992*, World Politics, vol. 52, no. 1, 1999, pp. 1–37.
Pal, Pratapaditya and Dehejia, Vidya, *From Merchants to Emperors: British Artists and India, 1757–1930* (Cornell University Press: Ithaca and London, 1986).
Plato, *Complete Works*, ed. John Cooper (Hackett: Indianapolis, 1997), especially *Ion*.
Proust, Marcel, *In Search of Lost Time, Volume VI*, trans. Terence Kilmartin revised by Joanna Kilmartin (The Modern Library: New York, 1993).
Reid, Jennifer, *Religion, Postcolonialism and Globalization* (Bloomsbury: London, 2014).
Rieff, David, *A Bed for the Night: Humanitarianism in Crisis* (Simon and Schuster: New York, 2003).
Rosen, Charles, *The Classical Style: Haydn, Beethoven and Mozart* (W. W. Norton: New York, 1998).
Rushdie, Salman, *Midnight's Children* (Modern Library: New York, 2006).

Said, Edward, *Orientalism* (Pantheon: New York, 1984).
Sands, Phillipe, *East West Street* (Vintage Books: New York, 2017).
Santayana, George, *The Sense of Beauty, Being the Outlines of Aesthetic Theory* (Scribner's: New York, 1905).
Sartre, Jean-Paul, "Existentialism is a Humanism," in *Existentialism from Dostoyevsky to Sartre*, ed. Walter Kaufmann (Meridian Books: New York, 1956).
Savile, Anthony, *The Test of Time: An Essay in Philosophical Aesthetics* (Oxford University Press: Oxford, 1985).
Schaper, Eva, ed., *Pleasure, Preference, Value: Studies in Philosophical Aesthetics* (Cambridge University Press: Cambridge, 1983).
Schiller, Fredrich, *On the Aesthetic Education of Man: in a Series of Letters*, edited and translated with an introduction by Elizabeth M. Wilkinson and L. A. Willoughby (Clarendon Press: New York and Oxford, 1982).
Smith, Adam, *The Theory of Moral Sentiments* (Kindly Edition).
Smith, Adam, *The Wealth of Nations* (Kindle Edition).
Steinberg, Leo, "The Philosophical Brothel," October, no. 44, Spring 1988, pp. 7–74.
Steiner, George, *The Death of Tragedy* (Hill and Wang: New York, 1968).
Stern, Irma, *Paradise: The Journal and Letters (1917–1933) of Irma Stern*, ed. Neville Dubow (Chameleon Press: Johannesburg, 1991).
Stiglitz, Joseph, *Globalization and Inequality Revisited: Anti-Globalization in the Era of Trump* (W. W. Norton: New York, 2017).
Taylor, Charles, *Hegel* (Cambridge University Press: Cambridge and New York, 1978).
Terminski, Bogumil, "The Evolution of the Concept of Perpetual Peace in the History of Political-Legal Thought," *Perspectivas internacionales*, vol. 6, no. 1, 2010, pp. 277–91.
Thompson, Leonard, *History of South Africa*, revised and updated by Lynn Berat (Yale University Press: New Haven and London, 2017).
Tomlinson, John, *Globalization and Culture* (University of Chicago Press: Chicago and London, 1999).
Warburg, Aby, *Images from the Region of the Pueblo Indians of North America*, translated with an Interpretative Essay by Michael Steinberg (Cornell University Press: Cornell and London, 1995).
Wilkins, Burleigh T., "Kant on International Relations," *The Journal of Ethics*, vol. 11, no. 2, 2007, pp. 147–59.
Wittgenstein, Ludwig, *Philosophical Investigations*, trans. Elizabeth Anscombe (Macmillan: New York, 1953).
Wollheim, Richard, *Art and Its Objects* (Cambridge University Press: Cambridge and London, 1968).
Wollheim, Richard, *On Art and the Mind* (Harvard University Press: Cambridge and London, 1974).
Wollheim, Richard, *Painting as an Art* (Bollingen Series, Princeton University Press: Princeton, 1987).

Index

aboriginal art 72–74, 76, 78–81
  dreamtime 74, 79–80
abstract expressionist art 74, 124
Achebe, Chinua 151–2
Addison, Joseph 141
aesthetics 1–12, 19, 31, 51, 72,
    82–3, 89, 104, 107, 117,
    122–3, 127, 133–5, 141,
    148, 155, 158, 160, 162,
    175, 177, 179, 181–2, 188,
    190, 194–6
aesthetic concepts 72–83
  aboriginal paintings 73–4
  thick aesthetic concept 74
  spiritual value 74
  walkabout 75
  weights to shared
    concepts 82–3
  aboriginal art 78
aesthetic judgment 161–96
  aesthetics today 195–6
  challenge of diversity 176–9
  delicacy of taste 169–74
  Hume's elitism 174–6
  Kant's subjectivist
    approach 181–6
  kantian formalism 186–90
  of David Hume 163–9
  of taste 161–3
  problem of objectivity 169–74
  standard of taste 176–9
  Ted Cohen, writing of 179–81
  universalizing humanism
    190–5
*Aesthetics, Arts and Politics in a
    Global World* 31
*Aesthetics: Lectures on Fine
    Art* 115

Africa 6–8, 27, 33–4, 38, 40–1,
    63, 99–100
African art 15, 46, 63
African National Congress (ANC)
    38, 48, 124
Ainslie, Bill 36
Altmann, Maria 95
amateur culture 34
America 3, 6, 8, 13, 24, 31, 68–71,
    89, 96, 100, 130, 132, 138
ANC. *See* African National
    Congress
Anderson, Benedict 8–9
Anglo-Indian landscape 149
Annan, Kofi 59
Apartheid Sophiatown 35
Appiah, Anthony 64, 66, 68, 70,
    72, 80, 85, 90–4, 97, 100–1,
    163, 181
Aristotle 134–5
Arnold, Matthew 10
art 107–32
  end of 127–32
  Hegel's colonial vision of 107–9
  Hegelian twist 118–27
  history of 114–8
  in South Africa 123–7
  meaning of 107
  medium of 107, 109–14
art history 107–32
art market 2–4, 13–15, 24, 33, 35,
    37, 49, 73, 130
The Art of Life 36
Asia 5–6, 38, 52
assembling reminders 103
austerity 31–2, 34–5
avant-gardes 16, 18, 21–2, 110,
    127, 130–2, 195–6

INDEX

Baartman, Saartjie 93
Ballen, Roger 45
banking 3
beauty of sublime 77
Beijing 2
Belonging 8
Benjamin, Walter 148
Bergen-Belsen images 27
Bernstein, Leonard 103–4
Bicycle Wheel 120
black arts 36–7, 47–8
Bloch-Bauer, Adele 95
Brecht, Bertolt 43
Breton, Andre 75–6
Brillo Boxes 119
British Museum 11
Brücke, Die 33
Burke, Edmund 141

Cabanne, Pierre 111
Candide 104
cannibalizing practices 54
Cape of Good Hope 6
Cape of Storms 6
Cape Town National Gallery 47–8
Cape Town 2, 14, 33–4, 36, 41, 45–6, 47, 169
capitalism 2, 6
"Cathedral to Labor" 43
Cavell, Stanley 1
Cecil Skotnes 36
Chatwin, Bruce 75
China 3, 5–6, 14–15, 33, 39, 42, 61, 66, 71, 73, 129–130
Chinese Cultural Revolution 103
Chinese globalization 5
Chinese opera 62, 103–5, 177–8
Chinnery, George 149
Cohen, Ted 177
Collingwood, Robin 1
colonialism 5–6, 8, 13, 31, 53–4, 55, 61, 85–8, 92, 96, 107, 109, 133, 140, 152, 154, 179, 181
Conrad, Josef 151

Constable's Wivenhoe Park 149
contemporary art 1, 12, 31–7, 40–1, 44, 49, 73, 95, 107, 122, 126, 129, 132
convulsive beauty 75–6
Coppola, Francis Ford 132
cosmopolitan task 193
cosmopolitanism 3, 51–6, 58, 60–6, 68, 71–3, 79, 83, 85, 97, 100–2, 104–5, 133, 135, 152, 155, 158, 163, 177, 180–1, 192, 195
  colonialism 53–4
  demands of 55
  Heauton Timorumeno 52
  human dignity 65
  linguistic diversity 65
  problem of 64
  rights of people 65
  universal stance 64
Cosmopolitanism: Ethics in a World of Strangers 64
Critique of Judgment 142
Critique of Practical Reason of 1788 191
Cukor, Georg 55, 180
culture
  art 91
  attitude 90–1
  collective guilt 98
  "cost-sharing" relationship 100
  curation and presentation of objects 99
  decolonization 92, 98
  deep feeling of offence 97
  demand for return 94
  empowerment 99
  global curation 99–100
  largesse 91
  moral debt 99
  moral right 98
  national debt 98
  negotiation 95
  objects stolen 93
  postcolonial states 97–8

repatriation 95
settler society 98–9
stewardship 91
cultural capital 9
cultural property 85–90

da Gama, Vasco 6
Da Ponte 146–7
da Vinci, Leonardo 82
Daily Telegraph 8
Daniell, William 149
Danto, Arthur 1, 13, 114, 118–22, 127–8, 130–1
"dark continent" 7
Davidson, Donald 62, 68
Declaration of Independence 137
Demoiselles 154
Derrida, Jacques 1
Dewey, John 1
Diaz, Bartolomeu 6
Die Antwoord 45
Diogenes 51–2
Don Quixote 169, 172
Duchamp, Marcel 111–13
Dumas, Marlene 41

Eckstein, Soho 17
'École Internationale de Théâtre Jacques Lecoq 17
economy 1
ecstatic sublime 77
Egypt 11, 149
"Einsam" (alone) 33
Elgin marbles 11, 93–4
Emanuele, Vittorio 92
England 7–8, 11
English 3, 6–9, 11, 16, 61, 65–6, 139, 168
Enlightenment Eurocentrism 64
Enlightenment legacy 58
Eurocentric beliefs 48, 60, 86–8
Europe 3, 5–8, 10–14, 22, 31–5, 53–4, 56–7, 59, 73, 77, 85–6, 89, 93, 96, 99–100, 107–8, 129, 132–4, 138, 148, 149, 154–5, 162, 177, 192–4
"Existentialism Is a Humanism" 57

fake news 69–71, 134
Fantasia 17
Feni, Dumile 36
figural solidity 153
Final Constitution of 1996 38
Fine Arts Association of Cape Town 36
Finnish art 63
First Amendment rights 69–70
"flexible capitalism" 15
fordist capitalism 2
Foucault, Michel 1
Foundations of the Metaphysics of Morals of 1785 191
France 8, 11–12, 15, 90, 93, 149
Franklin, Benjamin 35
free speech 69–70
Freedom of Speech 70
French 7
French Revolution 127, 129, 138
The Fundamental Constitution of the Carolinas 138

GEAR. *See* Growth, Employment and Redistribution Act
"genius" 102
genocide 58–59, 71
Gittoes, George 26–9
global art world
  art markets 13–14
  breakout 26–31
  decentering of art markets 14
  drawing and sketch 28–9
  international markets 14–15
  multimedia art 20–4
  new product 15–16
  political art 24–6
  problem of voice 16–20
  quality of invention 29
  speed of drawing 28

INDEX

global culture 108, 176
globalization 1–13, 16, 31–2, 38–9, 51, 60–1, 63, 73, 129, 133, 149, 156, 178
  access 4
  art markets 4
  banking 2
  blogs 3
  branding 4
  communication 2
  economic growth 4
  goods 6
  health care 2
  history of 5–12
  homogeneity 4
  investment 2
  in manufacturing 2
  in production 2
  opportunity 4
  service industries 2
  trading relations 5
  trading route 6
  voice 4
  websites 2
"Glorious Revolution" of 1688 138
The Godfather 132
Golden Age 10
Gracyk, Theodore 177
Grain Silo 41, 43–4
Grand Tour 148–9
Grant, Cary 55
Green, David 41
Growth, Employment and Redistribution Act (GEAR) 38
Guggenheim 46
Guyer, Paul 141

Habsburg Vienna 11
Harvey, David 15
Haven, Dexter C. K. 55, 180
Heart of Darkness 151
Heatherwick, Thomas 42–5
Hegel, G. W. F. 1, 31, 66, 107–123, 126, 127–9, 133, 135
  colonial vision of 107–9
  idea 107–9
  idealizing notion of art 122–7
heritage 9–10, 44, 85–6, 88–100, 175, 178, 181
"Herwitz Gallery" 95
Hitchcock, Alfred 112
Hodges, William 149
hoodia 100–1
"Hottentot Venus" 93
human diversity 60–3
  aesthethic differences in 62–3
  hard ethical issues in 61
  specify differences in 62
human rights 27, 29, 58–60, 64, 66, 71, 83, 129, 138
humanitarianism 58–9, 64, 71, 129
Hume, David 55, 102, 139–40, 142, 145, 162–78, 180–1, 188, 195
hunters and gatherers 100
Hwang, David Henry 103

Imagined Communities 9
In Search of Lost Time 185
India 3, 6, 14, 3, 73, 91, 93, 95–6, 125, 130, 149–150
Indian wall carvings 177
intellectual property 100–1
  cultural ownership and 101
  invention in 101
  knowledge of 101
  ownership in 102
  patent in 101
Interim Constitution of 1994 38, 124
International Monetary Fund 38
Italian opera 104–5

Jamestown colony of 1613 52
Jefferson, Thomas 137
Jews paintings 94
Johannesburg Art Foundation 36
Johannesburg Art Gallery 48
Judeo-Christian tradition 191–2

Judgment 134, 140
Justice Kennedy 70

Kant, Immanuel 51, 55–8, 60, 62, 66, 83, 91, 102, 117, 122, 127, 129, 133, 140, 142–3, 145, 159, 162–3, 181–4, 186–8, 190–3, 195–6
Kentridge, William 16–18
Khoi-San 93, 100–1
Khumalo, Sydney 48
King James II 138
Klimt, Gustav 95
Krauss, Rosalind 20
Kumalo, Sydney 36

Lake Albert 7
Lake Congo 7
Lake Tanganyika 7
Lake Victoria 7
Lanzmann, Claude 27
Latin America 6
Lauterpacht, Hersch 59
Le Demoiselles d'Avignon 154
Legae, Ezrom 48
Lemkin, Rafael 59
Lennon, John 57
Ligon, Glenn 41
"Liking What's Good" 179
liquid capital 4
Liszt, Franz 149
Little Red Riding Hood 45
Livingstone, David 7–8
Locke, John 137–8
locus classicus 107
London 2
Los Angeles 2
Louvre 11, 46
Lualaba River 7
Luxembourg 2

MacPherson, C. B. 138
Macron, Emmanuel 90
Magaziner, Daniel 36–7

Making Theory/Constructing Art: On the Authority of the Avant-Gardes 1
Mandela, Nelson 38, 93, 124, 126
Manet, Edouard 32–3, 118
"maps of locomotion" 75
Market economy 133
The Marriage of Figaro 146
Marx, Karl 1, 10, 133, 161, 175
Mehretu, Julie 41
mercantile capitalism 6
Mezzogiorno 148
Midnight's Children 16
mise-en-scène 24
modern art 31–4, 36–7, 96, 118, 120, 130
Montaigne, Michel de 54–5, 56, 67
moral disagreement 66–71
   autocratic religious state 67
   child-rearing 66–7
   cosmopolitanism and 68
   democratic public sphere 71
   free speech vs. the giving of offense 69
   Ghanaian vs. American forms of parenting 68
   individual rights 68
   moral concept 66
morals 51, 55–6, 62, 82–3, 85–6, 117, 142, 158–60, 181, 190–2
Morocco 149
Mozart 72, 142, 146–7, 187
Muller, Max 151
Musée de L'Homme 152
Musee du Quai Branly 90
Museum of Anthropology 93
museums 4–5, 9, 11–12, 14, 24, 26, 31–2, 34, 37–49, 80, 85, 90, 93–6, 99–100, 118–19, 131, 146–50, 153–6
Mutu, Wangechi 41

National Gallery of Modern Art 32
"National Sorry Day" 99
national sovereignty 8, 129
nationalism 4, 8–11, 33, 38–9, 56, 60, 70, 133, 133, 136, 156, 169, 181
natural rights 58, 89, 116, 137–8, 142
"naturals" 52
Nazi Nuremberg rally 159
Ndaleni Art School 36
neoliberalism 3
New York 2
New York Herald 8
Nietzsche, Friedrich 9–10, 78, 123
Noh Theater 177
Norval, Louis 37, 48

"Of Cannibals" 54
Of the Standard of Taste 163
Ofili, Chris 41
"ohne Liebe" (without love) 33
oil 3
"On the Very Idea of a Conceptual Scheme" 62
"Orientalism" 109
Orientalist knowledge system 151
ownership 85

paintings 17, 20–1, 28–30, 32–4, 36, 74–5, 80, 82, 85, 88, 90, 94–5, 111–12, 114–16, 131–2, 147, 149, 152–3, 159, 166, 177, 179, 189
Panza, Sancho 169
Paradise 33
Paris 152
Peabody Essex Museum 95
Pechstein, Max 33
perpetual peace 56–60
  concept of humanity 58–9
  cosmopolitan standpoint 57
  crimes against humanity 59
  example 57–8

humanitarianism 59–60
moral universality 58
morality 57
"phallocentrism" 112
The Philadelphia Story (1940) 55, 180
Philosophical Investigations Part II 52
Picasso 152–4
plastic art 29–31
Plato 134–5
politics 1, 3–4, 9, 11–12, 20, 24, 26–7, 47–8, 51, 57, 60, 69, 73, 77, 79–80, 82, 92, 99, 110–111, 117, 122, 125, 139, 146, 157–60, 169, 181
Polly Street Art School 36–7
Polo, Marco 5–6
"possessive individualism" 138
pre-Raphaelite romanticism 149
Progressive Artists Movement 32, 96
"proletariat" 10
protestants 8
Proust, Marcel 184–5
Psycho 112

refugees 2, 28, 58–9
renaissance 80, 82, 115, 121, 141, 147, 153, 159, 177, 179, 189, 196
"retina" 111
Ricardo, David 139
Riefenstahl, Leni 159
Rodchenko, Alexander 22
romantic companions 2
romanticism 10, 79, 149
Rushdie, Salman 16
Russia 3, 11, 14, 18, 22, 71
Rwandan genocide 29, 60, 71

Sachs, Albie 43
Said, Edward 109, 151
Salon des Refusés 33

Santo Domingo 6
Sartre, Jean-Paul 57, 194
Schat, Gabriel 78
Schiller, Friedrich 158
Sebidi, Helen 36
Second Treatise of Government of 1689 137–8
Second World War 8, 24, 59, 91, 96, 131
Sekoto, Gerard 35
"sensis communis" 83
Shanghai 2
Sheng, Bright 103
Sherman, Cindy 24–6
Shimin, Wang 82
Shoah 27
Shusterman, Richard 177
Silicon Valley 2
The Silver River 103–4
simply art history 128
Smith, Adam 139
social philosophy 6
The Songlines 75
Sontag, Susan 27
South Africa 38
  art markets 37–49
  comptemporary art 49
  cramped market 39
  excess of demand in 40
  foreign investment 38
  hegemonic globalization 39
  globalization 38
  museums 37–49
    design 42
    lacks funding 48
    lacks representativeness 46–7
    list of construction workers 43
    membership for citizens 42–3
    tax-free collection 46
    texts 43–4
  national revitalization 39
  nationalism 38
  problem of voice 39–40
  state of insufficiency 37
  universities 40
South African Constitution 69
South African Society of Artists 36
South-West Africa 6
Soweto Uprising of 1976 36
Spain 6–8
Speke, John Hanning 8
Stable Gallery 119
Stanley, JohnMorton 7–8
Steenberg Winery estate 48
Steinberg, Leo 154
Stern, Irma 33–4
Street Scene of 1942 35
Surrealism 75–6
synergy 51, 102–5
Syria 2
system of biennales 4

Taj Mahal 91, 114
taste 133–60
  art 155–60
  autonomy 144–7
  beautiful and sublime 142–4
  cosmopolitanism 155–60
  imagination 140–2
  individual liberty 137–40
  modern art 152–5
  museum 148–52
  native object 152–5
  pleasure 140–2
tax-free region 4
technology 129
Terence, Kilmartin 52, 56
"the guardians" 79
"automatic pen" 77
Things Fall Apart 152
Third Critique 193
Third Estate ofEurope 3
Thomas, Dylan 143, 149
"To Perpetual Peace: A Philosophical Sketch" 56
Treaty of Westphalia of 1648 8, 11, 58, 129

INDEX

Triumph of the Will 159
Trump, Donald 46, 91, 180
Truth and Reconciliation Committees 38, 123–4
Turkey 149
Tutsi forces 59

UNESCO. *See* United Nations Educational, Scientific and Cultural Organization
United Nations Educational, Scientific and Cultural Organization (UNESCO)
United Nations 58–60, 91
United States 2, 4, 14, 31, 61, 103
University of Fort Hare Museum 47
utopian future 111
Utrillo, Maurice 33

Venice 6
Verdi 92, 103, 178
victorianism 10
Villa d'Este 148
Virginia 6

visual forms 105–6
visual properties 120–1

Ward, Eleanor 119
Warhol, Andy 118–21, 130
Waterfront Corporation 40–1
Watson, Judy 79–80
West Side Story 104
"Western Civilization" classes 174
Wiley, Kehinde 41
William III 138
William Kentridge
  Felix in Exile 17
Wittgenstein, Ludwig 52, 58, 78, 102, 155
Wollheim, Richard 1, 155–6
World Bank 100–1

Xhosa concepts 68–9

"Years of Pilgrimage" 149

ZAR 175 43
Zietz MOCAA
  Zeitz, Jochen 40–9